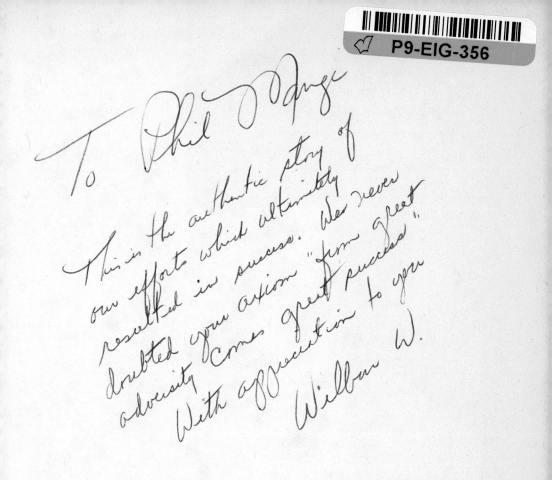

To Phil Mange

This is the authentic story of
our efforts which ultimately
resulted in success. We never
doubted your axiom "from great
adversity comes great success."
With appreciation to you

Wilbur W.

One Day
at
Kitty Hawk

Wilbur Wright preparing the catapult takeoff track for a flight, France, 1909.

ONE DAY
at
KITTY HAWK

The Untold Story
of the Wright Brothers
and the Airplane

John Evangelist Walsh

Thomas Y. Crowell Company
New York   *Established 1834*

Copyright © 1975 by John Evangelist Walsh

Designed by Ingrid Beckman

Manufactured in the United States of America

Library of Congress Cataloging in Publication Data

Walsh, John Evangelist, 1927-
    One day at Kitty Hawk.

    Bibliography: p.
    Includes index.
    1. Wright, Wilbur, 1867-1912. 2. Wright, Orville, 1871-1948. I. Title.
TL540.W7W3   629.13'092'2 [B]   75-12740
ISBN 0-690-00103-7

    2   3   4   5   6   7   8   9   10

Other Books by
John Evangelist Walsh

THE SHROUD
The Story of the Holy Shroud of Turin

STRANGE HARP, STRANGE SYMPHONY
The Life of Francis Thompson

THE LETTERS OF FRANCIS THOMPSON

POE THE DETECTIVE
*The curious circumstances behind
the Mystery of Marie Roget*

THE HIDDEN LIFE OF EMILY DICKINSON

For Younger Readers

THE SINKING OF THE U.S.S. MAINE

THE MAYFLOWER COMPACT

THE PHILIPPINE INSURRECTION

Preface

I am loathe to snarl with argument the threads of what is, to my inward vision at least, a supremely compelling tale, all the more fascinating for its being true. Thus, rather than plague the reader with frequent displays of evidence, I have presented the story for the most part as a continuous narrative. All the evidence, however, all the sources, on which my conclusions are based, will be found fully arrayed at the rear of the book. And I herewith give the reader assurance that every detail in my text is firmly anchored in these sources, down to the smile that lit the features of the elder Wright on hearing that his sons had flown.

Necessarily, these Notes are a bulky accumulation, containing as they do a good deal of random information that may be of interest or value. But they need not intrude their sometimes thorny technicalities on any reader who chooses to avoid them. Here and there, I have rescued from the Notes some more pertinent bit of fact and have footnoted it in the text. These are points that I felt should not be permitted to lurk undetected in the crowd.

For my own pleasure, I should here like to record the fact that my interest in the Wrights and their airplane goes back some twenty years, to a time when it would never have occurred to me that I might someday try to tell their story. That task, as it seemed to me then, could be adequately done only by some rare being who combined high talent as a writer with the detailed knowledge possessed only by a professional aeronautical engineer. It was not until later that I began to see the truth: that such professional knowledge would tend to be a handicap, even a severe one, in any attempt to evoke the primitive bright simplicity of the brothers' work. Such was quite evident in all that had been written about the Wrights by professional men, where the viewpoint invariably was one of looking backward through an almost impenetrable screen of modern technology.

How much better it would be for a writer to approach the Wrights' story, I thought, armed only with a deep interest and a willingness to learn—as the Wrights themselves, without special knowledge, had approached the problem of flight. A writer could then, to some extent, follow their thought as it grew, actually learn with them, relive the whole unparalleled, day-by-day adventure.

With this in mind, some eight years ago I began my studies, and promptly made two discoveries. The first was that the brothers' work, from the hazardous glider experiments to the finer scientific detail, was easily within the grasp of a layman. This was heartening. The second point, never bargained for, was that the story of the Wrights, as it is presently understood, bore about the same relation to the full truth as, say, a cameo bears toward the person whose image it carries. That was dismaying. It meant that much of what had been written about the brothers over the past seven decades was untrustworthy—including, I note with some sadness, the official biography.

My task had grown and expanded. I would have to dig anew into the beginning of things, and before the beginning. No one's unsupported word could be accepted for anything. There must be experiment with likelihood, a weighing of probability, and a final reliance only on demonstrable fact. It was then that I realized that I had become like the Wrights themselves in their search for the secrets of flight.

But I will say no more here.

Dumont, New Jersey　　　　　　　　　JOHN EVANGELIST WALSH
February 1975

Contents

The imagination voyaging
through chaos and reducing
it to clarity and order
is the symbol of all the
quests which lend glory
to our dust.

> J. L. LOWES,
> *The Road to Xanadu*

We need to have our
true story told in
an authentic way.

> WILBUR WRIGHT
> in a letter of 1908

1

The Long Silence

In an upstairs bedroom of an ordinary frame house on quiet Hawthorn Street in Dayton, Ohio, Wilbur Wright lay dying. Gripped by typhoid fever, he had suffered recurring periods of burning delirium and had been put under opiates. Around his bed prayerfully watching the lean, hawk-nosed face for signs of returning strength, were gathered his three brothers, Reuchlin, Lorin, and Orville, his sister Katharine, and his eighty-four-year-old father, a retired bishop of the United Brethren Church.

The family was not alone in its vigil. Daily, newspaper reporters came quietly to the front door to ask in hushed tones if there had been any change. Less than nine years before, together with Orville, his younger brother, Wilbur had made history's first powered airplane flight. It was not quite four years since the two had unveiled a developed, practical airplane to the wondering eyes of the world.

For a week the fever had fluctuated, one day seeming about to pass off, then rekindling the next, bringing incoherent mutterings and the need for forcible restraint as the patient struggled to leave the bed. Two doctors were in attendance and, while there was little that medicine could do then against typhoid, even after weeks of uncertainty it still appeared that he would recover. Then he suddenly began to sink and at dawn on May 30, 1912, Wilbur Wright breathed his last. He was just over a month past his forty-fifth birthday.

The funeral took place from the First Presbyterian Church in Dayton, where twenty-five thousand people filed past the body. The family had wanted private services but had given in to the urgent requests of the city fathers. Burial, with only the family present, was at Woodland Cemetery just outside the city limits.

With the announcement of Wilbur's death, telegrams and letters of condolence by the hundreds began to arrive at Hawthorn Street. Obituary notices appeared in papers across the nation and in most other countries, all lamenting the irreparable loss to the fledgling science of aeronautics. This outpouring, even though Wilbur himself had always remained aloof and was in his private life little known to the public, was only natural, to be expected. One of that unique team of brothers whose work had opened a new era in history had passed away.

Yet in many of the stories and obituaries there was something else, something that went beyond what might have been expected. As a bright thread gleaming in some old tapestry, there ran through the newspaper coverage the settled belief that it was not the two brothers together but Wilbur, and Wilbur alone, who had uncovered the fundamental secrets of powered flight, Wilbur who had been the masterful guide of all the brothers' work. Orville had been no more than his valued assistant.

In the days of the Wrights' early fame it had been evident to most people that not every step could always have occurred at the same time to both men. The true division of credit was a matter of real curiosity to the public and the question had often been asked. Yet in describing their work the two had never specified which, if either, had contributed what, nor would they say what portion or element of the invention was the work of which brother. Purposely obscuring their individual contributions, they had talked of their work in terms of "we" and "us." They had even refused to say which of them had been the pilot on the first flight.

Now, with the older brother dead, newspapers and magazines, in headline and story, unhesitatingly made a choice between the two. Wilbur was identified not only as the dominant brother but as the true "inventor of the airplane." He was called "Father of Flight," and "Conqueror of the Air," and pointed to as "the man who made flying possible." President William Howard Taft, in a statement issued from the White House, hailed him as "the father of the great new science of aeronautics." In all of this, where Orville is mentioned at all, he is offhandedly identified as Wilbur's younger brother, sometimes without being named. He is assigned the role of helper, important for his mechanical ability and his daring in the air. Nowhere is he presented as deserving of a full share of the scientific credit.

One account filed by a Dayton reporter was explicit: "It is not known how they divided their labors, but it has always been thought that perhaps Wilbur . . . was the student and scientist of the two . . . Orville backing him up with his mechanical skill." *The New York Times* stated flatly that Wilbur Wright had done "more than any other man to make the modern conquest of the air possible," and even Wilbur's father, in the privacy of his diary, seemed to reflect something of the general belief. In words that imply something beyond the mere exaggeration of grief, Bishop Wright sadly recalled the qualities of the son he had lost: "In memory and intellect there was none like him."

Just how the newspapers had managed to reach this sweeping certainty about Wilbur—a certainty that yet seemed in some way limited—when the brothers themselves had provided no clear information on the matter can only be guessed. Orville, himself, stunned by his brother's sudden passing, remained silent. Soon, as attention shifted to the living member of the team, this widespread belief in Wilbur's primacy began to fade from memory.

Left unwritten at Wilbur's death was the book in which he had planned to set down the full story of the invention of the airplane, including its dim beginnings, all the hesitant gropings and sudden insights, along with full technical details. His busy life as president of the Wright Aeronautical Company, however, and his hectic prosecution of half a dozen lawsuits against patent infringers had repeatedly delayed its start. The task then devolved upon Orville— who took fully thirty years to tell the story, in the meantime blocking similar efforts by others. Surprisingly, in Orville's version it was not the older brother but the younger one who deserved, if either of them did, to be called the discoverer of flight. But this is only one of the puzzling items in the younger brother's fairly puzzling subsequent life.

It is often said that Orville, dispirited by sorrow, became a "recluse" after Wilbur's death. While the word is too strong, it is a fact that within three years of Wilbur's passing, Orville did make some drastic changes in his life. He sold the Wright company to a syndicate of eastern businessmen, retaining for himself not a single share of stock, and was never again, in fact, to have any business connection with airplane manufacture. He then opened a small private laboratory for aeronautical research but during the fifteen years or so of its existence the contribution it made to the field was negligible (a 1913 award for an automatic stability device concerned an idea the brothers had worked on together as early as 1904).

From the year of Wilbur's death, Orville virtually disappeared from any active or significant role in the tumultuous world of early aviation. So effacing did he become that, while he outlived his brother by thirty-six years, his death in 1948 came as rather a shock to a world that assumed he had died long before.

It was in 1915 that Orville made his first attempt to get a book written. Many publishers and friends, and especially his sister Katharine, urged him not to postpone the job. Professing distaste even for letter writing, Orville turned to a newspaper friend, Earl Findley, a former New York *Herald* reporter. Given only controlled access to the voluminous files of correspondence, diaries, and notebooks, and lacking experience in serious research or book authorship, Findley soon decided he needed help. With Orville's approval he called in another young writer friend and between them, working about six months, they completed the manuscript.

Submitting their work to Orville, however, the two eager young authors met with a crushing disappointment. Gruffly, Orville refused to allow publication. He was suffering from sciatica at the time and was bedridden. On finishing his perusal of the manuscript he called his secretary and said bluntly, "Tell them I'd rather have

the sciatica." The secretary dutifully, not to say insensitively, relayed Orville's remark to the anxious authors.

Findley was later to give different reasons for Orville's dislike of
the manuscript. At one time he said it was because the narrative
was "too personal." At another time he went further, stating crypti-
cally that the real cause of the suppression was "due to his own
honesty and a disagreement with Orville." What the disagreement
may have been remains a mystery.

Thereafter Findley always carefully preserved the manuscript,
at one time keeping it in a box under his bed, but apparently making no further effort toward publication. His last traceable appearance in this connection took place in 1940 at a meeting with
Charles Lindbergh, and was recorded only because Lindbergh happened to make a note in his diary. Discussing the Wrights, Lindbergh expressed his concern that their story had never been adequately told. Findley confessed that the story had indeed been
told, and he recounted something of the disagreement with Orville.
"I could see that he had been badly hurt by the whole affair," wrote
Lindbergh, "so badly hurt that it is still somewhat painful to discuss the matter." The wound must indeed have gone deep, since
twenty-five years had not healed it.*

With the rejection of Findley's effort, Orville closed up his files
and put them under the care of a private secretary. In the years following he now and then gave assistance to writers for magazine
articles or parts of books but these were superficial efforts, most
often rehashes, and very little information appeared that had not
been available long before. To those who still urged him to do a
book he usually replied that he couldn't write well himself and he
didn't trust other writers to be accurate enough. Understandably,
this remark sounded odd to listeners since Orville was friendly
with or known to most of the leading aeronautical writers in the
country, any one of whom would have accepted such a commission
with delight. Once, Lindbergh relayed to Orville an offer from a
highly qualified author but met only indifference. Undaunted, a

---

* The Findley manuscript, never published, is still in existence but is unavailable for
study. A curious situation later developed when a rewritten version of it *did* find its
way into print, over Orville's objections. See the Notes.

month later Lindbergh managed to introduce the writer to Orville in person. Ruefully he recorded the fact that he had enjoyed "no more success than before."

Just before the start of World War II Orville at last found a writer he felt he could trust. This was Fred Kelly, an Ohio newspaperman the brothers had known for years. In 1943 a book finally appeared: *The Wright Brothers: A Biography Authorized by Orville Wright.* If Orville had found a writer he could trust, he had not found one who could write on the level required for a subject of such historical importance (a judgment that holds true even granting that the book was intended for the general public rather than specialists). Yet this verdict probably does some injustice to Kelly. While the book plods along, at times on the juvenile level, leaving many vital questions unanswered and showing no sign of the research in depth that the topic cried out for, this may reflect the control exercised by Orville.

At the book's publication, three decades had passed since the death of Wilbur and it had been forty years since the first flight—years in which the science of aeronautics had made such astonishing progress that its misty beginnings seemed to belong to quite another and far distant epoch. Though there were people then alive who had known Wilbur (not intimately, since few had been allowed that privilege), the world's living memory of the older brother had faded nearly to oblivion. No one seemed to recall the once general belief that the genius behind the airplane had been his. Consequently, almost no one was surprised to learn that it was not Wilbur but Orville himself who had supplied all the initial theorizing, the original scientific insight, by means of which the elusive principles of flight had been uncovered. Nor did it seem a distortion that while Wilbur is allowed an equal share in the working out of the theories propounded by Orville, and in the actual experimenting, he remains in Kelly's pages a strangely unfocused and shadowy figure.

Throughout the Kelly book, Orville is shown to have taken always an equal, more often a greater, part in the invention of the flying machine, as well as in its later development. He is also presented as the one whose public flights first brought a practical airplane to the attention of the world. All in all, it must have appeared

to Kelly's readers that the true inventor of the airplane had not died
in 1912, as Wilbur's obituaries had stated, but could still be
glimpsed sometimes walking the streets of Dayton, a white-haired
old man in his seventies who preferred a secluded life and who was
no longer actively connected with aviation.

Publication of the authorized biography did not loosen Orville's
hold on the precious hoard of papers. All requests by writers to
consult them were refused. Orville and his secretary were the only
ones ever to touch a single document. The Library of Congress and
the Smithsonian Institution both offered themselves as repositories,
invitations that Orville for a variety of reasons refused. As he
neared his seventy-seventh year he still had not made arrangements for permanent care of the collection. Then in 1947 he was
felled by heart trouble, from which he doggedly struggled back.
Three months later he was struck again. For a week he lingered
and on January 31, 1948, he finally succumbed. His death was announced in newspapers around the world, not always on the front
pages (bigger news that same day was the assassination of Ma-
hatma Ghandi).

Orville's will left the disposition of his papers in the hands of his
executors, with no indication of preference. It was known that he
had been thinking favorably of the Library of Congress, however,
and in 1950 the papers were sent there, still under restrictions. By
special arrangement they would be kept closed to the public for
ten years. In the meantime the Library was to prepare the more
significant documents for publication, under a financial arrangement with Oberlin College, Katharine's alma mater, to which Orville had left a large sum of money.

In 1953 two volumes were brought out. With this, the matter of
priority between the brothers—by now, of course, questions on the
topic were no longer even asked—received another peculiar twist.
While the editor of the volumes in his commentary continued to
bracket Wilbur and Orville as equals, it was, or should have been,
fairly clear to any careful reader that the older brother had been,
at the very least, the controlling intelligence and had exercised absolute dominance over all the work, even down to deciding when
it was safe for Orville to attempt his first glider flight.

Further, it was beyond doubt that the initial interest in flying had come from Wilbur, and that for the entire first year of study and experiment he had worked in isolation—"one man alone and un-aided," he described himself.

Patient analysis of the mass of data contained in these two vol-umes, *The Papers of Wilbur and Orville Wright,* makes it impos-sible, at last, to see the whole extraordinary outpouring as anything but the overflow from one full mind, rays of probing light from a single intense vision. Wilbur Wright may be a shadowy figure in the official biography, but in these original documents—so long withheld, so casually received when finally made available—he can be glimpsed once more both as the true "father of the great new science of aeronautics," and as the extraordinary, driven genius that he was.

In 1911 the brothers purchased a large tract of land in the ex-clusive Oakwood suburb of Dayton, and contracted to have an im-posing pillared mansion erected as their family's new home. Here they would rule over the new industry of aviation, leading and guiding its inevitable progress. But this part of the dream was not to be. With the building only half completed, Wilbur died.

It was Orville who, in 1914, moved with his father and sister into the big house, to preside over it as master for more than three dec-ades. The father died in 1917 and the sister left to marry in 1927 (dying only two years later). Thereafter, for twenty years Orville had the house to himself as—gradually, and no doubt with growing certainty as the years slipped away—he also assumed, and allowed a grateful nation to bestow on him, the major role in the invention of the airplane.

Yet he must have been aware during those years of another pres-ence in the silence of those elegant rooms—the admonishing ghost of the brother who by dying early had been deprived of his full measure of fame. "The spirit of his brother, Will, is ever present in these surroundings," wrote one astute visitor in 1927, sensing in the atmosphere something more than fond memory. "To see and talk to Orville one has the definite feeling of his brother's presence. His must have been a strong personality for it hovers around his brother like an aura."

Perhaps it would be an arid task, so long after the fact, to attempt disentangling the brothers' work, were there not still another issue involved, one of even greater moment than the matter of priority between the two. The fact is that the same curious process that has obscured their respective roles has also thrown a pall over the invention of the airplane itself. Thus, an event that many people view as the most remarkable single achievement in the history of invention, a feat that triumphantly realized "man's oldest dream," altered the course of world history, and helped open the pathway to the stars, is today known only in outline, a distorted and fragmented outline, which in some ways amounts very nearly to downright falsification.

Further, that same obscuring process has also left in shadow the more than four years that intervened between the first flight and the memorable day when the brothers gave their developed airplane to the world, years in which the airplane was perfected, *in secret*, and then coolly withheld from public view while the brothers searched for a sure way to earn their fortune. During those years —while scientists still called human flight absurd, while other men struggled to lift cumbersome machines a few feet off the ground, while all the world wondered if the rumors about the Wrights could be true—the brothers possessed a practical airplane, one capable of carrying two men at a speed in excess of forty miles an hour.

It is the detailed truth of the manner in which all these marvels were accomplished that I have tried to recover, from the tangle of manipulation no less than the silts of time. That this can still be said nearly three-quarters of a century after the first flight is in itself incredible.

2

Wilbur Wright's
Lost Decade

Most of the great inventors and discoverers have been driven by the desire for renown and the chance to gain a fortune. A few have had deeper reasons, reaching into the circumstances of their lives and personalities. Wilbur Wright was one of these few. His search for the secrets of flight began solely as a last desperate effort to lift himself out of a shattered existence.

The plain fact, never quite understood before, is that Wilbur Wright, between the time he left high school, at eighteen, and the time, at twenty-six, when he joined his brother in opening a bicycle shop, had never been gainfully employed, had never earned a living. During those eight years he had remained aimlessly at home, an invalid as the result of a sports accident. And his entry into the bicycle business brought no joy. It was a sad acceptance of what promised to be a melancholy future, a bleak compromise, devoid of the challenge he had once eagerly sought from life.

Born in 1867 on a farm near Millville, Indiana, by 1885 Wilbur was a senior at Steele High School in Dayton, where his father was then assigned. A good student, he was also an incessant reader, particularly of such romantic fare as the novels of Scott, but also serious history, science, and even theology (he was in time to gain some amateur competence as a theologian). Physically, he was spare, never weighing more than 140 pounds and standing about five feet ten inches. An excellent all-round athlete, he took part in baseball, hockey, and the primitive, very rough football then being played. He was also a gymnast, one of the best in the Dayton area, it is said.

His plans, even this early, seem to have taken definite shape: he was to attend Yale Divinity School to prepare for the ministry, and there is reliable information that he already had his eye on a local girl, a classmate at the high school. Then about March of his senior year there occurred the accident. It was to change his life completely.

While playing hockey with his school varsity against a team made up of the sons of officers from a nearby army installation, a stick swung wildly by an opponent smashed into his face, leaving his mouth a mass of bloody pulp and knocking out nearly all his upper front teeth and many lower ones. He was attended by an army surgeon and taken home with his head swathed in bandages. In time, care and false teeth restored his face, the false teeth perhaps developing that tight-lipped smile so often in later years described as "enigmatic." He soon showed some unlooked-for complications, however. A chronic stomach disorder appeared and, more seriously, heart trouble.

For a long period afterward he was kept at home, a semi-invalid, growing ever more discouraged and nursing a secret fear about his heart. "It seemed to everyone," reported an early writer who talked to the family, "that the boy was handicapped for life." Wilbur gave up his plans for the ministry, and though he found himself increasingly drawn to science he made no effort to prepare for such a career. He had gradually reached the morbid conclusion that his weakened constitution destined him to an early death. He did not want to waste time or money, as he said, in a vain pursuit of futile hopes. "Several times in the years that are past," he would later wanly recall, "I have had thoughts of a scientific career, but the lack of a suitable opening, and the knowledge that I had no special preparation in any particular line, kept me from entertaining the idea very seriously."

His days he filled with reading and with work around the house. The rest of the family, while at first sympathetic, eventually came to feel that his disability was increasingly more emotional than physical. His growing tendency to withdrawal and long periods of

silence gave them cause for real concern. They talked of this peculiar twist in their brother's life with puzzlement and even annoyance. The older Reuchlin, who had married and moved to Kansas,
in November 1888 voiced his brotherly impatience in hyperbolic
style when he inquired by letter of his sister, "What does Will do?
He ought to do something. Is he still cook and chambermaid?"

Mostly, at this time, Wilbur was taking care of his ailing mother,
who had long been struggling against consumption. In 1887 she became enfeebled and was bedridden (the cooking and household
duties, from this time at least, were handled by a hired girl). Wilbur had always been her favorite and he now assumed the whole
burden of her care, bringing her downstairs to the parlor in the
morning and, when she was too weak to walk, finding the strength
in his own weakened frame to carry her up at night. His father, by
now a bishop and away from home much of the time, was later to
say that Wilbur's devoted care had prolonged his mother's life by
at least two years. She died in July 1889, aged sixty-one.

Mrs. Wright's influence on her handicapped son seems to have
been of more than usual importance. The little that is known of her
indicates that she was a clever woman, decisive in character, even
possessing some mechanical aptitude (exercised in the kitchen and
on the children's toys). On Wilbur, especially during the bleak
years of his invalidism, she lavished motherly encouragement. "She
seems to have had a great belief in the latent power of Wilbur,"
wrote one man who later interviewed the Wrights' close neighbors.
It has fallen to the lot of few mothers to nurture a child whose intellect was destined to alter the face and pace of life the world
over. To Susan Koerner Wright the world may owe more than it
knows.

No other women figure importantly in Wilbur's life after the accident, at least there is no record of any, and this has been seen as
the natural result of his fervent commitment to the flying problem,
which in truth occupied all his time and attention from the age of
thirty or so. He himself once wryly replied to a questioner that he
"could not support a wife and a flying machine, too." It was his invalidism, perhaps, and not just his concern over the airplane that
played the decisive part in this social isolation. But some stray recollections by a young man who worked in the bicycle shop and later
on the Wrights' planes, offers a hint that it may bear some relation

to his melancholy memories of the mother who had wasted away under his eyes.

"Will kept saying he didn't have time for a wife," recalled the young man, "but I think he was just woman-shy—young women at least. He would get awfully nervous when young women were around. When we began operating at Simms Station on the outskirts of Dayton in 1904, we always went out on the traction cars. If an older woman sat down beside him, before you knew it they would be talking, and if she got off at our stop he'd carry her packages and you'd think he had known her all his life. But if a young woman sat next to him he would begin to fidget and pretty soon he would get up and go stand on the platform until it was time to leave the car."

This vignette shows, at least, the extent to which his brooding had thrown him in on himself, perhaps shows as well how the constriction of his heart and personality served as a main strand in the bonds that would hold him so relentlessly to his work on the problem of flight, that great quest more than filling the emotional void.

Mrs. Wright's death made little change in the generally somber mood of her son's life. While Orville dropped out of high school to become a printer's apprentice,* while Lorin and Katharine were attending college, Wilbur's aimless, homebound drift continued. That he often sank into something like despair can be judged from a later remark of his, that unvarying tranquillity led only to a fearful boredom. "Most enjoyment in life," he is quoted as saying, "consisted of relief from discomfort. To try to be always comfortable and happy was therefore a mistake, for if one succeeded life became unbearably monotonous."

Still, his seclusion was not absolute. With his brother Lorin he belonged to a social and athletic club whimsically named "The Ten Dayton Boys," and made up of former schoolmates, which seems to have met once a week. He took no part in the athletics but served as club secretary. The entire membership formed itself into a glee club in which Wilbur was remembered for "his fine bass."

Orville, who had acquired a printing press of his own and had

---

* Orville quit high school, according to his niece, Ivonette Miller, because "there were too many required subjects . . . in which he was not interested." Existing records, including Kelly, supply little further on the point.

opened a job printing shop, now made a venture into the newspaper business with a small neighborhood weekly of four pages, *The West Side News*. Its circulation was never more than four hundred, home-delivered every Saturday by the Wrights themselves and a friend or two. After about a year Orville ambitiously, if unwisely, converted the paper to a four-page neighborhood daily, which expired within a few months. While Wilbur wrote for and helped edit both of these papers he knew only too well that such dilettantish journalism did not constitute a full-time occupation. It took little of his time and brought a minuscule financial return. Whether he ever thought of going seriously into the profession is not known, though it is unlikely. Of other occupations for Wilbur there is no record, beyond a brief stint as "folder" of the church bulletin edited by his father (done by an ingenious machine Wilbur had put together himself).

In December 1892 the brothers opened a small bicycle shop for repairs and rentals. This was a sensible move that took advantage of the "safety bicycle" craze then sweeping the country (wheels of equal size and chain-driven, as opposed to the old high-wheel variety). It was an undemanding situation for Wilbur but he went into it without enthusiasm and even without intention to remain. The renewed activity, however, seems to have somewhat revived his spirits and his dampened ambitions and by September 1894—a decade after the hockey accident—he began to think again of college and a career.

Writing to his father who was traveling in pursuit of his pastoral duties, he explains that he has lately felt much better, has become restless, is unhappy in business, and thinks he might like to become a teacher. "Intellectual activity is a pleasure to me," he remarks, "and I think I would be better fitted for reasonable success in some of the professions." This new attitude pleased his family and the father quickly replied with words of encouragement, promising also to help with the necessary funds. But Wilbur did not return to school and nothing further is heard of the plan. Instead he continued with his uncongenial place in the shop, his intellectual desires undiminished but frustratingly unfueled. While it may be no more than a coincidence, it should be noted that it was about this time, or shortly after, that the problem of human flight first began to interest him.

So much of significance, and no more, may be gleaned from the scanty records regarding Wilbur's early life and character. It is little enough. The essential man himself remains, and perhaps will always remain, elusive. The only way to form a more intimate idea of his mind and personality is to draw on those who knew him in later years, and who were qualified to speak.

On several points all who knew him are agreed. Wilbur's reserve in personal contact, and his aversion to small talk, were not the result of mere shyness. These things flowed naturally from a spirit of self-possession, a rigid independence, qualities that often struck those who met him as coldness or arrogance, even at times fanaticism, and that were reinforced by his clipped, laconic manner of speaking. "When he had something on his mind," remembered a niece, "he would cut himself off from everyone. At times he was unaware of what was going on around him." Most striking was the intellectual cast of his dark, lined face, thin and sharp, almost emaciated, with its high forehead made even higher by premature baldness.

One French reporter, who had spent many weeks in dogged pursuit of Wilbur, was captivated by the silent American. "This man is strange and cold," he wrote in wide-eyed fashion, "but of a coldness that is smiling and sympathetic. He is tall, thin and severe—a man that is tempered like steel. The countenance is remarkable, curious—the head that of a bird, long and bony, and with a long nose. The face is smooth-shaven and tanned by the wind and country sun. The eye is a superb blue-gray, with tints of gold that bespeak an ardent flame, for Wilbur Wright is a fanatic."

Another Frenchman, Léon Bollée, a prominent manufacturer who was to become connected with the Wright company, was effusive on the diversity of Wilbur's talents. "Mr. Wright will go down in history as one of the most remarkable men of his age," Bollée said at an interview. "Not only does he possess a startling mechanical genius, but he is, apparently, fully versed in most branches of learning." Bollée may have overstated the case, but there is no doubt that the breadth of Wilbur's intellectual interests came as a surprise to more than one of his acquaintances. Genius in any line, it was thought, particularly a mechanical one, would throw all alien subjects into shadow. "Wilbur did not suffer in this respect," insisted Griffith Brewer, one of the few to become friendly with him. "On subjects of which I had some knowledge he could always add some information, and even in my special work I learnt some points from him."

Adding to this impression of mental capacity was Wilbur's manner and even appearance. Most descriptions of him echo the words of one English reporter, who recalled the "fine-drawn, weather-beaten face, strongly marked features, and extraordinarily keen, observant, hawklike eyes . . . one felt instinctively that here one was faced by a truly remarkable and outstanding personality." Softening the aloofness of this portrait was a saving vein of humor, especially evident within the framework of home and family but apt now and then to be let loose in public. As one Dayton friend recalled, he seemed a man "who would apparently say something rather dry and droll, if he said anything at all."

The picture of Wilbur Wright that emerges from a study of contemporary opinion, it can be seen, brings once more into the light a truly singular personality. Hardheaded, widely knowledgeable, personally reserved, never failing to impress those who met him as in some way set apart, he was yet "without a trace of vanity."

No such comments as these can be found for Orville. The younger brother was liked by all who met him, was admired for his technical skill and his competence as a pilot, but he elicited no strong response as being in any way extraordinary. Voluble, outgoing, with a mustached freshness of countenance, Orville quickly made friends wherever he went. When he appeared in public with Wilbur, however, it was his charismatic brother who received—albeit unwillingly and uncomfortably—the attention.

It is the ultimate irony that the image of these two has become confused in the public mind, their personalities and even appearances blended until, for most people today, they are nearly indistinguishable. The obliterating power of time could go no further.

Certainly it is strange that Wilbur's lost decade should have faded from the record, stranger still that there is no more than a veiled hint of it in the official biography. As a result of the accident, writes Kelly, Wilbur was "unable to engage in much outdoor activity" for several years. This reticence was hardly fair. The full story would have provided an inspiring narrative, for it is now clear that Wilbur's

drive toward solution of the flying problem did not spring from ordinary ambition. It was, beyond any doubt, a last effort to salvage
his life, to give scope to talents that had seemed destined to wither
unfulfilled. In an early letter to his father, he intimates as much. He
is not, he says, taking up the investigation for profit, but still, "I
think there is a slight possibility of achieving fame and fortune
from it."

In the same letter he explains why he has settled his hopes on the
flying problem, a task that might very well have seemed beyond
him. It is not because he feels a special affinity for it but because
"it is the only great problem which has not been pursued by a multitude of investigators, and therefore carried to a point where further progress is very difficult." The question of human flight, being
still in an exceedingly primitive state, did not seem to require the
years of formal preparation that are always needed in fields where
much has already been done. Imagination, a feeling for fundamentals, a systematizing bent, an analytical inclination—these were the
unteachable qualities, Wilbur knew, that had always been counted
most precious in any pioneering scientific quest. These, and sufficient desire. In his own mind he had long been aware that he possessed just such qualities. Now the desire, too, had begun to smolder.

3

The Dream Begins

It was after he had spent more than two frustrating years walking daily from the Hawthorn Street house to the little brick bicycle shop on West Third Street, to fill dreary hours fixing broken chains and patching inner tubes, that thoughts of flight first stirred in the brooding mind of Wilbur Wright. Fittingly for a man who gave most of his free time to books, the initial spark came from something he read, a magazine article provocatively entitled, "The Flying Man."

The article told of the work of Otto Lilienthal, a forty-six-year-old German engineer, who had achieved something then unheard of: using a rigid plane of wings resembling those of a bat, below which he hung by his arms, Lilienthal had succeeded in sustaining himself in the air, in making a true glide, not once but hundreds of times. In September 1894 his work and the theories underlying it were described in *McClure's Magazine,* a popular periodical of the day which prided itself on supplying the latest in all fields. A series of fascinating photographs showed the frail, graceful craft soaring against the sky, sometimes at an altitude of thirty feet, with the dark figure of its inventor clinging beneath it.

Only once did Wilbur make public reference to the moment when the idea of man in flight struck permanent fire in his soul.

The news of Lilienthal's feat, he said, had renewed in him "a passive interest which had existed from my childhood." In this he was recalling, partially at least, an incident of his eleventh or twelfth year concerning a toy his father brought home one day. A small device of bamboo and paper resembling a miniature helicopter, it had rotary wings powered by a rubber band. Wound up and released, it would shoot up to the ceiling, hover momentarily, then fall slowly to the floor as the power diminished with the untwisting of the rubber band. The youthful Wilbur was entranced by the toy and attempted to make a larger version of it only to find that it would not fly. (Not until much later would he understand why: a doubling of the dimensions required not twice, but eight times the power.)

The story of the toy helicopter, so often cited as prophetic, has an appropriate charm but no real significance—the toy was very simple in construction and materials, and undoubtedly hundreds of boys tried to enlarge on it. Until the advent of Lilienthal, nearly twenty years later, Wilbur thought no more of flying things. He must have been familiar from boyhood with the romance of ballooning, which in the public mind was then invested with more glamour and excitement than space flight is today. Certainly he had read of the spectacular exploits of the famous balloonists, probably he also knew something of the long and fruitless efforts to make balloons steerable. Interestingly, none of this exerted any hold on him.

The topic of powered, heavier-than-air flight, while it was always of intense concern to a few, had at this time caused hardly a ripple among the general public. Occasionally an article in the popular press might carry confident predictions by recognized scientists as to the immanence of the "flying machine." As often as not these were flatly contradicted by other scientists, many of high standing, who patiently detailed the reasons why hopes of human flight were little better than an absurdity.

Grant the impossible, argued one typical opponent, and say that a machine might manage to get itself off the ground. Say that the pilot might even manage to control it as it went "darting through the air at a speed of several hundred feet per second!" Grant all that, yet "it is the speed alone that sustains him. How is he ever going to stop?" Present-day familiarity with the airplane makes that question appear silly; in its own day, before anyone in the world had actually seen an airplane, it was not so easy to answer.

The argument was a muted one, in any case, and a good part of the otherwise occupied public could not even visualize the concept of heavier-than-air flight, or quite understand how it differed from lighter-than-air. Balloons or flying machines, they were all "air-ships."

These discussions in the press were almost always hypothetical, with little of practical experience to bolster either side. Only now and again would some unknown inventor cause a passing flurry of interest by designing and patenting and, sometimes, actually building a machine. Mostly, these involved highly fanciful, thoroughly unscientific birdlike designs, with flapping wings meant to be moved either mechanically (muscle power exerted on a gear arrangement) or by steam engine. Since the founding of the United States Patent Office, plans for nearly two hundred of these flapping-wing contraptions had been registered. Of the few constructed, none ever gave the least sign of a desire to leave the ground.

There were soberer minds at work on the problem, of course, but their studies progressed slowly, if at all, usually without much public notice. Still, in the twenty years before Wilbur began his studies, on no fewer than four occasions, full-size, fixed-wing, propeller-driven airplanes were built and tried, all unsuccessfully. The only one of the four that Wilbur could have read about as it happened was the prodigious attempt of Hiram Maxim in England. From the reports reaching America, it must have seemed to Wilbur—and to everyone else—that the age of flight had arrived.

Maxim, one of the most brilliant engineers and inventors of the day, was the designer of the first efficient machine gun. This, together with improvements in gas generating plants, steam engines, and vacuum pumps, had made him wealthy (and, it has been claimed, he very nearly beat Edison to the electric light). When he took up the problem of flight he placed himself, perhaps inevitably, among those who believed that the secret lay in the motor. He was convinced that power to give and maintain speed through the resisting air was the first and almost the only fundamental requirement. Matters such as the sustaining function of the wings and the balance controls were, to him, of secondary importance, easily to be achieved. He also felt that previous experimenters had been hampered by working on too small a scale. Consequently, seized by an irresistible urge toward gigantism, he designed and had built a huge experimental apparatus weighing fully four tons.

It consisted of a wooden platform, eight feet wide by forty long, mounted on wheels and carrying a large steam engine of no less than 300 horsepower. On the platform there were also a water tank, pumps, generator, and a "steering cabinet," with enough space left over to accommodate a pilot and two passengers. Spread over this platform, on steel tubing, were the fabric wings, a crazy-quilt combination of shapes and surfaces that extended a full twenty feet on either side and forty feet from front to back. The outer ends of the wings rose slightly in a modified V-shape, an old idea which was supposed to give automatic stability. Attached to the wings at front and back were smaller horizontal surfaces meant to act as crude elevators for controlling the fore-and-aft attitude. Looming at the rear were pusher propellers, two of the largest ever built, each measuring eighteen feet from tip to tip.

Designed as an experimental rig to be run on a track, with outriggers engaged to a guide rail to prevent the wheels from rising more than a few inches, Maxim gave this astonishing apparatus its first real test in August 1894. News of the heartening result, as it appeared in *The New York Times*, was strangely brief, but there was no mistaking its import. "Maxim Has a Flying Machine," announced the headline. The two-paragraph story stated that the inventor and two passengers "have traveled 500 feet with it."

A few days later the *Times* carried the news that "Maxim's Flying Car" was in the process of being adapted to large-scale air travel. This was corrected by Maxim himself, who explained that his first purpose was not to use his invention for passenger service, but as a "military observer." And with that confident pronouncement, Maxim and his wonderful machine disappeared, finally and entirely, from the aeronautical firmament. Balked in his further experiments, he gave up, having expended something like a hundred thousand dollars.

The truth about Maxim's "flight," which the public was not to learn for some time, was rather different. The machine did rise its few inches—probably the first time in history that a full-size, heavier-than-air machine had lifted from level ground under its own power (but *only* lifted and *not* in free or sustained flight). After it had proceeded a few hundred feet one outrigger broke through the guide rail and the obstreperous monster threatened to rear up out of control. Maxim hastily cut the engine and the machine settled roughly to rest, askew on the track and badly damaged.

Though it was a dead-end effort, Maxim's work did demonstrate, even if fleetingly, the simple fact that air pressure could actually lift such an enormous weight as eight thousand pounds, something only surmised before. It also brought renewed attention to the propeller as means of propulsion and hinted at the possibilities of the elevator for longitudinal control (both of these were old ideas, having first been tried in connection with balloons).

But Maxim also introduced a confusion that was to persist for a long time, even in aeronautical circles. Almost any surface, even one devoid of aerodynamic qualities, if pushed or driven at a positive angle (leading edge raised) against the wind or air with enough force, will leave the ground and will hop or jump some distance before coming to earth. Such a jump, depending on the size and design of the surface, the strength of the winds, and other factors, might easily cover several hundred feet. This of course does not constitute a "flight," since true flight requires sustaining power after the original impetus has been expended. While that point may be easily appreciated now, in the beginning, when all things aeronautical were new, it was not always understood.

Whether Maxim's experiments, misguided and abortive as they were, interested Wilbur beyond the normal curiosity felt by most people is doubtful, and another year was to pass before he encountered the reports of Lilienthal's gliding. While the German had been at work long before Maxim began, from the start he had taken a different, more modest approach, beginning with a minute study of birds and bird flight. From his painstaking investigation, covering perhaps twenty years, he had evolved a form of wing that would sustain his weight, allowing him to descend in safety from a fifty-foot hilltop in graceful, more or less straight-line glides, some of nearly a thousand feet.

The essential discovery that made this possible, explained the writer in *McClure's,* was "the gentle parabolic curve" across the upper surface of the wing from front to back, which Lilienthal had freely copied from the birds. It was this delicate bulge that endowed the wing with lifting power, though exactly how or why Lilienthal could not say. While curvature in the wing was not entirely a new idea, it was obscure and doubtful. In the article Lilienthal is heard complaining that "there are still prominent investigators who will not see that the arched or vaulted wing includes the secret of the art of flight."*

In the bird's wing, he added, this essential curve is always a parabola, rising more or less abruptly at the front edge and gradually diminishing toward the rear. But, Lilienthal went on, "the simple parabola differs so little from the arc of a circle that I adopted the latter curve as the more practicable." He had even been able to determine the desired proportion for the greatest depth of this arc: it should be just one twelfth of the straight-line breadth of the wing, front to back.

His own wing, spreading from tip to tip, more than twenty feet, was "made almost entirely from closely woven muslin, washed with collodion to make it impervious to the air, and stretched upon a ribbed frame of split willow." Protruding backward from the wing there was a flimsy rudder consisting of two parts, a flat, horizontal blade, and a vertical one shaped rather like a large palm leaf. Both of these surfaces were immovable and had nothing to do with steering. Together, claimed Lilienthal, and acting automatically, they prevented "sudden changes in the equilibrium," keeping the glider and its pilot heading into the wind. Balancing was done by a skillful shifting of his dangling body, which altered the location of the center of gravity as needed. To a very small degree, he could change the direction of his glide but was unable to effect a real

* It is difficult, perhaps impossible, to say who first thought of using wing curvature in connection with human flight. The curve in the bird's wing had been noticed, of course, even in ancient times. The poet Ovid in the first century refers to it in his description of the artificial bird wings made by Daedalus for his son Icarus.

turn; circling flight was entirely beyond him and was never even attempted.

His method of starting the apparatus was properly birdlike. Standing on top of a hill with his wings folded behind him, Lilienthal would make a short run against the wind. When he reached the hill's sloping brow he would launch himself with a leap, at the same time spreading the wings, which were snapped to their full breadth on meeting the air, "whereupon he sails majestically along like a gigantic seagull."

So satisfied was Lilienthal with his performance, stated *McClure's*, that he would soon add a diminutive motor, to be run on the vapor of carbonic acid. This motor he intended to link to a small outer portion of each wing, providing power for flapping them in the manner of birds, for propulsion. He didn't bother to explain why he favored the flapping wing over the propeller. The fact itself (always ignored by modern extollers of the pioneering German, most often in connection with deprecation of the Wrights) is the best illustration of the maze of difficulties facing all who in the primitive years concerned themselves with the flying problem.

While hopeful of attaining some measure of true flying ability, however, Lilienthal was "far from supposing that my wings possess all the delicate and subtle qualities necessary to the perfection of the art of flight. But my researches show that it is well worth while to prosecute the investigations further."

With this article in *McClure's* the American press began to carry more frequent reports on Lilienthal, stimulating more minds than Wilbur's. (Inevitably, of course, not everyone was able to see the significance such gliding held for the future. By some, Lilienthal was dismissed as an eccentric with a new toy, and a dangerous one at that. He was derisively called "a flying squirrel," who could come down but "couldn't go up.")

Aside from admiration for the German's ingenuity and daring, what struck Wilbur most forcibly was the great inadequacy and danger of his control method, as well as the severe limits it placed on further experiment. Wings heading into the wind, Wilbur knew, even moving through still air, would not always tend to remain level, but with every gust or change in pressure on one wing or the other would lose lateral balance. About the same would hold true for longitudinal balance.

Lilienthal's way of dealing with this problem was consistent with his unvarying effort to imitate the birds. His body hung by the arms, on a special framework, below the wings, as the bird's body occupied a position lower than its wings. In each case, Lilienthal believed, gravity was the factor that determined balance. In flight, if his left wing began to rise he would kick his legs to the left, the sudden extra weight of his body bringing the wing down to the level again. The same simple maneuver would control the other wing as well as the longitudinal balance. The position also afforded advantages in starting and, especially, in landing, where the process became much like that of a parachute.

As a rough experimental tool, Wilbur realized, the method was valuable but it would work only for wings of fairly small size. In larger wings, if the disturbance was too sudden or too violent, the shifting of seventy or eighty pounds could hardly be expected to overcome it. Under the best of circumstances, moreover, the success of the method depended on a high degree of skill and agility. If anything further was to be learned from glider flight larger wings must be tried, yet that could hardly be done until some means were found to give more positive control.

Even at this early date, Wilbur's mind was reaching toward a logical formulation of the problem itself. As he later expressed it, the control factor must have the potential to increase in effectiveness in the same ratio as the disturbing factors.

Wilbur was pondering these things, reading the very sparse flight literature to be found in the Dayton libraries, when word came that his conclusions about Lilienthal's control had proven tragically correct. Early in August 1896, in an unusually high flight, the German's glider nosed over, resisting all his frantic kicking to right it. "The apparatus worked well for a few minutes," reported *The New York Times* with a minimum of technical understanding, "and Lilienthal flew quite a distance, when suddenly the machinery of the apparatus got out of order, and man and machine fell to the ground." The courageous aviator's neck was broken in the crash and he died the next day.

Meanwhile, another outstanding aeronautical feat had been accomplished, this time by an American. Wilbur was aware of it and he later said that it had "great influence" on his decision to enter the field himself.

Professor Samuel Langley, an astrophysicist of world renown and head of the Smithsonian Institution, three months before Lilienthal's death had succeeded in putting into the air for a sustained flight a large, unmanned model airplane. While it was not the first attempt at model flight, this was the first time in history that one had actually flown, and the event was very widely reported.

Looking rather like a monstrous dragonfly and weighing nearly thirty pounds, Langley's model had two sets of wings, set in tandem, that spread fourteen feet from tip to tip. It was powered by a tiny steam engine and driven by two pusher propellers. In May 1896, it was launched by catapult from the roof of a houseboat on the Potomac River. Controlless, except for a rudimentary tail and the same slight V-shape in the wings that Maxim had used, the model curved gracefully through the still air, then settled to the surface undamaged.

The full story of this historic, if limited, achievement was told by Langley in an illustrated article he wrote for the June 1897 *Mc-Clure's*. Reading it, Wilbur would have found much to spur him on, but he would also have found a great deal to discourage a neophyte. Langley's triumph had by no means been an easy one.

Fascinated by bird flight ever since his boyhood, Langley in 1886, at the height of his fame as a scientist, had defied ridicule to begin serious experimenting. Like Maxim, he believed that power was the answer, but unlike Maxim he felt that the principles of flight should first be established through study of unmanned models. It had taken him a full ten years of work, both in the laboratory and outdoors with models, before success finally came. Those ten years, even with the help and advice of other scientists, mechanics, engineers, and craftsmen, were largely a record of failure, with now and then a small technical advance, just enough to keep hope alive. At one point in his *McClure's* narrative, while he is describing the interminable frustrations of that decade, perhaps grown weary with his own steady recital of woes, he pauses to ask, "Has the reader enough of this tale of disaster?"

Then at last came the long-awaited triumph. The model, dubbed by its inventor an "aerodrome," was catapulted from the houseboat. "For the first time," wrote Langley, "the aerodrome swept continuously through the air like a living thing, and as second after second passed on the face of the stopwatch, until a minute had gone by, and it still flew on, and as I heard the cheering of the few spectators, I felt that something had been accomplished at last . . . at the end of a minute and a half (for which time only it was provided with fuel and water) it had accomplished a little over a half mile, and now it settled rather than fell into the river with a gentle descent. It was immediately taken out and was flown again with equal success, nor was there anything to indicate that it might not have flown indefinitely except for the limit put upon it."

A reader with even a casual interest in Langley's achievement would have been curious to know what, exactly, had been established. Had the model yielded up all the necessary secrets of flight? Was Langley about to enter on the construction of a full-size machine? Was man about to fly? Langley's claims in this regard were confident and in no way modest. He explained that in his opinion the model flights, brief as they were, had proved the "practicality" of the flying machine, which had for so long been "a type for ridicule." As for building a full-size version, his assured tone implied that there would be little difficulty in the way of such a move. But he had no room in the article to discuss larger machines, or to explain how "they may be built to remain for days in the air, or to travel at speeds higher than any with which we are familiar."

Surprisingly, Langley himself was not to be the one to carry this great effort to a conclusion. He had brought to a close the part of the work that seemed to be specially his, he explained, and for the next stage "it is probable the world may look to others." He gave no reason for thus seeming to bow out at a critical moment. Most readers would have guessed that he was speaking out of an utter weariness with the whole business. "Perhaps if it could have been foreseen at the outset," he confessed, "how much labor there was to be, how much of life would be given to it, and how much care, I might have hesitated to enter upon it at all."

But Professor Langley did not bow out. A secret agreement with the United States War Department, hastily made early in 1898 when a clash with Spain over Cuba seemed imminent, provided him with fifty thousand dollars and all necessary assistance in order to construct a true flying machine for use by the army. Six more years were to pass while Langley, having no doubt of ultimate success, labored to translate the techniques and dimensions of his model to larger reality.

That part of the story must wait, however. For at the very time that the eyes of the world were focused on Langley's first full-scale power tests, in December 1903, the then unknown Wright brothers would be poised in lonely obscurity on the sands of Kitty Hawk, ready to launch their own first attempt at powered flight. And in a way that has not been realized, Langley would play a crucial part in the Wrights' plans.

The Langley model flights of 1896, though they did supply further encouragement, had no effect on Wilbur's own rapidly forming ideas. He had, in fact, already made up his mind about the one choice that faced all those who would dabble in aeronautics. Power or control? Were the skies to be conquered by mounting a motor on wings that had, hopefully, been made automatically stable, and getting up into the air? Was the secret of flight indeed one of sufficient "motive power"? Or should the initial approach be more cautious, taken in stages, first learning in glider experiment how wings might be made to answer the dictates of a pilot, and when all was ready apply a motor? Wilbur unerringly chose control, and though that may now seem obvious, in Wilbur's time when all was cloudy conjecture, the pathway to success was not so clear.

For over two years after the death of Lilienthal, Wilbur did little about his interest in flight except read the few things he could find on the subject and spend many of his free hours, especially on Sundays, observing birds of all sorts. He even found a favorite spot for this birdwatching, a rugged location just outside Dayton called the Pinnacles. Here he would lie on his back for hours peering through field glasses at the wheeling, soaring creatures that so effortlessly, so mysteriously, commanded the invisible forces of the atmosphere.

It is arresting to picture this intense, silent man of thirty, quietly dreaming of human flight while most of the other young men of Dayton—of the world—dreamed only of a spanking new buggy and a fine span of horses (the rattling, sputtering horseless carriage was then only for the very rich; few Americans had even seen one); when entertainment in the gaslit homes was provided not by the radio, which was then unheard of, but by the piano and the scratchy gramophone; and when the newest proof of progress was the friction match.

4

Something in
the Wing Tips

In the spring of 1899 Wilbur began delving into the flying problem in earnest. Typically, his approach was an orderly one, a careful survey of all that had already been done or thought on the topic. For guidance as to study materials, and no doubt because of Langley's connection with it, he wrote to the Smithsonian Institution. In his letter, while boldly announcing his staunch belief in the inevitability of human flight, he was careful to display a proper deference. "I am an enthusiast, but not a crank," he cautioned. ". . . I wish to avail myself of all that is already known and then if possible add my mite to help on the future worker who will attain success."

The Smithsonian's answer was prompt. About June 6 a package arrived at the Wright home containing four pamphlets and a list of suggested books. The pamphlets, reprints from Smithsonian publications, included technical works by Langley and Lilienthal. More stimulating than these, to Wilbur, was a short treatise called *The Empire of the Air*, by Louis Pierre Mouillard, a French engineer and ardent early apostle of glider flight.

Wilbur was later to say that Mouillard's pamphlet was "one of the most remarkable pieces of aeronautical literature" ever published. His reading of it, he admitted, filled him with new inspiration. It was not inspiration of the technical kind, for Mouillard had been a failure when it came to actual gliding. Rather, it proceeded from the infectious tone with which the Frenchman expressed his beliefs.

"If there be a domineering, tyrant thought," Mouillard insisted, "it is the conception that the problem of flight may be solved by man. When once this idea has invaded the brain it possesses it exclusively. It is then a haunting thought, a walking nightmare, impossible to cast off." Mouillard wrote in 1881, a time when there were very few people in any country who would listen to talk of balloonless flight. His main purpose was to pierce this crust of incredulity.

"O blind humanity," he exhorted, "open thine eyes and thou shalt see millions of birds and myriads of insects cleaving the atmosphere. All these creatures are whirling through the air without the slightest float; many of them are gliding therein, without losing height hour after hour, on pulseless wings without fatigue; and after beholding this demonstration, given by the source of all knowledge, thou wilt acknowledge that aviation is the path to be followed."

Mouillard's conclusions were based on years of observations of the great soaring birds, those that are found only in the hot regions of the world, notably the *Gyps fulvus,* the large tawny vulture of Africa (Mouillard lived for many years in Egypt). These magnificent creatures could stay in the air for hours, hardly moving their wings, but when Mouillard published his work little was known about them in Europe or America, as also little was known of the giant condor of Peru or the astonishing albatross with its ability to hover at its ease in the sky for days. Even the great California condor was then virtually unknown to science.

In the always fascinating realm of the might-have-been, it thus can be said that geography itself contributed to delaying the invention of the airplane. If the spectacular example of these huge birds, these living prototypes, had been daily before the eyes of European scientists it is more than likely that the manned glider would have made its appearance—who knows how many centuries before? (Using only wood, cloth, and cord, the glider might of course have been invented at any time. Psychology, not lack of materials or ability, must explain its oversight.) And if the glider had been a commonplace when the internal combustion engine appeared, then crude airplanes would quite likely have limped into the skies over France or England or Germany perhaps thirty years before the triumph at Kitty Hawk. In that case the perfected airplane would exist today as the product of many men's minds, instead of being born almost entirely out of one man's genius and desire. And the history of the world for the last century, too, would have been different. But that is all might-have-been.

Wilbur—now himself a prisoner of that haunting thought—had his already glowing imagination even further heated by Mouillard's ringing words. When, in later years, certain French aeronautical circles arrogantly and falsely claimed that the Wrights had stolen important ideas from Mouillard, who was then dead, Wilbur effectively deflated the claims but did so gently, never losing his admiration for the prophetic Frenchman.

The books recommended by the Smithsonian included *Progress in Flying Machines,* a valuable historical roundup by Octave Chanute, and an annual publication ambitiously called *The Aeronautical Journal,* of which three numbers had been issued, those for 1895–97. This journal attempted to make available to experimenters all that had been done, and was being done, on the problem of flight. It did not discriminate, and in its pages could be found rumor as well as fact, theory as well as experiment, treatises on flapping wing flight as well as dissertations on propeller power, the writings of Maxim, Langley, and Lilienthal, even some of Leonardo da Vinci's.* Wilbur soon procured these books and a number of other writings and settled down to a feast of study. What he learned more than surprised him.

While serious interest in heavier-than-air flight, he found, reached back at least four hundred years, to the pioneering but abortive studies of da Vinci, and had attracted the attention of many outstanding inventors and scientists—Alexander Graham Bell and Edison, to name two of the better known—little of proven worth

---

* A great deal of nonsense has recently been written about da Vinci's place in the history of flight, including the claim that if he had had a motor he could have flown. Actually, da Vinci knew nothing of the basic principles of flight, never even envisioned the possibility of a glider. For further comment see the Notes.

had been established. Until the daring Lilienthal had floated on his wings, no one had ever been able to sustain any kind of apparatus in the air. Over the centuries a number of men, with more ambition and courage than knowledge, had tried. The only result had been broken limbs and permanent discouragement.

Before Wilbur's own century all hopes of powered flight had centered on the flapping of wings, mechanically or by use of a steam engine. It was a remarkable Englishman, Sir George Cayley, a wealthy dabbler in sundry scientific matters early in the nineteenth century, who took the indispensable first step toward freeing aeronautical thought from slavish imitation of the bird.

Dimly, Cayley perceived that the two functions combined in the bird's wing—those of sustaining and propelling—might, for man's purpose, be separated. Some sort of rigid surface or plane, he thought, might provide the lift, while propulsion might be managed by separate appendages for flapping. He even tried once or twice to build unmanned gliders, but these depended on a wing that was almost square in shape and showed little promise.

Considering the time when Cayley began his work, the ingenuity with which he pursued his studies, and the ease with which he repeatedly glimpsed truths that would find their development only much later, he is an impressive figure. Today he is legitimately seen as the man who first put aeronautics on a scientific basis, even if gropingly. But he, too, became lost in a maze of conjecture. To the end of his life—he died in 1857—he continued designing machines meant to be propelled by wing flapping.

It was only as the nineteenth century neared its midpoint that the idea of the now familiar fixed-wing, propeller-driven airplane was conceived, envisioned whole in one imaginative burst, by another Englishman, William S. Henson. A manufacturer of lace by profession, and with no discernible credentials as either mechanic or scientist, in 1842 Henson created a considerable public stir by announcing that he was forming a company to build "aerial carriages." These futuristic contrivances, he assured investors, would transport passengers to the far corners of the earth, not quite in the twinkling of an eye but still with heady speed—twenty-four hours from London to Peking was one blithe estimate.

Elaborate drawings, in detail, of the machine Henson planned to manufacture were printed in newspapers around the world. Of really ingenious design, based largely on the ideas of Cayley and others, the plane was to have a streamlined cabin slung beneath a single fifty-foot wing. For steering, it sported an upside-down rudder and there were to be two four-bladed propellers worked by a steam engine. This marvel would take off, explained its inventor, not from level ground but from a long down-ramp run. In flight it would use its engines and propellers only to gain altitude for gliding. Unfortunately Henson had gotten a little ahead of himself and he soon found that it was a great deal easier to conjure up an aerial carriage, and draw a picture of it, than to make it fly. His grand ambitions came to grief when his small-scale experimental models refused to behave. Henson himself soon faded from view.

His original ideas about propeller propulsion, however, undoubtedly derived from the efforts being made in his own day to fit propellers to balloons, did not even set the style for the future. Most experimenters continued to feel that human flight must imitate the birds even in this respect. Still, after Henson aeronautics did receive an increased amount of attention, much of it ingenious if not quite fruitful laboratory work.

It was yet another Englishman, Francis Wenham, who in 1866 first insisted on the importance of the curve or vaulting in the upper surface of the wing. It was also Wenham who first brought home the fact that the fixed wing, instead of being one very broad unmanageable surface, might instead be made shorter with two, three, or even four surfaces set above each other. This suggestion, which proved useless in the hands of its deviser, was carried further by the American, Octave Chanute, who reduced the multiple tiers to two, and imparted strength to the biplane formation by adapting a standard method of bridge trussing for its bracing. And it was a young Frenchman, Alphonse Penaud, who about 1870, while working with rubber band models, hit on the V-shaped wing as a means of providing automatic stability.

Despite these few tentative advances, *none of which at that time stood out from the mass of conjecture so clearly as they do now*, the total result of Wilbur's studies was to convince him that there was, in reality, no such thing as a "science" of flight. There was only a

Wilbur Wright.

Orville Wright.

ABOVE: The Wrights' first camp at Kitty Hawk, 1900. The tent, anchored by ropes to the tree, was pitched on the windswept sands just south of Kitty Hawk. It housed the glider as well as the brothers.

BELOW: The Wrights' first experimental glider being flown as a kite at Kitty Hawk, 1900. The protrusion in front is actually the forward elevator, here concealed by the angle. In the distance is the Atlantic Ocean and the white line of surf.

ABOVE: The workshed built by the brothers at Kitty Hawk, 1901. Wilbur Wright is standing. Seated l. to r. are three visitors: E. C. Huffaker, Octave Chanute, and George Spratt. The tent that served as living quarters can be seen to the left of the shed.

BELOW: Launching the 1901 glider from the top of the West Hill, with Wilbur as pilot. The helpers are William and Dan Tate, Kitty Hawk residents. Lifting the glider by its wingtip struts, they would run with it into the wind, then release it.

Wilbur Wright in a high glide at Kitty Hawk, 1901. His hands grasp the elevator levers while his feet control the wing-warping for lateral balance. The following year the warp control was linked to a hip cradle.

fearsome jumble of unsupported opinions, doubtful claims, un-
tested observations, wild guesses, and bare and often contradictory conclusions. He himself aptly described the situation as he
found it in June of 1899. It is a statement worth remembering now,
when the murky night out of which the airplane was born has
faded before the blaze of full knowledge.

> At that time there was no flying art in the proper sense of the
> word, but only a flying problem. Thousands of men had thought
> about flying machines, and a few had even built machines which
> they called flying machines, but these machines were guilty of al-
> most everything except flying. Thousands of pages had been written
> on the so-called science of flying, but for the most part the ideas set
> forth, like the designs for machines, were mere speculations and
> probably ninety percent was false. Consequently, those who tried to
> study the science of aerodynamics knew not what to believe and
> what not to believe. Things which seemed reasonable were very
> often found to be untrue, and things which seemed unreasonable
> were sometimes true . . . things which we at first supposed to be
> true were really untrue . . . other things were partly true and
> partly untrue . . . a few things were really true. . . .

The same materials that Wilbur studied are still available today,
and even a cursory look at them amply bears out the truth of that
statement. What Wilbur encountered in 1899 was perhaps the most
chaotic accumulation of hypothetical groping ever gathered around
a single scientific problem. Yet within a matter of only three weeks
from the start of his serious studies, he managed to solve the great
riddle of lateral control, firmly grasping the one essential secret that
would eventually bring the airplane to birth.

Wilbur's theory of lateral balance involved a simultaneous movement of the wing tips, a "torsion," as he called it. If the *underside*
of the *right* wing tip, while proceeding through the air, were to be
exposed at a slightly increased angle, the added pressure from beneath would make it rise. Similarly, if the *topside* of the *left* tip
were given more exposure, it would drop. Thus, if these movements were done simultaneously, the entire apparatus could be

made to revolve on itself. By reversing the process when necessary, a disturbance of equilibrium effecting either side could be
corrected and the wings held in any desired attitude.

This theory, so startlingly simple when once formulated, had occurred to him one day, he said later, while he was watching the
nervous flight of some pigeons. It resulted not from a direct sighting of the wing movements—no eye could follow such slight and
rapid flutterings on so small a scale—but by a species of deduction
that implies many hours of observation. He first became aware of
something stirring in his imagination when he realized that the os-
cillation of one pigeon's outstretched wings—the tilting from side to
side—was occurring with unusual speed, much too fast to be explained by a shifting of the bird's body.

"These lateral tiltings," he recalled, "first one way and then the
other, were repeated four or five times very rapidly; so rapidly in
fact as to indicate that some other force than gravity was at work."
What that force might be was a question that occupied him for
some unknown length of time. Then,

> the thought came that possibly it had adjusted the tips of its wings
> about a lateral transverse axis so as to present one tip at a positive
> angle and the other at a negative angle, thus, for the moment, turn-
> ing itself into an animated windmill, and that when its body had
> revolved on a longitudinal axis as far as it wished, it reversed the
> process and started to turn the other way. Thus the balance was
> controlled by using dynamic reactions of the air, instead of shifting
> weight.

Only one other time did Wilbur make direct reference to the
phenomenon he had visualized in the pigeon. In this instance he
noted it as a direct sighting in connection with the slower, lazier
flight of some large buzzards. "If the rear edge of the right wing is
twisted upwards," he explained in an early letter, "and the left
downward, the bird becomes an animated windmill, and instantly
begins to turn, a line from its head to its tail being the axis. It thus
regains its level even if thrown on its beam ends, so to speak, as I
have frequently seen them." A secondary method, he says in the
same letter, concerned the drawing in of one wing to reduce its
area, but this was of questionable worth. It was the torsion prin-

ciple, he was sure, that gave the birds their marvelous and minute control.

Quite likely, both of these incidents took place while he was roaming the Pinnacles, squinting up at the bird-filled sky, but he never said just when they happened or gave any other details of the circumstances. Consequently, in what exact manner the solution "came," or how long a period intervened between sighting and deduction, are questions that remain tantalizingly unanswered.*

Pursuing his preliminary studies in the summer of 1899, Wilbur found, to his relief, that the secret of lateral control by torsion of the wing tips was still a secret. While three or four men in the previous thirty years had indeed flirted with something like it in their technical writings or in experiments, it had always been in a vague, half-understood way. Not one investigator had ever seen it as a primary method in itself; nor had anyone used it or anything remotely like it in an actual experimental machine or model. Neither had anyone recorded any objections to it or uncovered any possible deficiencies. The way was open for Wilbur to proceed. He need only devise a mechanical embodiment of the principle. This, as he was now well aware, would be no easy task since lightness could not be sacrificed and strength of construction was a prime necessity.

At the very outset Wilbur was facing, in its pristine form, the very problem that still bedevils the aeronautical engineer—the eternal effort to find a proper balance between the power to lift and sustain, on the one hand, and on the other, the power to control and propel; the effort to diminish weight while increasing or at least not lessening power.

He was also thinking further ahead than the moment. The records make clear that from the very beginning Wilbur knew what Lilienthal, for all his ingenuity, did not know: that wings which were controllable in a glide, front-to-back as well as side-to-side, needed only a motor and a propeller to turn them into a true flying machine. And those two items, in the year 1899, appeared to present no great difficulties of achievement. As the last summer of the nineteenth century glowed across the land, there had coalesced in a most unlikely mind, and in a not very likely place, the basic elements of the airplane.

* Some speculations on this point will be found in the Notes.

Some six weeks after Wilbur began seeking a way to incorporate the torsion principle into a glider, the solution presented itself, suddenly and completely. It was still another of the instances, so numerous in the story of science, of an unconscious leap from the known to the unknown by way of some quite familiar and everyday thing. In this case, the familiar thing was a humble item that he had handled hundreds of times in the bicycle shop.

Toward the end of the third week in July—perhaps the morning of Saturday, July 22—Wilbur was at the shop alone, Orville having taken the day off to act as escort to his sister and one of her friends. The quiet of the shop was broken by the tinkling of the bell over the door and a customer entered wheeling a bike with a flat tire. Wilbur upended the bicycle on the floor, removed the tire, and saw that the inner tube was too damaged for repair. He reached to a shelf, took down a narrow box, pulled out a new inner tube, and in a few moments had the wheel repaired. The bell tinkled again as the customer left.

Wilbur picked up the empty inner tube box from the counter, intending to throw it in the waste bin. Something about the feel of it in his hands made him pause. Absently, his fingers had been squeezing at the corners, distorting the flimsy cardboard from its right-angle shape. He looked down at it and in that moment all the images of wings that had been soaring and tumbling through his dreams for months now suddenly ceased their agitation and faded away, leaving in their place one bright vision.

Instead of seeing in his hands an empty box—some two inches square by ten in length—he saw a perfect model of biplane wings, the upper surface connected to the lower surface by the perpendicular sides of the box.

He sat down at his desk, took a pencil, and drew a series of heavy vertical lines from top to bottom along each of the two sides, four in front and four in back, so that they had the appearance of struts. Then he tore off the end flaps, put the transformed box on his desk, leaned back and stared at it. Simple! Marvelously simple!

Picking up the box, he held one end in each hand. The fingers of the left hand tightened slightly: the cardboard was distorted so that the rear margins dropped a bit, exposing more of the under-surface. At the same time the pressing fingers of the other hand had distorted the right side of the box, but in reverse, so that the rear margins rose slightly, exposing more of the top surface. There in his hands, Wilbur thought jubilantly, was the embodiment of his torsion principle. And it was the biplane conformation, as reflected in the form of the empty box, that would make it possible.

Instantly Wilbur had seen that a set of wires arranged on small pulleys between two real airplane surfaces, connected by hinged struts or uprights, would easily accomplish the same warping effect that his fingers had given to the box. Thus the wing itself, made both flexible and strong, and with the addition of almost no weight, would carry the essential principle of balance within itself, just as did the wings of birds.

Anxious to make some quick test of his idea and to try a few details of construction, during the following weeks Wilbur worked at a feverish pace, paying little attention to the bicycle business. First he made a small model out of split bamboo—two wings, rigid in overall length but flexible enough for the slight twisting necessary, connected to each other by bamboo struts that were hinged at top and bottom where they met the wing edges, and braced by a truss of stout threads. For a day or two his eager hands gently flexed and twisted this model, his closely peering eyes searching for additional revelations. Still impatient, he then began work on a much larger model, one that could be flown as a kite. At this stage, he knew, all the theorizing in the world was not worth ten minutes of experiment, and he wanted to submit his idea to the natural action of wind.

Working late into each night, he completed the second model by July 27, less than a week after the incident with the inner tube box. Its wingspread reached five feet. Each cloth-covered wing measured about a foot from front edge to rear and was slightly "vaulted" or curved, as Lilienthal had prescribed. The warping action was to be controlled by cords reaching to Wilbur's hands on the ground.

Now the instinctive caution and desire for secrecy that was to become so marked a trait of his work made its first appearance. "I flew this apparatus about the end of July 1899," he later recalled, "in a field west of the city of Dayton. This field is now a part of the city, but at that time a retired place where I thought no one would intrude." Orville was not present at these tests, and except for two or three schoolboys who sauntered over to investigate the man with the strange-looking kite, no one did intrude. The tests gave complete satisfaction, the kite model always responding promptly to the warping of the surfaces.

Ironically, even at this very first of the series of experiments that would lead to flight, there was a near-accident, a small one but with hidden significance. With the kite aloft in a strong breeze, it unexpectedly nosed downward, diving directly at the boys. The movement was so sudden and the descent so rapid that they didn't have time to run, but threw themselves down on their faces, covering their heads. The kite skimmed harmlessly over them as Wilbur hastily backed off, yanking on the lead string.

While Wilbur did not realize it at the time, in this trivial fright he had had his first encounter with a phenomenon that was to cause him a great deal of difficulty at Kitty Hawk, threatening him with failure; a phenomenon that was in reality the very thing that had caused Lilienthal's glider to crash, killing him. It concerned the curvature in the wing.

Wilbur in his model had made this the arc of a circle, following the German's claim that the arc differed little in its action from the simple parabola that had been built by nature into the bird wing. Lilienthal was wrong. The difference between the arc and the parabola was fundamental. Lilienthal's failure to appreciate that fact had kept him from fully understanding that even in a parabolic curve there still might lurk subtle hazards. It was Wilbur who would establish this, both the fact of the danger and the reason for it, and he would do it by repeatedly risking his own life in the air.

5

Kitty Hawk 1900

On the evening of September 6, 1900, Wilbur Wright boarded a train in Dayton, taking with him a large trunk into which he had packed his disassembled first flying machine.* This was a full-size experimental glider which would also be used as a man-carrying kite.

In the trunk, in addition to a supply of tools and an assortment of metal fittings, were over fifty thin wooden rods, all about five feet in length. Thirty of these, to serve as the ribs in the wings, were curved slightly at one end to provide the necessary arch. Twelve of them, the struts that would connect the two wings, were perfectly straight and all were precisely machined to a smooth finish. The rest were spares, in case of breakage, a possibility that Wilbur had to admit was not unlikely.

There were also a number of spools of wire, made of fifteen-gauge spring steel (about $\frac{1}{16}$ inch thick), as well as a bulky, carefully folded bundle of smooth white cloth known as French sateen. Only one component of the machine was not in the trunk, the long spars needed to form the leading and trailing edges of the wings.

* The Wrights, following the usage of the time, used the word "machine" to describe their gliders, as well as the later powered planes. I have followed that practice, the context making quite clear what is meant.

These were planned to be eighteen feet long and Wilbur intended to pick them up in some lumberyard near his destination.

Traveling alone, he was bound for an isolated location off the North Carolina coast, a tiny hamlet on the unique elongated sandbar called the Outer Banks. Stretching for more than a hundred miles along the eastern edge of the United States, the Banks stand like a barrier reef against the stormy Atlantic. In their northern extent they lie fairly close to the Virginia shore, but at their middle the line of the North Carolina coast falls unevenly away to the west, creating Albermarle, Pamlico, and Roanoke sounds, calm and serene most of the time yet liable to be violently stirred by the oceanic frenzy that periodically sweeps across the loose, low-lying sands of the Banks.

Along the endless, lonely stretches of surf-pounded beach on the ocean side of the Banks, at intervals of seven miles, stood government lifesaving stations, whose personnel day and night scanned the waters offshore for ships in trouble. The lower Banks, especially around the Cape Hatteras area, presented some of the stormiest and most treacherous waters in the world; so many ships had been wrecked, and lives lost, that it was known as the Graveyard of the Atlantic.

Wilbur had chosen the spot after reading reports of wind velocities supplied in answer to his request by the Weather Bureau at Washington, and exchanging letters with one or two residents of the little Banks hamlet of Kitty Hawk. One of these, J. J. Dosher, who had charge of the U.S. Weather Bureau station there, explained that "the beach here is about one mile wide, clear of trees or high hills and extends for nearly sixty miles same condition. The wind blows mostly from the north and northeast, September and October . . . I'm sorry to say you could not rent a house here, so you will have to bring tents."

William Tate, Kitty Hawk's postmaster, was a little more particular. "You would find here nearly any type of ground you could wish," Tate wrote. "You could, for instance, get a stretch of sandy land one mile by five with a bare hill in center 80 feet high, not a tree or a bush anywhere to break the evenness of the wind current." Tate, as later became evident, had caught fire at the idea of having glider experiments in his own back yard, and he made an effort to be convincing. "This in my opinion," he insisted, "would be a fine place; our winds are always steady, generally from 10 to 20 miles velocity per hour."

Back in Dayton, Orville had been left in charge of the bicycle shop with the understanding that if business were not too heavy and a dependable replacement could be found, then he was to follow. If Orville was unable to get away then Wilbur was prepared to carry out his experiments alone, enlisting local help when necessary.

At Norfolk, Virginia, where he stopped over for a night, he met with an unexpected disappointment. The lumberyard could not supply the eighteen-foot lengths of spruce needed to form the wing edges; only sixteen-foot boards were available for sawing into strips. This meant that the carefully worked out specifications of the glider would have to be altered, reducing the total wing area by about thirty-five square feet, and this in turn meant that stronger winds than anticipated would be required to lift the machine. In addition, the sateen cloth wing covering, so meticulously prepared at home, would have to be cut down to the new size and resewn. Aside from the inconvenience and delay, the heightened wind requirements could conceivably rob him of practice time, since stronger winds were not to be expected daily.

Further aggravation awaited him at Elizabeth City, near Albemarle Sound, where he planned to hire a boat for the forty-mile trip to the Banks. The small settlements nestled far out among the dunes, it appeared, were strange territory even to North Carolina's coastal dwellers. Among those to whom Wilbur first spoke no one had heard of Kitty Hawk. And there were no boats available. It took a day and a half of inquiry before he was able to find a man who had some idea of Kitty Hawk's location and who also had a boat for hire.

Not the least of Kitty Hawk's attractions as an experiment ground was its isolation, so that the nearer Wilbur got to it the more satisfied he must have felt. The final leg of the journey would provide him with the ultimate confirmation of its seclusion. What should have been an afternoon's sail became instead a two-day odyssey, and it was only by good fortune that Wilbur and his trunk did not find a last resting place at the bottom of Albemarle Sound.

On Tuesday, September 11, he engaged a small, flat-bottomed schooner, supposedly used as a fishing boat by its owner, Israel Perry. To reach the boat from Elizabeth City, Wilbur, his baggage, the lumber, and a boy who served as deck hand were cramped into a leaky skiff for the three-mile row downriver. The water lapping the gunwale of the overloaded skiff, along with the leaks, made it necessary to bail constantly.

Climbing onto the deck of the schooner, Wilbur saw with disgust that the condition of the skiff had been prophetic. The boat's sails were rotting, all the ropes were badly frayed and worn, and even the rudderpost was half decayed. He looked into the cabin and found that it, too, was dirty and vermin-infested. Had the day not been fair, with a light west wind blowing, he would have turned back. A five- or six-hour run over the placid waters of the sound, he thought, would not put too much strain on the decrepit craft.

By mid-afternoon the schooner was underway, its tattered sails cringing before the slight breeze. It was almost dark before the boat left the river and entered the sound, the waters of which stretched to the horizon with no sign of land. Soon the breeze freshened and shifted around to south by east, making progress doubly difficult and whipping the surface into choppy waves. The schooner labored forward but went sliding frequently to leeward, its light load and flat bottom offering little resistance to the crosswind. Steadily the weather roughened as the schooner, rolling and pitching, sprang a number of leaks and began to take on water by the bow. As midnight neared, the wind was at gale force. With his boat being tossed at the mercy of the angry waters, Perry decided not to try for Kitty Hawk but to make a run north for shelter.

Suddenly, with a roar the foresail ripped loose from its boom and fluttered wildly on the mast. Wilbur and the boy made their way forward on the dangerously slanting deck, scarcely able to see for the darkness. They managed to haul in the canvas and lash it down. A few minutes later there was another roar as the mainsail also tore loose from its boom. After another struggle, Wilbur and the boy were able to secure it, but now they had only a small jibsail left, and if that went the schooner would be helpless. The three on board knew that their aged boat was not equipped to ride out such fury.

With no choice left, Perry took a dangerous gamble. He swung the stern into the wind, praying that the sudden shift would not capsize him. Groaning and heeling, the schooner managed to stay upright and then scudded erratically to the north, taking on water and shuddering in the pounding sea. It was after one o'clock when the exhausted party slid into the shelter of land. They had been battling the storm for nearly four hours.

The battered schooner lay to under the shelter of the Point until the afternoon of September 12, then with sails patched up and only a slight breeze blowing, it ventured into the now calm waters of the sound. By dusk Wilbur could make out a flat shadow of land capping the entire length of the horizon and at nine the schooner entered serene Kitty Hawk Bay. A short while later it tied up at a small, deserted wharf on which stood a general store, now unlit and shuttered. It was too late and too dark to go anywhere, so Wilbur spent another night on board, sleeping on deck.

Next morning early he unloaded his trunk and lumber, waved good-bye to Perry, and inquired at the store for the home of William Tate. A boy named Baum agreed to take him there and after a walk of a quarter-mile over a road of hard-packed sand, he arrived at Tate's. The house was a severely simple two-story structure with unplaned siding, whose bare, unpainted boards had faded to a mottled gray that blended well with the uninterrupted sweep of ocean, sand, and sky.

Tate, his wife, and their daughter welcomed Wilbur and, on hearing that he had not eaten for two days, Mrs. Tate promptly served up a large plate of ham and eggs. Describing his voyage from Elizabeth City, Wilbur explained that there had been no time to think of eating, and if there had been, the dirty condition of the cabin would have banished even the most robust appetite. A small jar of jelly, slipped into his bag by his sister before he left home, had sufficed him.

While eating he looked round the room and was not surprised to find the interior in perfect keeping with the building's outside. There was no plaster on the board walls, which were bare of pictures, and the ceiling was raw, unvarnished pine. There were no carpets and only the necessary furniture. "There may be one or two better houses here," he remarked to his father in a letter a few days later, "but this is much above the average. You will see that there is little wealth and no luxurious living." Impressed by the austere life lived by the Banks people, he went on in the same letter to report that "the ground here is a very fine sand with no admixture of loam that the eye can detect, yet they attempt to raise beans, corn, turnips, etc., on it. Their success is not great but it is a wonder that they can raise anything at all."

Tate made his living, Wilbur soon found, as did most of the other Bankers, by combining various small occupations with seasonal activities as a fisherman. Tate served as the village postmaster and was also a commissioner of Currituck County. At that he had a good deal of free time, since the leisurely fishing season on the Banks ran for only about three months, starting in October. He readily agreed to lend Wilbur a hand whenever needed and confessed to being fascinated by the prospect of what he called "scientific kite flying."

After a restful night's sleep, Wilbur borrowed Tate's horse and small cart and hauled his trunk, baggage, and lumber up from the wharf. At a little distance from the house he set up a canvas lean-to and in its shelter began to assemble his glider.

His purpose on this trip was primarily to test the efficiency and range of his balance controls and to obtain practice in their use. The wing warping for lateral balance appeared, in concept, to be without flaw. The technique he had settled on for longitudinal control, however, was still an unknown quantity. He had decided to use an elevator—a small, horizontal surface, placed at the front rather than the rear, the better to prevent sudden dives—or as it was called in the parlance of the time, a "horizontal rudder." While not new to aeronautical experiment, knowledge of the elevator's function was still almost entirely theoretical; the actual technique of its operation no one knew.

Wilbur was well aware that proper use of both of these controls —should they in fact prove satisfactory—would depend on trained skills and these could be developed only by exhaustive practice. The skill of the pilot, he realized at a time when very few other experimenters had grasped the point, would play a major part in successful flight. In this, he had come face to face with the fine-edged dilemma that haunted all aeronautical pioneers.

A true flying machine could not be achieved without experimental free flight, in which the machine would be entirely committed to the uncertain embrace of the air, and with an operator in full control. Only when man and machine were able to spurn the earth, riding free for however long and returning in safety, could it be said that man had flown. Yet an operator could hardly trust himself aloft until he had gained the indispensable skills, and this he could not do until he had at his disposal a true flying machine on which to learn. Nothing quite like this situation had existed with regard to any other invention in history. Because the airplane would carry man into an alien, virtually unknown element, it was necessary for him to proceed in two opposing, directly contradictory, directions at once—he had *simultaneously* to invent the airplane and learn to use it. Let him seriously miscalculate in either direction and he would find awaiting him the possibility of serious injury and sudden death.

Wilbur's approach was to take each area alternately and by piecemeal. He would first fly the glider as a man-carrying kite, tethering it by a rope to a small wooden tower (a "derrick" he called it). The wind, blowing directly at the front of the glider and opposing the pull of the rope, would lift it to a height of perhaps fifteen feet. Stretched at full length in the center of the lower wing Wilbur would work the wing tips, for lateral control, by a lever at his feet. The lever to work the elevator, for vertical control, would be held in both hands.

Thus, with a minimum of hazard, he expected to spend hours every day in the air, testing the controls, learning their use and sharpening his skills. There was still danger, of course. The wind could not be expected always to blow evenly, and a strong gust could upset the glider in a flash, even hurl it abruptly to the ground.

Wilbur's father had expressed some such fears, for Wilbur assured him in a letter that "I do not expect to rise many feet from the ground, and in case I am upset there is nothing but soft sand to strike on. I do not intend to take dangerous chances, both because I do not wish to get hurt and because a fall would stop my experimenting, which I would not like at all. . . . Carelessness and overconfidence are usually more dangerous than deliberately accepted risks."

Only when he felt that he had gained some proficiency in control did Wilbur intend to attempt free glides, and these would also be taken in stages. He would launch himself first from very slight slopes, interested only in perfecting a landing process. No experimenter before him—not Lilienthal nor any of his imitators—had ever landed a glider while lying at full length on the lower wing, allowing the wing itself to make first contact with the earth. Such a technique had been pronounced too dangerous, for it seemed to deprive the pilot of all hope of slowing his speed before touching down.

A glider running to earth at even a moderate speed might easily crack something or flip over—with the operator's neck, head, and face taking the brunt of any such accident. Yet the position of the operator, Wilbur knew, was critical. With his system of control, a body dangling below the wings was simply a useless impediment, adding some five square feet of resistance, when the effort to diminish resistance paid heed to even a few square inches, down to studying the best cross-section for the thin struts that held the two wings together.

When he had worked out a proper landing technique, he then meant to try glides a little longer and higher, testing his skill at the controls in free flight. If all went well he would gradually lengthen his glides by starting from higher up and flying in stronger winds. Once at this point, with the question of equilibrium solved and his piloting skills honed, he would be ready to consider putting a motor on his wings, and then the airplane—human flight!—would be a reality. "When once a machine is under proper control under all conditions," he confidently wrote home, "the motor problem will be quickly solved."

Whether Wilbur thought he could achieve complete equilibrium during this one trip to Kitty Hawk is uncertain, but that he thought he might do it, and hoped he might, is clear from his letters, even as he mildly demurs. He does not, he explains to his father, "have any strong expectation of achieving the solution at the present time or possibly any time." Modestly, he hedges but leaves the door open to the possibility that he just might arrive back in Dayton with the proud announcement that he will now proceed to mount a motor on his wings.

The plan to fly the machine as a man-carrying kite, hooked to the derrick, was based on the apparent fact that one fundamental problem had already to a degree been solved, or so it appeared—that of the proper size and form of wing that would be able to ride the air in brief glides with an operator on board. The success of Lilienthal and his imitators had seemed to demonstrate this. Already in general circulation were standard tables of air pressures, showing what size wing could be expected to bear what weight. It was on the basis of these tables that Wilbur had constructed his own biplane wings.

Calculating such factors as his own 140 pounds, and the average strength of the winds at Kitty Hawk, he had decided on a wing area of 200 square feet, the machine itself to weigh not more than fifty pounds. This would give about one pound of load to one square foot of wing area. To lift and sustain this weight a wind of eighteen miles an hour would be needed. Now, however, because the spread of each wing would be slightly less than planned, he concluded he would need a wind of perhaps twenty-five miles per hour to lift the glider and hold it nearly horizontal against the pull of the rope. A minute sloping of the wings in the air, backward from the leading edge, was also planned for—about three degrees, in Wilbur's estimation.

The curvature or arch in the upper surface of the wings (he had by now learned to refer to this feature as "camber," the French word for *curve* which had been adopted by aeronautical writers, and which is still in use) was not the arc of a circle but a parabola. Neither was it the deep 1-in-12 recommended by Lilienthal, but a shallower compromise between the German's beliefs and some others—about 1-in-22. Wilbur had no precise reason for choosing a less pronounced camber, aside from some vague opinions he had read asserting that a deep camber somehow made a wing less stable.

It had been only when he came to the actual work of making the ribs, bending the thin wooden rods in a vise after steaming them, that he found himself faced with another question not answered by the literature. Where along the length of the rib should the greatest depth of curvature be applied? Flush at the front? A little way back? Lacking all knowledge of the true function of camber, his decision was hardly more than a guess. He placed it about three inches from the front edge.

Working long hours every day in his lean-to, slowly and with infinite pains, Wilbur put his machine together. For each wing he formed an oblong with the spars, then filled in with the ribs, spacing them about a foot apart. An essential part of the design was simple strength of construction, to reduce the chance of the machine's coming apart in the air when buffeted by strong winds or of sustaining damage in a rough landing. To this end, he worked with great care, actually testing every single piece of wood and every metal fitting, from the tiniest to the largest, that went into the machine.

This meticulous workmanship of Wilbur's was a personal ideal that was foreign to nearly every other experimenter of the time and it contributed in no small measure to his eventual success. He was never to abandon this ideal of confident self-reliance, this desire to see with his own eyes, to feel with his own hands, to accept nothing on trust, to check and recheck. Even by itself, this was an approach that set him apart from such men as Maxim and Langley, who were mainly thinkers, supplying designs to be constructed for them by hired workmen. In later years, when Wilbur had finally brought the airplane before the eyes of the world, this attitude was never relaxed, and his everlasting, unswervable attention to detail became an amazement to everyone who was allowed to be near him.

After about ten days the two wings were completed, ready to be joined by the struts. He then had to pause in order to shorten and resew the sateen covering. This he did in the Tate home, using Mrs. Tate's sewing machine, with the lady herself hovering about ready to help where she could and shaking her head at this sad waste of so much fine dress material. While he was at this task a letter arrived from Orville saying he would, after all, be able to get down. This was welcome news since Wilbur had begun to see that, for some of the experiments, at least two helpers would be necessary and so far he could count only on Tate.

On September 28 Orville arrived, bringing a large tent and a supply of foods, especially sugar, scarce on the Banks. The two planned to live and work in the tent, which was also large enough to house the finished glider. The next four days were occupied in setting up the tent a short distance south of Kitty Hawk, and in completing assembly of the machine.

The two wings, now encased in sateen, were joined by the five-foot struts, six at the front edge and an equal number set about a foot in from the rear edge. All were hinged at their extremities, where they joined the wing, to permit the movement necessary for warping. Next came the wire bracing, Wilbur's ingenious variation of the Chanute truss, which gave the glider great strength and permitted retightening of the whole assembly by taking up slack in only two wires, one at each end. Then followed the most critical operation of all, the threading in of the warping wires on a series of small pulleys. Finally the small, nearly square surface that would serve as the elevator was set on two wooden rods protruding from the center of the lower wing and reinforced by two more rods leading down from the upper wing. There was no tail of any kind, Wilbur having decided that the experience of others had proved its uselessness.

By the morning of Saturday, October 6, the glider was completed, the wooden tower erected, and the results of a year and a half of study and planning were ready for the first test. In the simple mechanism and simpler lines of the machine, now resting on the sands outside the tent, its bright wings reflecting the unclouded sun of a promising day, reposed all Wilbur's secret hopes for a new life.

The wooden tower had been put up on a level stretch of sand a short distance from the tent. The brothers lifted the glider, one at each tip with Tate helping in the middle, being careful to keep the leading edge dipped to ward off the wind, and carried it to the tower. The wind was a strong one, blowing about twenty-five miles an hour, as measured by a hand-held anemometer borrowed from the Kitty Hawk weather station.

Before sending the glider up to ride on the tower rope, Wilbur wanted to get some preliminary feel of the unique experience he had in store. A narrow section in the middle of the lower wing, about eighteen inches wide, had been left open and it was along this cavity that the operator was to ride, face down. His elbows would rest on the wing's leading edge, his hips on a wooden rung, his feet in contact with the warping lever.

Ducking under the wings, Wilbur brought his head and shoulders up through the opening. Orville and Tate each had a tight grip on ropes attached near the wing tips. Leaning forward, Wilbur put his weight on the wing, then lifted his feet. When he was comfortable the ropes were payed out slowly. The wind easily lifted the machine to a height of about fifteen feet.

Almost immediately the glider began to buck, the front dropping abruptly, then as quickly rising again as the full force of the wind struck the lowered rear edges, the whole apparatus wavering wildly from side to side. After a few moments in this blustery chaos, Wilbur's voice rose above the wind. "Let me down! Let me down!" he shouted anxiously. The men hauled on the ropes, grasped the wing tips, and forced the glider to the ground. Wilbur crawled off, a little sheepish at having shown fright. "What's the matter?" asked his brother. "I promised Pop I'd look after myself," Wilbur mumbled.

His fright, generated more by surprise than by actual fear, had been real and for the first time he was able to appreciate fully a remark that Lilienthal had made in the *McClure's* article. "No one can realize how *substantial* the air is," the German flyer had wisely insisted, "until he feels its supporting power beneath him." That the fright was also to some extent prompted by Wilbur's old concern for what he believed was a weakened heart is more than probable.

He climbed aboard again, this time with the glider held closer to earth, scarcely above the heads of the two helpers. The machine still rode unsteadily but the violent movements were not repeated, the wind pressing mostly against the underside of the sloping wings. Gingerly, he manipulated the warp and elevator controls. With a sense of satisfaction, he felt the machine subtly responding, rising or falling slightly by the nose, tilting a little first to one side then the other. After a half hour or so of this tentative practice he announced he was ready for the tower.

With the stout tower rope attached to the center of the lower wing and with Wilbur aboard, Orville and Tate allowed the glider to climb on the breeze until it stabilized at about the height of the tower—some fifteen feet. They then slackened their ropes and the machine floated free, held more or less stationary by the tower rope. It was an exhilarating experience for Wilbur as he worked the con-

trols, the ground shifting and dancing beneath him, the wind rushing against his narrowed eyes and whistling past his ears, enclosing
him in a very private world all his own.

His handling of the warping and elevator controls was still very
rough and instinctive. Having to think about and manipulate both
of these simultaneously, he soon found, demanded an instant touch
that was yet far beyond him. Still, the promise he could feel in the
machine was exciting. Then, gradually, it became apparent that
something was wrong.

During those moments when the wind blew evenly, allowing
the kite to hang approximately in one spot, it could be seen that
the wings were not being sustained in the expected attitude—nearly
parallel to the ground with a three-degree upward pitch at the
front. Instead, they sloped sharply into the wind, the whole apparatus riding at an angle Wilbur guessed must be at least twenty
degrees. Occasionally the wind gusted, exceeding thirty miles an
hour, but even then the angle of slope was reduced no more than
ten degrees or so. The glider still hung at an impossible angle for
flight, badly interfering with the response of the controls.

Wilbur stayed at the tower for about three hours, coming down
intermittently for rest and study. Then, in a disconsolate mood, he
called a halt for the day. The three men hauled the glider back to
the tent, where the brothers sat on the sand in earnest discussion.

What could be the defect, they wondered. Was the camber perhaps too shallow? The proportion used for it had, after all, been
only an educated guess. Was the sateen wing covering excessively
porous, allowing the wind to force its way through and dissipating
the lifting pressure? Were the wings themselves too small in area for
Wilbur's weight? But the wing area had been calculated from the
standard tables, and Wilbur was sure he had made no error. Could
it be possible that the tables themselves were wrong, the tables so
laboriously put together over the years by Lilienthal and others?
There was no way to answer these questions with certainty at that
moment, and Wilbur climbed into his cot that night forced to face
his initial disappointment, a severe one. His first day of practice at
the tower would also be his last, on this trip anyway.

The continuous hours of practice he had looked forward to were
now out of the question. To sustain the glider in a proper attitude,

winds of perhaps thirty-five or forty miles an hour would be needed. Not only was it unlikely that there would be many days with such winds, but if they did come, it would be little short of insanity for him, lacking all experience, to go up in such a powerful blast. In any case, the most pressing problem now was to pinpoint the source of the difficulty and it was not at all clear to Wilbur just how he should go about doing that.

The next day was Sunday, during which the brothers customarily did no work; this was a rule they observed out of respect for their father and almost never infringed. On the three following days they were out with the glider again, Wilbur determined to extract as much information as he could, concerning both lift and control, by improvising tests.

Curious to find just what weight the glider would carry, he had it lifted head-high in the wind, which was blowing about twenty miles an hour. On the lower wing he loaded some chains borrowed from Tate. The limit proved to be seventy-five pounds, just about half the loading promised by the original calculations. Other tests demonstrated the welcome fact that, in one respect at least, he had improved on his predecessors. The resistance set up by the mere framing of his machine—determined by such things as its general conformation, the gap between surfaces, breadth of the wings from front to back and the shape of the struts—was much below that achieved by anyone before him.

Further encouragement was gained on Wednesday morning when he sent the unmanned glider up on the tower rope and worked the controls from the ground by cords. Both the warping and the elevator operated with satisfying precision; they were able to make the apparatus perform "some feats which almost seem an impossibility," as Orville reported to Katharine (regrettably leaving the feats unspecified). Then an accident occurred which promptly threw the two back into their despairing mood of the previous Saturday.

Having hauled the glider down from the tower and placed it on the ground to adjust a rope, the brothers turned away momentarily —and looked back just in time to see their fifty-pound machine jerked up from the sand by the wind, tossed helter-skelter twenty feet through the air, and smashed down with a sharp cracking of

wood and rending of fabric. It had happened so quickly that neither brother had had time to move. The two stared glumly at the
heap of cloth and sticks, now looking like anything but a flying
machine, then dragged the remnants back to camp and "began to
consider getting home."

The next morning, as Wilbur poked at the wreck, things began
to look a little brighter; perhaps it could be repaired sufficiently to
make the few further tests he had in mind. The patching up—re-
placing the broken parts with spare pieces—proved to be less difficult than he had imagined, though the job still occupied four or
five days. The brothers worked inside the tent except when they
went up to Tate's to use the sewing machine on the fabric. Once or
twice a day they took time out for a walk along the beach, inevitably reverting to the vexing question of the machine's lift deficiency, but making no progress toward its solution.

The weather was fair during this time and on these walks Wilbur couldn't help noticing the multitude of birds—alone, by twos
and threes, and in flocks—that filled sky and landscape as if in innocent mockery of his ambitions. There were hawks and sea gulls
dipping and wheeling everywhere. At the edge of the surf, sea
chickens skimmed down to hop along the wet sand in search of
food, then scampered before the oncoming water. There were ma-
jestic bald eagles, with wingspreads exceeding five feet, while buzzards by the dozen soared lazily over the dunes and the bay. A
sight to beguile and charm the spirit, to Wilbur this world of birds
was only depressing. "Will is 'most sick of them," Orville wrote his
sister.

Just when they were ready to resume, they were again delayed,
this time by a real nor'wester. It was October 17 before they could
again venture out of their tent, having taken refuge for nearly two
days from the howling sand-laden winds that shook the top and
sides of the tent "till they sound like thunder."

During the storm Orville took advantage of the enforced idle-
ness to write a long, chatty letter to his sister. In it he provides an
intimate glimpse of life on the Banks.

But the sand! The sand is the greatest thing in Kitty Hawk, and
soon will be the only thing. The site of our tent was formerly a fer-

tile valley, cultivated by some ancient Kitty Hawker. Now only a few rotten limbs, the topmost branches of trees that then grew in this valley, protrude from the sand. The sea has washed and the wind blown millions and millions of loads of sand up in heaps along the coast, completely covering houses and forest. Mr. Tate is now tearing down the nearest house to our camp to save it from the sand. . . .

A mockingbird lives in a tree that overhangs our tent, and sings to us the whole day long. He is very tame, and perches on the highest bough of the tree (which however is only about ten feet high) and calls us up every morning. I think he crows up especially early after every storm to see whether we are still here. . . .

The sunsets here are the prettiest I have ever seen. The clouds light up in all colors in the background, with deep blue clouds of various shapes fringed with gold before. The moon rises in much the same style, and lights up this pile of sand almost like day. I read my watch at all hours of the night on moonless nights without the aid of any other light than that of the stars shining on the canvas of the tent. . . .

I believe I started in to tell what we eat. Well, part of the time we eat hot biscuits and eggs and tomatoes; part of the time eggs and part tomatoes. Just now we are out of gasoline and coffee. Therefore no hot drink or bread or crackers. The order sent off Tuesday has been delayed by the winds. Will is 'most starved. But he kept crying that when we were rolling in luxuries, such as butter, bacon, corn bread and coffee. I think he will survive. It is now suppertime. I must scratch around and see what I can get together. We still have half a can of condensed milk, which amounts to six or eight teaspoonfuls. . . .

Wilbur's interest had now shifted to the problem of longitudinal control, particularly in its inherent or automatic aspects—he was still very much aware of the difficulty he had met with in trying to work both warping and elevator controls at once. If some measure of fore-and-aft stability could be made self-acting, he thought, then by so much would the operation of a flying machine be simplified.

For two days he improvised tests with the glider, seeking to uncover some one factor that might serve as a point of departure.

The effort only left him in greater confusion and with a new respect for the complexities involved.

There must be some way, he felt, to achieve, fore and aft, something of the same built-in balance that the V-shape of the wing provided for lateral stability. Perhaps if the elevator were to be set at a negative angle—with the leading edge dipped—then the downward pressure exerted on it by the wind would in some degree offset the upward pressure on the leading edge of the wing. If so, at some point, through some limited range of movement, these two opposing pressures might be expected to balance each other, keeping the machine in level flight and freeing the pilot to give his attention to other matters. While in strict logic the idea seemed correct enough, he soon found that the machine would not behave according to such nice reasoning.

With the glider aloft in a twenty-mile breeze, carrying seventy-five pounds of chain, and with the brothers hanging onto the ropes, it would frequently drop suddenly by the nose, almost as if it had been forcibly pulled earthward by something underneath. This was mystifying and seemed to negate the theories that explained the travel of the center of air pressure on a wing. Supposedly, the greatest upward pressure was in the wing's forward half, beginning at about the center, and traveling forward as the wing's angle of attack decreased. It was hard to see how this lifting force could be so suddenly and completely canceled, yet that is what was happening. The lift was being wiped out entirely, allowing the downward pressure on the elevator to tumble the whole machine over its leading edges.

Nothing Wilbur did or could think of supplied him with a clue to the mystery. He switched the glider's position so that the elevator was at the rear rather than the front, set it at different angles, and even went so far as to haul the machine to the top of a small dune, gently launching it free and unmanned in the breeze, not caring whether it was damaged in landing. He repeated this last, rather desperate test a number of times, hastily splinting broken struts when necessary, and peering intently for any revelatory quirk. "When we got through," Orville recorded, "Will was so mixed up he couldn't even theorize."

Departure from Kitty Hawk had been set for Tuesday, October 23, but Wilbur was reluctant to leave without gaining some feel of the machine in free flight. To go back to the bicycle shop without having once ridden on a moving glider, when he had started with such high hopes, would be the ultimate frustration. Since that first disappointing day he had not been aboard the machine and had had no chance to master the controls, so any real attempt at gliding was out of the question. Still, he decided, it should be possible on a gentle slope, without seeking either height or distance, and using only the elevator for longitudinal balance, to glide short distances in comparative safety.

With Tate's help the brothers carried the glider about three miles below the camp, to a section of the Banks called Kill Devil Hill, where the huge hundred-foot dune spread its undulating sides in a wide and gradual descent. The three men trudged with the glider a little way up the lower slope, on the northeast, the soft sand giving under their feet at every step. They placed the machine facing back down the hill. The wind was at twelve miles an hour, just about right. When combined with the glider's air speed it would produce sufficient lift. Stronger winds would have presented too many dangers of accident, even in the semiglides Wilbur intended.

Though he was already convinced of the feasibility of the prone position, his customary caution led him to make a test. Lying on the lower wing, he gave a signal to Orville and Tate. Each lifted a wing tip, slowly carried the machine into the wind, then released it a foot or so above the sand. It quickly sank down, made smooth contact and ran forward a few feet, kicking into Wilbur's face a fine spray of sand, then stopped. This was repeated a few more times, when he announced he was satisfied.

Starting from further up the dune, with Wilbur in position the two men grasped the spars at each end and began to run down the long slope. After covering a hundred yards of the yielding sand, the machine speeded up and the two could go no further. Orville and Tate released their holds and, as agreed, shouted to Wilbur that he was free. Hearing this, Wilbur instantly depressed the elevator to start the glider toward the ground. When let go, he had been only three or four feet above the slope, but so gradual was his descent, covering sixty yards or so, that the machine ran another thirty feet on the sand after touching down.

Compared to Lilienthal and the others it wasn't much of a glide but it was a start and none of those others had dared to take a prone position on their wings. "Although in appearance it was a dangerous practice," Wilbur explained soon after, "we found it perfectly safe and comfortable except for the flying sand, and the machine was not once injured, although we sometimes landed at a rate of very nearly thirty miles per hour." Wilbur already had a first to his name.

All together about a dozen glides were made that day, all very low and all by Wilbur, most of them very short, the free portion in no case covering more than a hundred feet. Especially satisfying was the action of the elevator in maintaining fore-and-aft balance. "The ease with which it was accomplished," he remarked afterwards, "was a matter of great astonishment to us." The writings of other experimenters had led him to expect much difficulty with it.

On October 23 the Wrights bid good-by to the Tates and boarded a boat for the mainland. Wilbur, especially, was departing with very mixed feelings. His six weeks on the Banks had established the worth of his basic controls, in itself a giant step. But controls were useless on wings that would not fly properly and the deficiency in lift was a source of real consternation. Also, he had really learned woefully little about the actual handling of those controls, having spent a ridiculous ten minutes on the kite instead of the fifty or so hours he had anticipated.

He had no thought of giving up or of pausing in his efforts; he was in fact already planning a return the next year with a new machine. The old one, useless for anything further it might reveal, he had given to the Tates. Not long afterward, most of the ribs, struts, and spars so carefully worked by Wilbur's own hands were feeding the Tate's kitchen fire, and their little girl was skipping along the sandy roads of the village attired in a bright new dress of French sateen.

6

Kitty Hawk 1901

A few days of quiet reflection at home, calmly sorting the results of his trip, were sufficient to restore Wilbur to his former confident mood. Having set out with revolutionary theories on many points, as he said, "We considered it quite a point to be able to return without having our pet theories completely knocked on the head by the hard logic of experience, and our own brains dashed out in the bargain."

At least part of his satisfaction must have been the fact that those weeks at Kitty Hawk had represented the first time in fifteen years that he had done anything of significance to himself, anything from which he could derive personal gratification. Equally important, he had subjected his heart to strenuous physical activity without detriment—he had not been thinking only of accidents when he wrote in an early letter that his interest in aeronautics might "soon cost me an increased amount of money if not my life."

His renewed optimism is evident in a series of letters written shortly after his return addressed to Octave Chanute, whose book Wilbur had read with much interest in the summer of 1899. He had, in fact, opened contact with Chanute just prior to the departure for Kitty Hawk in the hope of eliciting from the world-recognized authority some comment on his plans for experiment.

Chanute had answered him in kindly fashion at the time, with general words of encouragement and an invitation to submit further information after the trip. This initial notice from a man of Chanute's attainments, while it was pleasing to the unknown Wilbur, had probably also been something of a disappointment. In his letter Wilbur had fully described his warping technique for lateral control, obviously inviting a reaction from Chanute. But Chanute had not been moved to make any remarks on it, an omission that must have left Wilbur in some wonderment.

Chanute's international position of leadership in aeronautics had been well earned. A civil engineer of legitimate fame and some moderate wealth (he was a pioneer builder of bridges and railroads), Chanute's concern with the problem of human flight dated back nearly forty years, though he had taken no active part until the 1880's. Gradually, he had assumed the position of recorder and disseminator of information, writing widely on aeronautics in periodicals both specialized and popular. His 1894 book, *Progress in Flying Machines,* was the first comprehensive historical treatment of the field. On the appearance of Lilienthal, Chanute himself took up gliding—though he was then past sixty—aided by two assistants. He remained at the task for two seasons, achieving little. A generous and tireless dispenser of information and practical aid—he had already expended seven or eight thousand dollars in sponsorship of other hopefuls—he was the focus of inquiries and appeals from many parts of the world.

By 1900, for some reason Chanute had become convinced that the era of human flight was about to dawn. A year, he boldly predicted, might see the first motor-driven plane cleaving the skies. As to what might happen after that great event took place, he was not quite prepared to say. It seemed to him that no plane would ever fly at a speed much in excess of a hundred miles per hour, and it appeared that the new invention would never find much commercial use: sport and military observation, Chanute felt, were the probable limits of the airplane's employment.

Wilbur's first letter to Chanute after the return from Kitty Hawk was a detailed report of all that had occurred there. It included a suggestion, diffidently put forward, that the air pressure tables of the great Lilienthal were possibly in error. Particular stress was laid on the success of the elevator control; the efficiency of its operation, Wilbur wrote, had proved "a matter of great astonishment to us," openly implying his surprise that this technique had not been fully utilized before. The warp control had also proved eminently satisfactory after only "two minutes trial."

In his reply Chanute offered hearty congratulations, especially for proving that the prone position for the operator "is not so unsafe as I believed," but making no reference to the elevator or warp controls. "I shall hope to meet you," he added unexpectedly, "either here or at Dayton, to obtain further details . . . if your machine is not irrevealable I should much like to see it." Wilbur assured Chanute that he would be welcome at any time, though he cautioned that they could show him only a small model since they no longer had the full-size machine. Chanute's business, however, did not bring him into the Dayton vicinity until the following summer, and by then Wilbur had finished the design for his new glider and was full of plans for his second trip to Kitty Hawk.

Originally, the return trip had again been scheduled for six weeks or so in September–October. But so caught up was Wilbur in the promise of his new machine that he had decided, with Orville's concurrence, not to wait for the fall. That this decision implied a commitment beyond the immediate experiments can be seen in the fact that the brothers now hired a full-time assistant to work in the bicycle shop. And it was probably to this period that some words written years later by Wilbur refer. "We believed that if we would take the risk of devoting our entire time and financial resources," he recalled, "we could conquer the difficulties in the path to success before increasing years impaired our physical activity. We finally decided to make the attempt." That statement, it might be noted, contains two assumptions worthy of emphasis: Wilbur's vision was fixed on absolute independence from other investigators, and he recognized that the surest road to success lay in combining theory and practice—the theoretician himself should be the one to test his theories in the air.

The new man in the shop was a machinist named Charles Taylor, of about the same age as Wilbur, who had been known to the Wrights for two or three years. Though he could not have dreamt it at the time, fate had tapped his shoulder, for Taylor, too, was destined to make a contribution to the coming of the airplane. Before going with the Wrights, he had been employed by the Dayton Electric Company at a salary of $15 a week, and also ran a small machine shop in his home. It was there that he had first met the brothers when, from time to time, they brought him some bicycle work. Their offer of $18 a week, coupled with the fact that he lived only six blocks from the shop and, as he said, could cycle home for lunch, were sufficient inducements to make him forsake the security of the Electric Company. "Besides," he admitted, "I liked the Wrights."

Taylor was soon aware that the small shop's volume of business did not really require a third man, yet the brothers never mentioned any special reason for hiring him. "So far as I can figure out," he later concluded, "Will and Orv hired me to worry about their bicycle business so that they could concentrate on their flying studies." On June 15, 1901, at seven in the morning, Taylor reported for his first day at the shop and for the next eight years virtually ran the business, working a ten- or twelve-hour day. Three weeks after Taylor took over, the two Wrights left Dayton for Kitty Hawk, loaded with baggage and that one precious trunk.

In approaching the design of his new machine, Wilbur had still been faced with the dilemma that first presented itself at Kitty Hawk: in which element did the deficiency of lifting power exist— the shape of the wings, their total area, or something as yet unguessed? And in whichever it was, how should an improvement be made? Since there were no answers to these questions in the literature, the only recourse that suggested itself at that time was a small laboratory experiment that might afford some reason for leaning to one known factor or the other.

He put together two lengths of wood in a wide V-shape, attaching the point of the V to a vertical pivot that allowed it to swing right or left, the arms parallel with the ground. Next he made a number of small wing models out of wood, varying them in size and camber. These he tested against each other, two at a time, by mounting one on each extremity of the V, and exposing the instrument to natural wind. The wing models were affixed vertically, their lifts in direct opposition; the result was determined by how much one surface could push the other from the normal position.

As Wilbur readily admitted, this was an extremely crude device, giving only very rough and often equivocal measurements. Still, the results did seem to supply some confirmation of the suspicion that Lilienthal's tables were inaccurate and that much more wing area was required. There was also a hint that a deeper curvature would help to increase the lift.

The final estimate of the dimensions of the new machine—still hardly more than an educated guess—increased the wingspread by a full five feet and the front-to-back measurement by two. This gave twenty-two feet by seven, or an area well over 300 square feet, a larger surface than anyone had ever dared to use. For the camber Wilbur determined to go back to the Lilienthal depth of 1-in-12, but would move its deepest curvature a little rearward from the position where he had first placed it. Total weight of the new machine was nearly twice that of the first one, ninety-eight pounds. A wind of seventeen miles an hour, Wilbur estimated, would sustain it at the proper three-degree angle of inclination.

Enlargement of the glider brought with it the need for some further changes in the Kitty Hawk camping arrangements. The tent would no longer be adequate for housing both the glider and the Wrights, yet some sort of shelter for the glider was needed, and for the work of alteration and repair that would surely become necessary. A second tent might answer but it would have to be a very large one, and since there were certainly several seasons of work ahead, Wilbur decided on a simple wooden shed. He designed a structure seven by sixteen by twenty-five feet, with a low peaked roof, to be built of plain board siding on a framework of two-by-fours. A nice touch allowed both end walls to be swung out and up on hinges and propped. Alongside the shed they would put up the tent for living quarters. Orders for the shed lumber, cut to size, were sent ahead with directions to forward it to Kitty Hawk.

About a week before the date set for departure, Octave Chanute finally arrived in Dayton and his visit resulted in still further changes in the Kitty Hawk plans, not all of them welcome to Wilbur.

Chanute was a very different man from either of the Wrights, every inch the professional engineer of the day, his formal air enhanced by his white hair and a trim goatee. Affable, if perhaps a bit condescending toward these younger enthusiasts, he was ear-

nest in his efforts to be helpful. The Wrights liked him immediately.
He was just then, he said, having a new experimental glider constructed for him by an assistant. When he suggested that the brothers and he might combine their efforts at Kitty Hawk, Wilbur could
hardly refuse—though his reluctance in a letter written some days
later is not entirely disguised.

Chanute explained that, in reality, he had small hope for his new
glider. His assistant, E. C. Huffacker, had constructed it of paper
tubing in order to gain lightness. "If you were not about to experiment," he wrote, "I should abandon the machine without testing. . . . If you think you can extract instruction from its failure, I
beg to make the following proposition: 1. I will send Mr. Huffacker
and his machine to your testing grounds at my expense, and pay his
share of camp expenses. 2. He will assist you in your experiments,
in exchange for your assistance in testing his machine." Wilbur replied that he could not accept the offer "unless you feel that you
yourself are getting your money's worth."

A second proposal brought equally tenuous agreement from Wilbur. Concerned that the Wrights' dangerous experiments would
take place in the isolation of the Outer Banks, far from any medical help, Chanute offered to supply them with an assistant who had
some medical training. This was a young man named George Spratt,
another aeronautical hopeful and a graduate of Medico-Chirurgical
College. Spratt had at this time given up medical practice to devote
himself fully to laboratory studies on the problem of flight. He had
never witnessed any actual gliding, said Chanute, and was anxious
to do so. If Wilbur would accept him, Chanute would be happy to
have Spratt "serve under your orders," and would personally bear
all expenses.

Again Wilbur hinted that help was not needed. "We could not
permit you to bear the expense of his trip merely to assist us," he
responded, "if however, you wish to get a line on his capacity and
aptitude, and give him a little experience with a view to utilizing
him in your own work later, we will be very glad to have him with
us."

Wilbur's hesitancy at having his privacy invaded, or to link himself too closely with others in the field, was lost on Chanute, who
proceeded to make arrangements with both Huffacker and Spratt.

Since Chanute also gladly accepted Wilbur's invitation to join them at Kitty Hawk, the camp on the sandbar promised to be a fairly crowded outpost.

Just before leaving Dayton, Wilbur had the pleasure of noting his debut as an aeronautical author. The July issues of two small but highly regarded magazines, one from England and one from Germany, arrived in the mail, each containing a brief article by Wilbur on gliding flight. That was not the first appearance of the Wright name in print in connection with the subject, however. The June issue of *Cassier's Magazine*, a leading American engineering journal, carried an article by Chanute in which he brought the topic of "Aerial Navigation" up to date. At the article's close, after a survey of the more recent work, including his own, he turns a brief spotlight on the brothers—though failing to give any hint that the two unknowns had achieved something revolutionary in the matter of stability control:

> Since these experiments [Chanute's] a further advance has been achieved by Messrs. Wilbur and Orville Wright, who have produced a double-decked gliding machine in which the operator is placed in a horizontal position, thus opposing to forward motion one square foot instead of five square feet, when he is upright, and they have further reduced the resistance of the framing by adopting improved shapes, so that the aggregate head resistances are reduced to about one half of those which previously obtained.

If it seemed to a reader of that paragraph that the "further advance" made by the Wrights was properly to be regarded as an improvement on the practice of Chanute himself, and that the two were in some sense his protégés, the impression would not be wholly contrary to what Chanute himself had, even this early, begun to believe.

The name of Chanute is now tied inextricably to that of the Wrights, and attempts have even been made to assign him a principal part in their work. This is perhaps the chief of those murky but persistent myths that have affixed themselves to the Wrights' story, harmless in most cases and easily disproved, but in this instance calling for a statement of blunt truth. By the time Chanute met the Wrights he was already well past the zenith of his aeronautical abilities. Somehow, during his decades of study, he had let slip from him the amplitude of vision that should have lifted him above an interest in the mere accumulation of detail. He had, instead, become hopelessly enmeshed in the recording of an intricate web of aeronautical minutiae. Consequently, in his understanding of the larger dimensions of the Wrights' work he was seldom to be less than slow and was often obtuse. Sadly, in time he would prove a burden to them and an embarrassment, and the exasperated Wilbur would at last be driven to loose some rather frank complaints.

Chanute's real role with the brothers, important enough in its way, was as a provider of moral support, and in the summer of 1901 Wilbur was glad enough for his attention, even perhaps a little flattered.

When the Wrights arrived at Elizabeth City, on July 8, from where they would make the sail to Kitty Hawk Bay, the elements were again lying in wait for them. Along the Carolina shore and over the waters of Pamlico Sound was poured the full measure of nature's ferocity, creating a wild spectacle that exceeded anything in the memory of the oldest inhabitant. The brothers arose on the morning of the ninth to be greeted by a world rocking in the blast of an awesome hurricane. "We reached Kitty Hawk several days later than we expected," wrote Wilbur, "owing to the greatest storm in the history of the place. Anemometer cups gave way at 93 miles per hour so that is the highest speed recorded." (Actual speed, recorded elsewhere, was 107 miles an hour.) A week of drenching rain followed.

A strange coincidence, anyone might have said, for the brothers to be twice greeted by raging storms. Minds more prone to superstition, say the mariners of ancient Greece, would have known better—it was no accident, those old sailors would have insisted with knowing looks, that the storms came up just when they did, no accident that Aeolus, god of the winds, should have grown wrathful against the man who came to challenge his ancient domination of the skies. This Wright had better look out. Gods did not give up so easily.

The brothers reached Kitty Hawk on the eleventh, stopping overnight at Tate's. Next morning, despite the rain, they hauled their gear four miles south to the vicinity of huge Kill Devil Hill. The tent was put up hurriedly, then there came two more days of frustrating inaction, the hard rains halting all outside work and delaying the start of work on the shed. That task, carefully planned, required only three days of hoisting and hammering. The rough solidity of the structure rising lone on the gray sands, while it was dwarfed by the dune that gathered itself to a hundred-foot peak just to the south, must have given the brothers' quest a welcome touch of substance. "The building is a grand institution," Orville wrote proudly at its completion, "with awnings at both ends." Inside the shed, the very day it was completed, assembly of the glider was begun. By July 26 the new machine, its twenty-two-foot wings leaving little room at either end, stood ready for use.

During the entire week it took to put the machine together the brothers had been constantly harassed by an immense swarm of mosquitoes, brought out by the recent rains. They came "in a mighty cloud, almost darkening the sun," and for a time made both work and sleep an ordeal, on two or three occasions bringing the work on the machine to a halt. "We attempted to escape by going to bed," Orville recounted to his sister, "which we did at a little after five o'clock. We put our cots out under the awnings and wrapped up in our blankets with only our noses protruding from the folds, thus exposing the least possible area to attack. Alas! Here nature's complicity in the conspiracy against us became evident. The wind, which until now had been blowing over twenty miles an hour, dropped off entirely. Our blankets then became unbearable. The perspiration would roll off us in torrents. We would partly uncover and the mosquitoes would swoop down upon us in vast multitudes."

The use of netting and a ring of smoking fires around the camp, fed by old tree stumps and driftwood, made conditions barely livable. Then, the day after completion of the glider, the whole antagonistic horde simply disappeared.

By this time Huffacker and Spratt had both arrived, Huffacker bringing with him the small, collapsible Chanute machine; Chanute himself arrived a week later.

Spratt, a smiling, open-faced man of Orville's age, quickly proved
to be the perfect companion for life on the lonely Banks, bubbling
with enthusiastic talk of aeronautics and always ready with a quip
or a humorous story. During the three weeks Spratt was to spend
at Kitty Hawk, he and the two brothers would seal a friendship
based on mutual respect and admiration. Wilbur in particular, in
the depth and breadth of his knowledge, his peculiar quality of
alert self-confidence, made a great impression on Spratt. When,
however, Spratt later confessed he could not help envying Wilbur
his abilities, the elder Wright replied revealingly: "You envy me,
but I envy you the possession of some qualities that I would give a
great deal to possess in equal degree." Whether Spratt ever knew
that this was a wistful look back to the dampening, isolating effects
of those lost years is doubtful.

Inspecting the machine in the shed, Spratt was struck by the ingenuity and workmanship that had gone into it, but his keenest attention was focused on the camber. His own laboratory studies had
centered on this one feature and he had become convinced that a
curvature as deep as 1-in-12 was highly unstable and even dangerous. To Wilbur he offered the opinion that a wing with so deep a
camber could not be held in a proper attitude as the angle of attack decreased—as the wing came more nearly parallel with the
ground. Spratt was here touching on a problem that had as yet received very little serious study; even Wilbur had neglected it, being content to accept the tentative conclusions of Lilienthal and
others.

Ordinarily, as the attitude of a wing in flight decreased to smaller
and smaller angles of attack, the air continued to exert an upward
pressure from below, with the center of this pressure traveling
slowly toward the front edge. A wing with a very deep curvature
in its supper surface, however, radically altered this pattern. As the
angle decreased, the air impinging on the curved front edge exerted
greater and greater pressure downward. With the wing lowering
into the wind, at some undetermined angle this downward pressure
would overbalance the sustaining pressure from below, forcing the
leading edges of the wings—which were forward of the center of
gravity—to sink steadily lower. Depending on the form and depth

of the curvature, this displacement of pressure could be sudden and violent, causing a drop that might, when once begun, be uncontrollable.

Lilienthal had been the first to point to this reversal, though his warning had referred to a camber of 1-in-8, which had never been used in gliding. Neither he nor anyone else had been able to determine with any precision just what degree of camber combined both safety and efficiency, nor had anyone tried to find the angles at which the phenomenon began and ceased. It had been stated by some, in fact, that the condition was not always present and probably did not occur within those angles needed for gliding.

Spratt's ideas on the subject were definite, and he insisted to Wilbur that the camber he was using, 1-in-12, was unsafe, no matter that Lilienthal himself had used it. Wilbur replied that the danger had been "sufficiently guarded against," if indeed it existed at all in his machine, which he doubted. His elevator, he explained, had been placed in front of the wings precisely to prevent a tendency to nosedive. He was also trying something new in the wings themselves, he said, shaping the extreme front edges to a sort of blunt shield. This should at least ward off any too-sudden displacement of pressure. Spratt was suitably impressed, though not entirely convinced.

Early on the morning of Saturday, July 27, the day after assembly was finished, the machine was hauled endwise from the shed. The same plan as the previous year was to be followed. It would first be flown as a kite with Wilbur aboard to gain practice at the controls. On days when winds were too light for kite flying, he would attempt low glides.

That morning the men emerged from their tent to find the wind barely caressing the sands, blowing hardly ten miles per hour, less by a good five miles than the strength needed for kite flying. Wilber announced that he would begin the season by gliding. Since the machine was entirely new and considerably larger than anyone had used before, and since Wilbur's practice with the controls on the old machine had amounted to a bare ten minutes, his decision was a brave one. Whether it flowed from unusual impatience or simple confidence is hard to say. It would not be the last time that he would throw off the cloak of caution.

Carrying the machine, the men trudged halfway up the long, undulating slope of Kill Devil Hill. Wilbur climbed aboard the lower
wing, making a guess at how far forward he should position himself
in order to make his weight coincide with the machine's center of
gravity. Kite trials would have determined this exactly; now it
would need a series of short glides to fix.

The men lifted the machine a couple of feet above the sand, ran
forward and let go. The glider immediately settled to the ground,
having flown only a few yards. For the second attempt Wilbur
placed himself several inches further back, but the result was about
the same. The next two or three tries were aborted when the trailing edges of the wing brushed rises in the dune, the machine
plumping to a stop after skidding in a shower of sand. By the eighth
try Wilbur was a whole foot to the rear of his first position, something he had not expected.

For the ninth time the glider was released and now it kept going,
two or three feet above the sand, rising slightly, then falling, but
not touching down until it had sailed more than 300 feet. The onlookers, running down the hill, shouted their delight. When they
reached the machine, however, Wilbur was shaking his head. "The
full power of the elevator," he explained in some dejection, "had
been required to keep the machine from either running into the
ground or rising so high as to lose all headway." The previous year's
machine had not needed nearly so much elevator action. "It was
apparent that something was radically wrong."

And with that, in the face of "something radically wrong," Wilbur had the machine carried back up the hill, climbed aboard, and
prepared for another glide—this time in no doubt of the risk he was
taking.

Released, the machine sailed forward at a ground speed of about
twelve miles an hour—fifty feet, a hundred feet—then it began to
bear upward, higher and higher, fighting against the downward
pressure on the elevator. It was about thirty feet above the ground
and still climbing, though fast losing headway, when a cry from below reached Wilbur's ears. Someone, probably Spratt, running on
the sand underneath the machine, was frantically waving and
shouting. The warning, Wilbur later admitted, made him realize
his extreme danger. "This was the position," he wrote later, "from

which Lilienthal had always found difficulty to extricate himself, as his machine then, in spite of his greatest exertions, manifested a tendency to dive downward almost vertically and strike the ground head on with frightful velocity." It was, in fact, the position from which the German had fallen to his death.

Wilbur knew that his elevator, a device Lilienthal had not used, gave him the only means of bringing the glider to the ground under control. As his speed slowed, allowing the rear edges of the wings to drop, he quickly hunched himself forward a few inches to depress the front edges. At the same time he turned the elevator to full positive. This opened the elevator's underside to its maximum upward pressure and would, Wilbur prayed, offset the expected plunge. "The machine then settled to the ground, maintaining its horizontal position almost perfectly, and landed without any injury at all." Wilbur's matter-of-fact words disguise the heart-thumping excitement that must have gripped him in the fleeting seconds of that nearly flat descent to the sands. Stepping off, he was jubilant; his elevator had proved itself by overcoming "one of the very greatest dangers" in gliding.

His confidence increasing, and still anxious to locate the radical flaw in the design of the wings, he had the machine taken up the hill again. About ten more flights were performed that day by Wilbur, both long and short. One was an exact repetition of the flat drop; more dangerous, in fact, since this time the machine, after rising to unwanted heights, had actually begun to move backwards.

Despite the efficiency of the elevator, Wilbur had to confess that the day's experiments were severely disappointing. Aside from the trouble over control, the lifting power of the wings was not nearly what he had expected, only about one-third of what it should have been. And the angle of attack, instead of being about three degrees, was nearer six.

That night Wilbur jotted in his notebook: "At a speed of 18 miles, resistance (from all causes) of machine alone about 15 lbs. We estimate the drift of surfaces at $\frac{1}{12}$ of 98 lbs. $= 8$ lbs. Leaving a head resistance of 7 lbs. for framing. This would indicate that the unfavorable results in total resistance observed in gliding were due rather to drift of surfaces than to resistance of framing . . ." These figures had resulted from some brief, hand-held kite tests made that same evening. They indicated that the deficiency was not in the resistance set up by the "framing," the frontal area of the whole machine, but was due to some inadequacy in the wings themselves.

Once again Wilbur was led to express his "doubts of the correctness of Lilienthal tables of ratio of lift to drift." This was the third time he had recorded such misgivings, and very nearly in the same language. It was almost as if he was reluctant to believe it, unwilling to face its implications. Without the German's tables, so laboriously compiled over so many years, what could be used as a starting point in designing wings? Without Lilienthal, the study of aeronautics would be what it had been in Cayley's time a century before, an infant, unable even to lift its head.

Thoughts of gliding were now put aside—glides were useless anyway, with longitudinal control so difficult—as he concentrated on the vexing problem of camber. His first decision was to remodel the front edges, a task that occupied three or four days. The blunt shape had proved worthless and he would return to the smooth curve of the previous year. That done, he took the machine apart in order to test each wing separately.

With two ropes attached at the middle of the front edge, both leading to his hands, he had a wing lifted into the breeze, noting the angle at which it rode in winds of different velocities. No sooner had he started than he saw that he had stumbled on the simplest imaginable test for settling the nagging problem of the travel of the center of pressure.

In light winds, the front of the wing rode high, exerting a strong upward pull on the ropes. In winds a little stronger the pull was more nearly horizontal, tugging directly away from him. In winds stronger yet, the front edge dropped until the pull was forcibly downward, the center of pressure tending, as it were, to twirl the wing round its own center of gravity. Thus the center of pressure had indeed "reversed" itself, traveling backward from just ahead of the center of gravity to just behind it. And the critical moment of displacement seemingly had occurred at an angle of four degrees or so, well within those angles used for gliding. "This point having been definitely settled," wrote Wilbur, "we proceeded to truss down the ribs of the whole machine, so as to reduce the depth of curvature."

A long spar, laid across the ribs from wing tip to wing tip and tied down tightly, accomplished the makeshift alteration, giving a new camber of about 1-in-20. The deepest part of the curve, a little more than four inches, now occurred at a point one foot back from the leading edge.

With this shallower rise, Wilbur calculated, the center of pressure should not reverse itself so readily, since the diminished protrusion in the upper surface offered less area for the wind's action. All the conjecture and careful laboratory tests of other experimenters had not been able to track down the elusive movements of this pressure center. Standing in the natural winds sweeping in off the Atlantic, Wilbur had reduced the problem to its simplest form and resolved all doubts in a matter of hours. Following a simple hunch, he also reduced the area of the elevator and, only eleven days after his first disappointing glides, he was ready to fly again.

Thirteen times on Thursday, August 8, Wilbur cast off, high up on the slope of Kill Devil Hill, into a wind varying between ten and fourteen miles per hour. His own speed of ten to twenty miles per hour—depending on the angle of descent—when added to that of the wind, supplied the full degree of sustaining power that was lacking in the wings themselves. To his great relief he found that longitudinal control was vastly improved. Consistently, the angle of attack assumed a more acceptable four degrees.

His longest flight covered nearly 400 feet, the machine remaining in the air for fifteen seconds, but Wilbur did not think this glide the most rewarding. In one slightly shorter he had been able, by using a fairly steep start, to raise his total speed to over thirty-three miles per hour, and thence to glide for an additional 240 feet at a very shallow angle, only seven degrees. This took him well beyond the slope of the hill and he found himself skimming over the flats, the gray blur of the ground only two or three feet beneath his face, where he finally touched down in a gentle spray of sand.

It was a day of exhilaration for all concerned. Also a day of hard work. Climbing the loose sand of the dune after each glide, under the heavy burden of the glider, was a sweaty business in the glaring August sun, though the wind blowing up the dune did its part in lightening the machine's awkward weight. For Wilbur, though his thirteen glides had averaged only about ten seconds, and though the problem of lift deficiency remained to be solved, it was his first real day of unalloyed satisfaction. He was ready now to enter on a phase of gliding with which no one before him had ever seriously experimented. The next day, he determined, he would attempt to make a turn.

Ever since the time of William Henson's "aerial carriage" more than half a century before, all those concerned with aeronautics had assumed that a flying machine would make turns in the air in the same basic manner that a boat turns in water. To proceed to the right, the boat's rudder is turned to the right, the pressure on it forcing the stern to the left, thus slewing the bow in the opposite direction. Henson's rudder—which, like that of a boat, projected downward—was intended to bring about exactly this movement, and without much disturbance in the level attitude of the wings. It seemed reasonable to expect that air pressure on a rudder would act in the same way as water pressure, and thereafter Henson's concept had gone unchallenged.

Most experimenters had noticed, of course, that this was not the turning technique used by birds. Always, the bird seemed to begin a turn with a banking movement, in which one wing rose while the other dropped, the turn taking place round the lower wing. It had been noticed, too, that the sharpness of the turn bore some relation to the degree of tilt, a tight circle requiring a steep bank, a wide one being made with only a slight change. But these aerial acrobatics—all the wheeling, dipping, scooting—seemed to have a unique relation to the bird's life, necessary for its peculiar needs, possible only because of its finely adapted bodily structure. Such airy freedom, it was thought, would probably remain inimitable by man.

In any case, there was general agreement that a level turn in a flying machine, with the wings holding more or less parallel with the ground, would really be an improvement on the bird. Pilot, and eventually passengers, could then ride comfortably upright, avoiding the potential, if undetermined, dangers of topsy-turvy-dom.

Just when Wilbur began to think that the flying machine even in executing a turn should emulate the bird is not known. Certainly it could not have been long after the model kite trials in the sum-

mer of 1899, since it was the wing-warping principle itself that
made it possible to bank a glider. Wilbur could scarcely have failed
to note, very early, that the same action by which lateral balance
was maintained in the wings would, if sustained, also unbalance
them.

But at Kitty Hawk he knew that he could not attempt a deliberate upsetting of equilibrium until he had gained some familiarity
with the machine and its controls. The bird's banking movement
was a magical thing, smooth and simple. Whether it was, in fact,
quite so uncomplicated remained an open question. For all anyone
knew, there might be lurking within the bird's maneuver an instant hazard, conquerable by the bird only by virtue of some as
yet unobserved subtlety, either of technique or conformation. That
Wilbur was now ready to make a trial of his belief, with so little
actual gliding time behind him, once more reveals his growing
impatience.

The morning of August 9 brought clear skies, a bright sun, and a
northeast wind, ideal gliding conditions. When the party reached
the foot of the big hill, however, the wind had freshened sufficiently
to make Wilbur pause. The anemometer showed it to be slowing
at twenty miles an hour. "At first we felt some doubt as to the
safety of attempting free flight in so strong a wind," he later recalled, "with a machine of over 300 square feet. But after several
preliminary experiments we decided to try a glide. The control of
the machine felt so good that we then felt no apprehension in sailing boldly forth."

The glider was launched near the top of the dune. As soon as
Wilbur felt himself under good control, traveling at twelve miles
an hour about ten feet above the sand, he activated the warping
wires. Immediately the wings responded to the warp, the left side
sinking slightly while the right lifted. Almost imperceptibly, the
tilted glider began veering leftward, the ground beneath Wilbur's
narrowed eyes sliding away to the right and giving him a peculiar
feeling of disorientation. To the group watching the glider descend
in a gently curving path, the change of direction appeared to go
well. But as the flight passed the ten-second mark and was nearing
a distance of 300 feet, Wilbur became aware that the feel of the
machine under him was somehow different. It was turning all right,

but there was a vague instability coming over it. Quickly he brought the wings up level and within two or three seconds the glider touched down.

To Orville and the others, Wilbur found he could not quite describe his experience, beyond saying that the machine had not proceeded trimly, somehow skewing off course, though he was not even sure of that. He had been much too busy dividing his attention between the warping and the elevator controls, and keeping his eye out for a place to land, to take adequate notice of anything else.

A few minutes later they were back up on the dune and Wilbur was launched once more. On this flight, which covered about 200 feet, he did not try a turn nor did he do so on either of two succeeding flights; probably he was testing the controls to reassure himself that the previous day's glides had not impaired them. Then on the fifth flight of the day he again went into a turn.

At first it went smoothly. Then as he came nearer the ground he was again aware of that peculiar instability. He was just leveling out after some seventeen seconds in the air, bringing the left wing up, when he realized that his descent was too sharp. He grabbed at the elevator control but it was too late. The glider hit the ground, left wing tip first, then the front edges, finally bouncing flat and skidding erratically to a twisting halt in a heavy shower of sand. The momentum jerked Wilbur bodily from his perch on the lower wing and flung him headfirst against the cloth-covered ribs of the elevator. When the others ran up he was sitting on the sand, his hands to his face. Miraculously, he had suffered only a bruised nose and a battered eye, though the impact of his head and shoulders on the elevator had been hard enough to break two or three of its ribs.

While it was all still very hazy, Wilbur now had the glimmering of an idea as to what was happening. Against all reason, the machine displayed a tendency to face toward the side of the high wing while circling around the lower one, instead of facing in the direction of its flight path. This imposed on the craft a loose, slithering motion that threatened to send it into a reverse spin on its own vertical axis. The difficulty in discovering anything more specific about the cause was the obvious danger in sustaining the movement long enough to make observations. Yet there was no other way than gliding to study the problem. No experimental substitute for free flight could supply the same conditions.

The next two days, Saturday and Sunday, were spent in resting and discussion. Not even Chanute, however, in all his long experience had encountered such a problem. Neither he nor any of the others could offer a solution or even an explanation. Then two days of steady rain intervened. It was August 14 before Wilbur was ready to take to the air again.

He had by this time decided that long flights were unnecessary. Short, fairly steep ones, with the warp in operation from the start, would do as well and would give him a greater safety margin. Over the next three days he cast off a half dozen times, staying up less than seven seconds on each occasion, and covering less than fifty feet. There were anxious moments but no accidents, despite the fact that the last two or three glides were made in winds as high as twenty-seven miles an hour (a surprising risk for Wilbur to have taken at this period). By August 16 he had seen enough to confirm both his suspicions and his fears. "Upturned wing seems to fall behind," he noted briefly in his journal that night, "but at first rises."

The few words conceal his crushing disappointment. It was now obvious that the banking turn of the birds did indeed involve a secret element. "Our machine does not turn (i.e. circle) toward the lowest wing under all circumstances," he wrote a few days later, "a very unlooked-for result and one which completely upsets our theories as to the causes which produce the turning to right or left."

The defect itself he now understood: the very warping action which lifted the wing also created additional resistance which retarded its forward speed. While the speed of the lower wing remained constant, the high wing slowed more and more. This not only brought it down from its banked attitude, but pulled it opposite to its curving flight path, fighting against the momentum imparted by the initial bank. If continued, the conflict of these two forces would turn the glider into something very much like a bird with a broken wing, tumbling helplessly through the air.

With that, Wilbur announced the conclusion of his season's experimenting, giving as his reason the continued bad weather. It was not entirely the rain that prompted him, in the middle of August, to terminate his work, but a deepening disgust at the way his hopes, one after another, had been frustrated. The sense of doom in Wilbur at this moment was so heavy that it came very near to extinguishing the glow of ambition that had sustained him for three years. "When we left Kitty Hawk at the end of 1901," he wrote, "we doubted that we would ever resume our experiments . . . when we looked at the time and money we had expended, and considered the progress made and the distance yet to go, we considered our experiments a failure."

On the train that took the brothers back to Dayton, Wilbur sat in brooding silence, talking even less than usual. Once he roused himself to declare emphatically that if man ever did fly, "it would not be within our lifetime . . . not within a thousand years!" When the two reached home on the morning of August 22 Wilbur was sick with a cold. Katharine Wright could see by their unaccustomed silence that things had not gone well. To her father a few days later she reported: "The boys walked in unexpectedly on Thursday morning . . . haven't had much to say about flying."

7

The Promise of $P_{(tang.\ a)}/P_{(90)}$

As the weeks passed, Wilbur's melancholy sense of failure did not lessen. He believed that his dream was fading, that his future, after all, was to be bound by the few blocks between Hawthorn Street and the shop. The gathering complexities of "the present muddled state of affairs," as he morosely expressed it to Chanute, seemed beyond the ability of one man to solve in any reasonable length of time.

Looming before him was a series of interlocked difficulties of which other experimenters had had only the faintest notion. The lifting power of wings, far from being more or less settled as he had believed, had disintegrated into a parade of question marks. All previous calculations were suspect or definitely in error.

A wing's two main dimensions—span and chord—bore toward each other a finely tuned relationship in which the variations were seemingly endless. In birds, as Wilbur knew from his studies, the proportion of span to chord (the "aspect ratio," as students were then learning to call it) displayed a bewildering range of possible combinations. Some birds had wings whose sturdy span was only five times the chord measurement, while the delicate span of others stretched a full twenty times the chord, all of which was even further confused by the birds' widely varying body weights. When

80

the third main element of wing conformation, camber, was added to the span and the chord, complications multiplied rapidly.

The question of camber itself broke down into a further set of unknown quantities. How deep should the curve be in relation to the aspect ratio? Where along the chord should the deepest part of the curve be placed? Should the wing's leading edge be smoothly gradual or abrupt, and how abrupt? What degree of diminishing curve should the after part of the camber follow to the trailing edge? For that matter, did the trailing edge itself have any sort of important effect on lift or balance? And the wing tips, what shape was best for them—square, rounded, pointed, some combination of the three?

By this time Wilbur had also realized that the gap between the two wings must be considered. Experiment had hinted that the normal lift of a wing was, to some extent, decreased by superposing. But why this was so, and to what degree, and what the best gap might be for what manner of wing, were questions to which even an approach was lacking. With the different possible combinations of all these elements running into the thousands, Wilbur saw clearly that he might easily waste many years if he tried to build gliders by what amounted to guesswork. Conceivably, he might never reach his goal. And beyond all this was the aggravating defect in his turning theory, for which, as far as anyone could then tell, there might very well be *no* answer.

It all presented a thoroughly disheartening prospect, and the last thing, certainly, that Wilbur needed at this juncture was another pronouncement from the scientific hierarchy as to the absurdity of human flight. Yet that was the baleful greeting that awaited him on his return to Dayton, again in the form of a *McClure's* article. The magazine, having encouraged the public to believe that it might someday be flying, had now decided to give a hearing to the other side. The reputation of the spokesman it chose, Simon Newcomb, Ph.D., LL.D., easily matched, and overmatched, that of any believer.

An astrophysicist of enormous renown, Newcomb had been the first American since Benjamin Franklin to be honored with a place in the French Academy of Sciences, had once refused the directorship of Harvard Observatory, and at his death in 1909, after all his many honors had been detailed, he was referred to simply as "our Great Astronomer." Though Newcomb was a friend of both Bell and Langley, he most emphatically did not believe that practical mechanical flight was possible. In *McClure's* for September 1901 he made his views clear while being careful to speak in a properly open-minded way.

"Is the Airship Coming?" asked the article's title. That depends, Newcomb answered in a long opening dissertation on the ether and gravity, on whether man can find a way by which the force of gravitation itself "may be controlled and regulated." To the question whether this awesome event might ever come to pass, Newcomb could honestly reply that he did not know, though the impression is left that if it did it would not surprise him. Failing this, would a flying machine be feasible? Rather than deliver a flat no to that question, Newcomb marshaled his scientific logic. The immutable laws of physics, he summed up, made it impossible to design a wing whose sustaining power would be able efficiently to carry the total weight of the machine: "There would always be a distinct disadvantage in the ratio of efficiency to weight." Driving home this point he went on, still apparently with an open mind but in reality delivering a facetious negative:

> We may now see the kernel of the difficulty. If we had a metal so rigid, and at the same time so light, that a sheet of it twenty meters square and a millimeter thick would be as stiff as a board and would not weigh more than a ton, and, at the same time, so strong that a powerful engine could be built of it with little weight, we might hope for a flying machine that would carry a man. But as the case stands, the first successful flyer will be the handiwork of a watchmaker, and will carry nothing heavier than an insect. When this is constructed, we shall be able to see whether one a little larger is possible.

Even this did not close the matter, for still to be dealt with was the matter of gravity. Assume that, against all logic, mechanical flight was achieved. "A flying machine could remain in the air," warned Newcomb, "only by the action of its machinery, and would fall to the ground like a wounded bird the moment any accident stopped it." And such accidents, Newcomb felt, would be numerous and, in fact, unavoidable.

Wilbur in reading this article may have momentarily been even further depressed. The "ratio of efficiency to weight" was the very stumbling block that had defeated him. Yet, on reflection, Newcomb's opinions must in the end have actually brightened Wilbur's gray mood. Here was one of America's leading scientists talking nonsense about flying machines falling out of the skies the moment the engine stopped. The man, for all his erudition, obviously knew nothing of the true action of air pressure on wings, knew nothing of the real significance of Lilienthal's demonstrations or of Langley's model flights. As so often happens, Newcomb's vast competence in one field had made him arrogant in another, which he might properly have entered as a novice. Yet here he was, expounding in the pages of America's most popular magazine. With pardonable satisfaction, Wilbur might have told himself that, after all, his time had not been wasted. He already knew a great deal more about mechanical flight, its problems and potential, than did Simon Newcomb, Ph.D., LL.D.

It was not, however, until nearly two months after his arrival home that Wilbur's gloom began to drop from him, as he finally glimpsed a method for dealing with his impossibly tangled problem. The idea did not come with a rush, but gradually, haphazardly, and as an unanticipated gift of fate. The process began with an invitation from Octave Chanute.

As president of the Western Society of Engineers, Chanute made an effort to bring to its members significant developments in all engineering fields. Though the work of the Wrights was not the sort of thing to which the hardheaded engineers of the day were likely to respond avidly, Chanute judged that the time was ripe for some more formal recognition of aeronautics. A week after the return from Kitty Hawk he sent a note inviting Wilbur to be guest speaker at the society's next formal gathering, set for Chicago on September 18.

At first Wilbur was inclined to refuse. In his depression, he had no desire to appear before a distinguished group of professionals to discuss an effort that had, as it appeared, led nowhere. But his sister, seeing the project as the best means of lifting her brother out of his brooding, urged him to accept, saying it would do him good to "get acquainted with some scientific men." With satisfaction, Katharine reported to her father that she had finally "nagged him into going." That Wilbur may have had other, more personal, reasons for accepting is suggested by a study of the talk itself: believing that his work had come to a halt he wanted to put on record everything of value that he had learned. Perhaps, he seems to have thought, he could yet win some small place in aeronautics, perhaps his name might survive as a footnote when the airplane was finally brought to birth.

On September 2 he wrote to Chanute accepting, and warning that there wasn't enough time to prepare an elaborate paper. Then he began writing and for the next two weeks the Wright home was filled with aeronautical talk as the two brothers discussed and argued, sifting their experiences for pertinent details and essential points. "We don't hear anything but flying machine and engine from morning till night," complained Katharine in mock repentance of her success. "I'll be glad when school begins so I can escape." The finished paper ran to some ten thousand words; it would soon be recognized as the most important contribution to aeronautical literature since the writings of Cayley, nearly a century before.

On the morning of the eighteenth Wilbur arrived in Chicago, visited Chanute at his house, and that evening the two went together to the engineers' club. The affair had been made a "Ladies Night," and the audience of men and women, most in formal attire, numbered nearly a hundred. Wilbur, whose concern with clothes was minimal, had told Chanute that he would not appear in evening dress but he had still managed a degree of splendor by helping himself to Orville's wardrobe. "You never saw Will look so 'swell,'" his sister had remarked approvingly after seeing him off on the train.

Chanute took the podium. Before introducing Wilbur, he offered a few remarks on the subject of the evening. "Engineers have, until recent years," he began, "fought shy of anything relating to aerial navigation. Those who ventured, in spite of the odium attached to that study, to look into it at all, became very soon satisfied that the great obstacle in the way was the lack of a motor sufficiently light to sustain its weight and that of an aeroplane, upon the air." He went on to explain that, during the previous fifteen years, the situation had altered and there was now hope that power-ful, light motors, both steam and gas, could be designed. There was also another "important problem" yet to be solved, he added, that of safety or stability in flight. He then introduced Wilbur— who promptly proceeded to contradict his host.

Opening with a brief sketch of the difficulties others had encoun-tered, Wilbur observed that the achievement of stability "was the *first* instead of the *last* of the great problems in connection with human flight." Lilienthal, he said, was the first man who had really understood this, the first to show that actual practice in the air was not only feasible but indispensable. The danger involved was merely a condition that had to be accepted. Taking a piece of paper, he held it out at arm's length in full view of the audience, then let it fall. As it fluttered to the ground he explained:

> . . . it will not settle steadily down as a staid, sensible piece of paper ought to do, but it insists on contravening every recognized rule of decorum, turning over and darting hither and thither in the most erratic manner, much after the style of an untrained horse. Yet this is the style of steed that men must learn to manage before fly-ing can become an everyday sport. . . . Now there are two ways of learning to ride a fractious horse: one is to get on him and learn by actual practice how each motion and trick may be best met; the other is to sit on a fence and watch the beast awhile, and then retire to the house and at leisure figure out the best way of overcoming his jumps and tricks. The latter system is the safest; but the former, on the whole, turns out the larger proportion of good riders. It is very much the same in learning to ride a flying machine; if you are look-ing for perfect safety you will do well to sit on a fence and watch the birds; but if you really wish to learn you must mount a machine and become acquainted with its tricks by actual trial.

The balancing of a glider or flying machine, Wilbur went on, was in theory really very simple. "It merely consisted in causing the center of pressure to coincide with the center of gravity." But, in practice, between these two there was a mercurial "incompatibility of temper" that made the task of bringing them together an ex-tremely ticklish one that often resulted in injury to the operator. He described some of the balancing methods others had tried, then led into his own work at Kitty Hawk.

For the next hour or so, flashing photographs and sketches on a large screen behind him, he presented a concise technical history of his experiments. In the course of this he described the elevator and its function, revealed what he had learned about the travel of the center of pressure, and disclosed the secret of warping. This last, while it was not given in detail, was sufficiently clear to serve as a guide for others: "The lateral equilibrium and the steering to right or left was to be attained by a peculiar torsion of the main surfaces, which was equivalent to presenting one end of the wings at a greater angle than the other." A few minutes later he again referred to warping, calling it "a system of twisting the surfaces."

His great disappointment, he went on, had come with the discovery of deficiency in the wing lift. The reason for this, as it finally appeared, was a serious defect in the long-accepted Lilienthal tables of air pressures. As he made that statement to the assembly he felt a momentary twinge of doubt; it was no small thing to place himself on record as rejecting the conclusions of an honored name. What if, through some as yet unforeseen factor, it should develop that the German had been right after all?

Reaching the end of his talk he briefly discussed the problems that could be expected in the effort to mount motors on gliders, and then offered a far-seeing prediction about soaring flight. Someday, he said, with improved gliders, greater piloting skill, and an increased knowledge of those invisible currents of air that rose mysteriously from the earth, gliders would be able to "maintain themselves for hours in the air." That was a daring claim for the time, when the very nature and even existence of such rising air columns was still debated. (Thirty years later, soon after the rebirth of interest in gliding flight, the prediction came true.)

At Chanute's house, where Wilbur stayed overnight, he found that his friend was so pleased with the talk that he wanted to publish it in the *Journal* of the society. This was gratifying, but Wilbur hesitated, saying that he would feel more comfortable if he could first make a few simple tests at home to reassure himself about the extent of Lilienthal's errors. He would do this as soon as possible and make whatever revisions might be necessary in the manuscript.

Back in Dayton, Wilbur proceeded to set up a testing device somewhat similar to the wooden V he had employed the previous summer. This time he used a bicycle wheel, laid flat and with the tire removed, as a base. At one point on the rim he mounted a flat plane, and at another point, 120 degrees away, he placed a cambered aerofoil, both made of scrap metal from the shop. To allow the wheel to turn freely in the wind, the hub of the wheel was fixed on a spindle.

The device was first used in an open field on a windy day, but the wind was found to be too erratic, so he decided to try something different. He mounted his wheel device, flat, over the front wheel of a bicycle, on a special metal framework. He then rode the bike through the still air on windless days—incidentally providing the people on the sidewalks of Dayton with something to wonder about.

This was better, but it was still very rough, especially when measuring pressures with the model wing set at small angles of attack. It also quickly became apparent that the test was defective in that both surfaces, separated as they were, did not receive quite the same stream of air. He needed some device that would allow the two model surfaces to act against each other directly, in the same stream, and which would permit finer measurement.

What prompted his next move was another commonplace item which, in those days, could be seen rising by the dozen from the roofs of surrounding buildings, a weathervane. In place of the usual broad vane on the horizontal arm that took the wind's pressure, he attached his two model surfaces. One he angled so that the wind pressure would tend to swing it to the right, the other to the left. The position in which the two-pronged vane came to rest would be a resolution of the two opposing forces.

To obtain controlled conditions, he mounted this device at one end of a "trough" made of an old wooden box, and set up a fan to blow a steady stream of air against the vane. Tacked to the floor of the box beneath the model surfaces was a piece of paper (actually the blank side of old wallpaper scraps) and on these he traced the intersecting lines of the positions assumed by the model surfaces. Some simple calculations on the angles that resulted allowed him to form conclusions about their comparative lifting power. A single day's work with the instrument was sufficient to reassure him. "I am now absolutely certain," he wrote Chanute on October 6, only seventeen days after his return from Chicago, "that Lilienthal's table is very seriously in error."

Even as he wrote those words, however, the mere fact of Lilienthal's inaccuracies had become of secondary importance, for at some point while working with the vane, he had been granted—it is the apt phase—another vision. This new idea he also explained in the October 6 letter, his dry words disguising the deep excitement he undoubtedly felt. "The results obtained, with the rough apparatus used," he wrote, "were so interesting in their nature, and gave evidence of such possibility of exactness in measuring the value of $P_{(tang.\ a)}/P_{90}$,* that we decided to construct an apparatus especially for making tables giving the value of $P_{(tang.\ a)}/P_{90}$ at all angles up to thirty degrees and for surfaces of different curvatures and different relative lengths and breadths."

In plainer words, he had in one sweeping moment discerned the vast possibilities latent in an instrument that had lain neglected by science ever since its first tentative use over thirty years before— the wind tunnel.

Interest in wind pressures, and even crude experiments on them of one kind or another, went back probably to the fifteenth century, when mariners first began to approach ship design in technical terms (perhaps it was under the aegis of the remarkable Prince Henry the Navigator). What amount and shape of sail could best move what weight and shape of hull at what speed? But it was in connection with windmills that wind studies really began to take on the look of an exact science, and military men were soon making use of them to chart and improve the performance of artillery projectiles. Mechanical development at first took the form of a long arm whirling around a central pivot, with test surfaces at the extremity. It was Cayley in England, drawing on the work of two or three predecessors, who first made intelligent use of the whirling arm in aeronautics.

The next logical step was taken in 1870 by Francis Wenham,

* Generally, the lifting power of a curved surface at an angle to the wind, as compared to the pressure on a flat plane set at a ninety-degree angle—that is, full-face— to the airstream.

with other members of the British Aeronautical Society. Wenham brought an artificial wind to bear on a stationary test surface in a confined space, thus producing the pioneer wind tunnel. It was made of wood, some eighteen inches square and ten feet long. The purpose of Wenham and his associates was to obtain "data on which a true science of aeronautics can be founded," and while they did not quite do that, they did obtain some confirmation of the value of curvature and the higher efficiency of a large aspect ratio.

And yet, despite this promising example, and though in the next three decades half a dozen other experimenters made use of tunnels, no one had so much as guessed at the full potential of the process. Some who might have been expected to recognize its worth overlooked it entirely—Langley, for example, had actually returned to the use of the whirling arm for his experiments. It had been left to the uncluttered mind of Wilbur Wright to see that the use of miniature wings in a controlled wind could reduce the whole enormous problem of wing design to a simple question of mathematics.

Just prior to Wilbur's decision to use a wind tunnel, but in the same year, the most ambitious attempt of all was begun. Dr. A. F. Zahm, who had been experimenting in aeronautics for a decade, set up in its own building in Washington, D.C., a tunnel that was fully forty feet long and six feet square, with windows in the top and sides. A five-foot suction fan drew the air through the tunnel at a speed of twenty-seven miles an hour. Equipped with a variety of sophisticated measuring devices, Zahm began his work in the fall of 1901, at about the same time that Wilbur started making his own tunnel—a square wooden enclosure six feet long, with the interior sixteen inches on a side.

This was a coincidence that helps make clear just what it was that Wilbur did, for it was not the tunnel itself, its size or sophistication, that counted. What made the difference was the testing apparatus placed inside. The instrument designed by Wilbur proved capable of yielding fundamental principles never grasped before, as well as a wealth of accurate detail on wing properties and performance. Almost as if he were a magician waving a wand, with this flimsy-looking apparatus Wilbur finally brought order to the dizzying agglomeration of difficulties that had for so long stood in the way of powered flight.

The device, or "balance," as it was called, was constructed of materials picked up in the bicycle shop: hacksaw blades, bicycle spokes, and other bits of metal. It incorporated in its foot-square framework two tiers. Clipped to the upper tier, edge to the wind, was the model wing to be tested. The rushing air moved the wing to the right, in the direction of its curvature. Hanging from the lower tier was the flat plane, set "normal" to the wind, or head-on, so that the wind tended to force it back toward the left, opposing the pull of the model wing.

The flat plane, its area carefully calculated, was not used whole. To avoid serious deflection of the airflow it had been cut into four fingerlike pieces, all hung in a line. A dial pointer at the bottom of one pole gave a reading which could be quickly interpreted by trigonometric calculation.

The tunnel itself, sturdily built and free-standing, was patterned on the best work of other men. The airstream from the two-bladed fan (run by a two-cylinder gas motor, since the shop had no electricity) entered a funnel-shaped opening and, before reaching the balance, was straightened and controlled by a series of meshes and grids. Getting the wind to move steadily and true had proved unexpectedly troublesome. "We spent nearly a month getting a straight wind," wrote Wilbur later, "but finally were able to get a current whose direction did not vary one-eighth of a degree." A glass pane over the balance afforded the necessary view. The apparatus was set up in a corner of the Wrights' workshop, behind the store. Once in use, no large object in the room was permitted to be moved again. During the testing Wilbur always occupied the same position to the side, standing perfectly still while the fan was on. No one else was allowed near.

By October 16 the tunnel and the balance were both ready for use and here, again, Wilbur displayed an instinct for procedure that would have been commendable in an experienced scientist and that was remarkable in one who, devoid of formal training, was venturing into uncharted territory. His father later remembered how Wilbur "systematized everything," and nowhere did that habit prove of greater worth than in his dealing with the wind tunnel.

He had decided that rather than "work blindly on all sorts of shapes," he would divide his study into two stages. In the first he would probe the general field of wing aerodynamics, continually weighing the known against the unknown, surmise against what appeared to be fact, changing direction and emphasis as he learned, and pyramiding data. With this accumulated knowledge as a basis, he would design a series of model wings whose typical configurations would cover, he hoped, all the strategic points in that daunting array of possible combinations. If he was correct in his approach and did his work with care, he would then have laid open the whole secret of efficient wing design. After that it should be a comparatively simple matter, drawing on this treasure trove of theoretical formulas, to translate his miniature values into full-size reality. He would then have a glider with the lowest possible lift/drag ratio, one that would sustain his own weight—or any weight desired—and that of the machine at a proper attitude.

During five weeks, with the help of his brother, Wilbur made and tested some 150 model wings, taking great pains in measuring and cutting the bits of metal—oblong, square, curved, flat, thick, thin, sharp edges or blunt—precisely calculating and delicately hammering out the subtle curvatures. All the models were cut with a pair of tin shears from a sheet of twenty-gauge steel, $\frac{1}{32}$ inch thick. To vary the front edges when needed, small extra pieces were added by soldering. As these preliminary tests proceeded, he never ceased making "numberless small changes" in the balance and tunnel, in an effort to further reduce the margin of error that might arise from such things as friction, slippage, or fluctuation in the airstream.

This first stage reached its conclusion by the third week in November, and, without pausing, he began designing his series of typical shapes. He also devised a new form of balance, one that would provide a direct reading of the lift/drag ratio, thus eliminating a good deal of time-consuming calculation. On November 23 he made and tested a dozen surfaces—all with a span of six inches and a chord of one inch—and promptly found himself making discoveries that warned of the complications still to be faced.

Testing one model that had a parabolic curve of 1-in-12 against an arc of similar area and curvature, he found that up to an angle of eight degrees the lift of the parabola, as expected, was the greater. But above eight degrees, the arc became much the more efficient. And at the arc's maximum lift, about seventeen degrees, the registered pressure actually exceeded that on a square plane of equal area set full to the wind.

A week later some two dozen more surfaces had been prepared and tested, bringing to light further unpredictable results. Some surfaces that lifted most strongly when set at an angle below seven and a half degrees lifted least when set above that angle. One surface, with half-rounded tips and thickened front edges, increased its lift as the angle of attack rose to seven degrees, but above that point, surprisingly, the lift did not increase at all—at forty-five degrees the lifting pressure was no greater than it had been at the relatively flat seven degrees. Still another model when set at zero degrees had already attained more than half its maximum efficiency.

The most perplexing finding of all came when Wilbur was testing a flat plane, square in shape. On this, unaccountably, the pressure proved much greater at thirty degrees inclination than at forty-five degrees, a position in which a much larger area was offered to the action of the airstream. This caused him, as he said later, not a little "consternation," since it raised the possibility that his method or apparatus had some hidden defect. He interrupted his orderly testing of the typical series, devised a special recheck vane, and found that the original result—whatever reason might insist to the contrary—was quite correct.

It was such anomalies as these that later allowed Wilbur the luxury of commending his own foresight. "Accurately measuring the lifts of differently shaped surfaces at many angles," he explained in a letter to Chanute, "brings out peculiarities in their actions which averaging widely discordant data and testing a few angles only would not indicate."

In all, by the time he decided to halt this second stage of experiments, early in December, he had made systematic measurements of forty-eight different surfaces, each one tested at fourteen different angles, graduated from zero degrees to forty-five degrees. Counting miscellaneous efforts, in a two-week period he had recorded, studied, and evaluated well over a thousand readings, had begun to translate them into percentage tables, and to plot performance curves for all the surfaces on charts.

Since Wilbur's early test with the bicycle wheel, he had kept Chanute informed of his progress with the wind tunnel, at one point drawing from the veteran observer an admiring outburst. "It is perfectly marvelous to me," Chanute enthused, "how quickly you get results with your testing machine . . . you are evidently better equipped to test the endless variety of curved surfaces than anybody has ever been." Thus, when in mid-December Wilbur told Chanute that he was closing out the experiments, Chanute expressed much disappointment at the cessation of work that promised "important results"—somehow managing to overlook the fact that important results had already been attained.

The full extent of Wilbur's accomplishment with the wind tunnel was for many years neither known nor appreciated, only a few men, such as Chanute, having been let in on the secret. Even today it can be understood in all its dimensions only by those with technical knowledge, especially of the history of wind pressure studies. One such expert, in 1939, was the first qualified engineer to be allowed a close look at the original records and apparatus. The Wrights, he concluded, had been "far in advance of the contemporary art." So clear was the vision behind Wilbur's approach, so firm was his grasp of fundamentals, that in his typical series of model surfaces he had "included all but one of the important variables that have since concerned us in wing and aerofoil research . . . most subsequent research along this line appears mainly to have been in extension and refinement of this basic outline."

That opinion was offered at a time when the big, gleaming DC-3 had begun to revolutionize passenger travel, and just as the English Spitfire was about to streak to the defense of beleaguered Britain. And it remained largely true for another decade, until very high speed and supersonic jets brought a revamping of the whole basis of aerodynamics.

Still another expert, a few years later, was led to comment on the smallness of the Wrights' wing models and the short time taken up by the experiments. In light of these, he said wonderingly, "The accuracy of these conclusions is truly amazing . . . we must not overlook the fact that this was quite contradictory to and beyond the work of all other investigators who were 'better' equipped."

Responding to Chanute's dismay over the halting of the tests, Wilbur explained that in the six months since June, he had spent more than two-thirds of his time on aeronautical matters and "unless I decide to devote myself to something other than a business career I must give closer attention to my regular work for a while." Preparing for the spring rush in the bicycle trade, he meant, needed the fulltime efforts of himself and his brother as well as Taylor; by this time the business of the shop had expanded a little and the brothers were now selling their own make of bicycle, assembling it from ordered parts. Also, Wilbur added to Chanute, he wanted to take no chance of having untended business affairs interfere with the trip he was now planning to Kitty Hawk in the fall.

Chanute's reply to this must have surprised him. Perhaps, offered Chanute, he could arrange to have "some rich man" provide Wilbur with a subsidy, say $10,000 a year, to free him from the necessity of working for a living. "I happen to know Carnegie. Would you like for me to write him?" That was a very large sum for the time, probably more than double what the brothers cleared annually in their shop. Ten thousand a year just to keep at aeronautics the year round, and certainly Chanute would not have made the suggestion unless he was fairly sure of delivering; perhaps he had already mentioned it to Carnegie. It was, all things considered, an inviting prospect—but Wilbur was not tempted. With thanks, he declined, saying such an arrangement would only encourage him in a further neglect of the bicycle business, without giving him any assurance that he would have a livelihood to take the place of the shop if it were to fail.

Eminently levelheaded as he was, such business caution may have played a part in Wilbur's thinking. Yet it is now obvious that his decision to go on alone stemmed from a much more dramatic hope. As the last days of 1901 ran out, Wilbur had become convinced that he was, at last, on the threshold of success. The chance for fame and fortune that he had called "slight" the year before now loomed compellingly certain.

Flushed with the promise of the wind tunnel data, he boldly

stated to Chanute that he believed he was now enabled to make artificial wings whose performance in some respects would exceed natural ones—"superior to those of any bird in dynamic efficiency for soaring." A practical, powered airplane, he was sure, was now no more than "a very few years" away.

8

Kitty Hawk 1902

No raging Aeolus, but fair skies and a warm sun greeted the brothers' third arrival at Kitty Hawk. With heavily laden trunks, extra baggage, and a supply of long wooden spars, they reached the Banks on the morning of August 28, 1902, and went immediately to inspect the shed. This time Wilbur was prepared for a long stay, three or four months if necessary, so the camp would have to be made more livable as well as more convenient for the work ahead.

Trudging across the sands, their baggage loaded in a wagon, they were eager to begin assembling the new glider. Company was again expected in camp—Spratt, Chanute, and another assistant— and from his experience the previous year Wilbur had learned that the presence of guests drastically slowed down his work. He had hinted as much to Chanute but the hint had gone unheeded ("It was our experience last year that my brother and myself, while alone, or nearly so, could do more work in one week, than in two weeks after Mr. Huffaker's arrival"). To gain some time alone the best Wilbur had been able to do was to suggest a late arrival for the guests; they were all expected about the beginning of October. That left a month uninterrupted, little enough time for all Wilbur hoped to accomplish.

Coming up to the building, they saw that winter had not been

kind to it. Both ends now sagged two feet or more into large depres-
sions scooped in the sand by the winds, bending the roof into a
curve and loosening many of the boards. This was a discouraging
start, especially when they had planned to spend a few days adding
a small extension to the structure. Now many more days would be
lost.

It took over a week to make the shed livable. The ends were
propped on foundation posts, loose boards nailed tight, a ten-foot
extension put up, and sleeping, kitchen, and workshop sections
arranged inside. Finally, on September 8, the shed was in order and
assembly of the glider was begun.

That task was now more time-consuming. In addition to a new
conformation, Wilbur had also introduced many small refinements,
both structural and operational, making the machine a more sophisticated apparatus. As usual, every single piece and fitting was thoroughly tested and as each wing was readied the brothers determined its center of gravity by flying it as a kite. Two weeks after
starting, the graceful lines of the completed machine occupied
nearly one whole side of the shed's interior.

The new glider was not simply a scaled-up version of one of the
model surfaces tested in the tunnel. Carefully interpreting his mass
of data, Wilbur had chosen to amalgamate qualities derived from
three or four of the miniature wings. The most obvious change from
the previous years was in the span: from tip to tip the new wings
measured an inch over thirty-two feet, nearly double that of the
first glider and ten feet more than the second.

The chord, which the year before had been an ungainly seven
feet, was now slimmed down to five. This gave an aspect ratio radically different from that used in the first two machines—the span
was now six times the chord, instead of three—yet the weight of
the whole machine, 112 pounds, was only slightly increased. The
gap between the wings remained about the same, just under five
feet. The camber was the shallowest it had ever been, 1-in-24, and
it became even shallower as the experiments wore on, the steamed
ribs gradually losing their curvature.

The elusive problem of placement of the curvature's apex had
been resolved by a drastic shift rearward. It now occurred some
twenty inches back from the leading edge, or one-third the length

of the chord. In the Wrights' earlier machines, and those of all other experimenters, the greatest depth of camber had been located much further forward. The elevator was reduced in total area by three square feet and reshaped from its former near-squareness so that it had the appearance of a small wing jutting out ahead of the glider. The elevator did, in fact, in addition to controlling the fore-and-aft attitude, act as an auxiliary lifting surface.

Control of the wing warping had also been altered. Instead of levers at the feet, there was now a shallow cradle into which the operator, lying prone, would fit his hips. To this cradle were attached the warping wires, and a shifting of the hips, right or left, would activate them. Even in this, Wilbur's attention to detail was evident. The natural human response to an unwanted tilting of the wings, he knew, would be an involuntary movement away from the dropped wing and toward the high one. Taking advantage of this automatic response, he arranged the warp control so that movement of the cradle toward the high wing would give the desired increase of angle to the low one.

Only one feature was totally new: a tail. Set on spars extending nearly four feet back from the rear edges, a narrow, two-bladed vane rose vertically. Each blade was some six feet high and one foot broad. Strongly attached, the tail could not be moved in any way. It was with this device that Wilbur hoped to solve the turning problem.

Though fixed tails had been used on gliders by others, the conditions that had led Wilbur to adopt one had not existed before, so it was not simply a case of imitation, and the reasoning behind it appeared flawless. Since the turning difficulty he had encountered the previous year—the sudden reverse spin on a vertical axis —resulted from one wing losing speed while the other forged ahead, it had seemed to Wilbur that it was necessary only to retard the faster wing. With speeds equalized, or nearly so, a spin would be impossible.

Two methods for doing this had occurred to him. One was to build into each wing, at the tips, some device that could be actuated to provide additional resistance on either side. The other was a tail, which Wilbur, in the beginning, had discarded as more a trouble than a help. With a fixed vertical vane at the rear, set with its thin edge cutting unresistingly into the airstream, as soon as the glider should veer even slightly from its flight path, the surface of the vane would begin to receive pressure, forcing it back to the point of least exposure.

Preference for the vane had, again, been dictated by Wilbur's foresight, a concern for the needs not of the glider but of powered flight. A wing tip mechanism, he saw, would inevitably impair the efficiency of a propeller-driven machine: "every pound of resistance at the wing tips would cost an extra pound of push in the propeller." A tail, on the other hand, would give the needed correction at the expense of one pound or less of propeller thrust. A tail also had the supreme advantage of working automatically, leaving the already much-preoccupied operator to give his attention to the elevator, the wing warping, and scrutiny of the fast-rushing terrain. With this vertical tail, as Wilbur wrote Chanute, "We are convinced that the trouble with the 1901 machine is overcome."

At first this confidence seemed to be justified. On the afternoon of September 19, the same day it was completed, the glider was lifted into the wind for the first time, in a series of semiglides and kite trials. Even in these limited preliminaries, the new wings gave promise of being everything hoped for, both in sustaining power and control. Spirits buoyant, the brothers could hardly wait for the next morning to come and prayed it would bring with it strong winds and fair skies. September 20, they were sure, would become a red-letter day on their long road, the first of many they would spend in the following weeks soaring over the gray wastes of the Banks, as no man had ever soared, learning all the tricks of wind and machine, and refining their skills. When next they saw their home in Dayton, they fully expected to be the world's first qualified pilots, needing only to mount a motor and propellers on a modified glider in order to bring human flight to the world.

But it did not work out quite that way. In the search for control there was yet one more barrier to be crossed, and it would prove the most dangerous and perplexing of all.

The brothers rose early on the morning of September 20 to find the wind blowing at about eighteen miles an hour, just what was needed. With Tate's help they carried the machine to the big hill where Wilbur began the day with a series of short, straight-line glides. If the machine proved itself in flight, he would then allow Orville to begin training; up to now he had taken all the risks himself, refusing to let his brother go aloft while there was any likelihood of accident.

Quickly, it became evident that the wind tunnel data had produced a machine whose dynamic efficiency went far beyond that ever claimed or achieved before. Even in the first tentative glides it easily maintained a proper attitude and descended comfortably on a very shallow trajectory, many times at an angle of seven degrees, leaving Wilbur with the feeling that it could easily do even better.

Growing bolder, Wilbur now cast off from higher up the hill, trying for distance, and intending to make a small turn, putting the tail to its first real test. After sailing smoothly for 200 feet he shifted his hips a few inches, dropping the right wing and sending the glider into a slight bank. Without warning, the left wing leaped even higher "in a decidedly alarming manner," tilting the glider dangerously to the right. If there had been no cradle to sustain him, Wilbur might easily have been thrown down the sloping wings and out of the machine. As it was, in his confusion he could only think of getting back to the safety of the ground. Even as he depressed the elevator he knew he had made a mistake, forgetting that the elevator's mechanism had been changed.

As if it were a bucking horse, the glider nosed up abruptly, rearing to an angle of forty-five degrees, still inclined on a downslope to the right, and gradually slowing. At a point perhaps twenty feet above the ground, as its undersurface met the full force of the wind, it came almost to a dead stop in the air. Recovering himself, Wilbur slammed the elevator handle to full negative position and at the same time threw his body forward to add weight to the leading edge. Slowly nosing down, the machine gradually gathered headway, still in a bank to the right. No longer in proper contact with the cradle, Wilbur could do little to correct the tilt and for the first time he felt real fear.

The glider, in addition to its forward progress, had also taken on a loose, side-slipping motion, dropping faster and faster toward

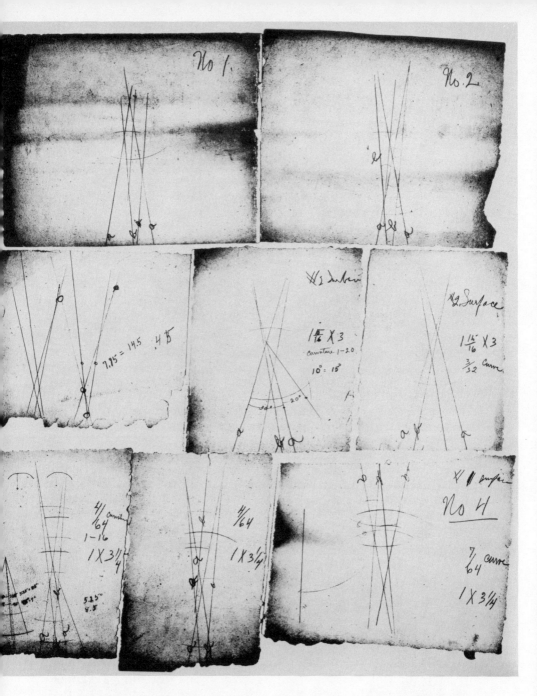

Old wallpaper scraps bearing results of the Wrights' earliest wind-pressure experiments, in which they used a modified weathervane. The intersecting lines represent various positions of model wings. These preliminary tests revealed the vast possibilities latent in a wind tunnel.

ABOVE: The balancing device from the wind tunnel. On the top tier a model wing rises vertically. The metal strips hanging from the bottom tier provide the flat-plane area against which the model wing was evaluated. The dial at the bottom of the left pole supplied a reading.

BELOW: The Wrights' wind tunnel (a reconstruction). A motor-driven fan at the right blew air through a series of grids against model wings on the balancing device at the left (the side in this reconstruction has been cut away to show the device). A glass pane in the tunnel's top, over the balance, allowed readings to be taken. The rack atop the tunnel contains a series of model wings.

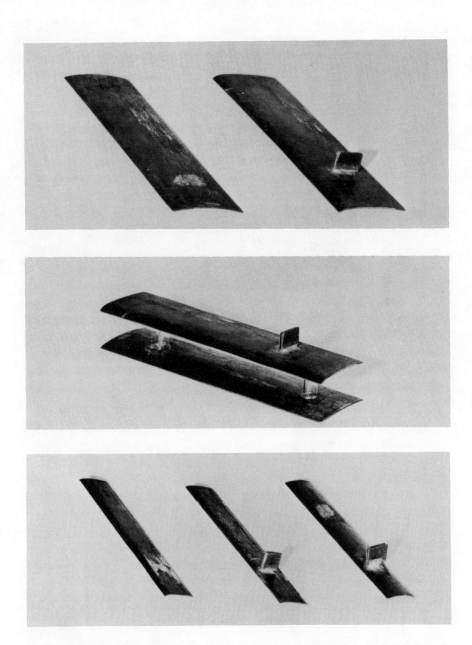

Some of the model wings used in the wind tunnel. All were cut by the brothers from sheet steel and shaped with a hammer; all had a span of about six inches.

Interior of the workshed at Kitty Hawk, 1902; Wilbur at rear. Along the right side is stored the old 1901 glider. Jutting from the rear wall is the brothers' dining table, still holding plates, cups, and the remains of a meal.

the right wing. Plummeting down, the tip of the wing struck the sand, the glider swung around it as on a pivot, then smashed flat in a bouncing twist while Wilbur held on grimly, ducking his head to escape the cloud of sand that was kicked up. Coming down flat, as it did, the machine suffered no damage. Wilbur, too, was unhurt.

Wilbur's analysis of the accident placed all the blame on himself, his confusion and lack of familiarity with the new controls. He had also encountered a crosswind from the left, he reasoned, and when the left wing rose this crosswind had suddenly gusted, throwing the already rising wing out of control. After a rest, he had the machine carried back up the hill and the gliding continued.

In all, Wilbur made twenty-five glides this day, most of them well under 200 feet and most without incident. A number of turns were made without mishap, the tail nicely performing its expected function. Despite his one near-crash landing, Wilbur was well pleased with the day's work. The machine was everything he had hoped for, though it was also clear that it needed some practice to fly properly. On their next gliding day, he told his brother, he could begin.

The twenty-first was a Sunday and the next morning brought rain, so it was September 23 before the glider was again taken out; it was to be mostly a day of practice for Orville. A small change, in the meantime, had been made in the glider's conformation: the wing tips now drooped slightly, hanging some four inches lower than the center of the span. This, Wilbur believed, would reduce the disturbing effects of side gusts.

With Tate, the two went to the small hill west of the big dune. Here Orville first climbed aboard a glider, being carried down the hill by Tate and Wilbur at the wing tips in short semiglides that were gradually lengthened. He proved an apt pupil, displaying an instinct for the right move and a deft touch at the controls. In the afternoon the party moved over to the lower slopes of the big dune, where slightly longer and shallower glides were possible. It was a premature move, one that the brothers almost immediately had reason to regret.

After warming up with a half-dozen short, straight-line glides, in which the warp control was made inoperable, Orville was then permitted to launch out on his own with the warp activated. He accomplished a steady flight of 160 feet at an angle of seven degrees, landing smoothly. Next Wilbur took the machine up, sailing out to 200 feet but experiencing a peculiar disturbance not felt before. Five or six times in the course of the glide the machine had swayed sharply from side to side, "sidling one way then the other." These oscillations had not seriously interfered with the glider's progress, but neither Wilbur nor Orville could find an explanation for them. Now, for once, Wilbur's customary caution failed him. Despite the unexplained development he allowed Orville to go up again.

Sailing out from a lower slope of the hill, Orville had the glider under good control. When the wings began to tilt as an oblique wind hit them, he applied the warp, expecting to right the balance. Instead, the high wind jumped higher, the nose lifted, and Orville found himself drifting backward. Then the glider tilted forward again, came speedily round in a tight circle, touched down on one wing tip, and plumped heavily to the sand. To his brother, Orville explained that the trouble really was his own fault. He had not applied the warp in time and then had momentarily forgotten to use the elevator.

Following a couple of uneventful glides by Wilbur, in which he made half-turns to both left and right, Orville again went up, promising to be more attentive this time. But almost immediately after launch he was once more in difficulty.

Sailing along at a height of about thirty feet, Orville became uncomfortably aware that "one wing was getting a little too high and that the machine was slowly sidling off in the opposite direction." He shifted his hips a little to activate the warp and bring the high wing down, but not knowing quite what to do about the strange "sidling." Abruptly, instead of righting itself, the glider was thrown into a rapid confusion of movement: the high wing jumped still higher, the nose lifted, checking the speed, and the whole machine began to slip sideways. The two men on the ground saw what was happening and began to call out warnings and advice. "Our shouts of alarm," recalled Wilbur, "were drowned out by the howling of the wind."

Hopelessly out of control, buffeted by shifting gusts, the glider slowed more and more, hung helplessly for a moment in the rending wind, then was flung backward toward the side of the hill. Orville had time only for a frightened glance behind him before impact.

Of all the anxious moments the brothers encountered in their experiments at Kitty Hawk, this was the most appalling. The glider, with Orville clinging desperately to the lower wing, thudded dully into the hillside, shivering as its spars cracked and the fabric tore, rolled down a few feet, and came to rest in a sunken heap. Wilbur and Tate raced toward it, fully expecting the worst. As they approached they saw Orville stir, then struggle up from the center of the wreckage, shaken but unhurt. "How he escaped injury," Wilbur said later, "I do not know. But afterward he was unable to show a bruise or a scratch anywhere, though his clothes were torn in one place." The three could hardly believe Orville's luck in emerging whole from the accident—and somewhere above the clouds a certain jealous god must have also been shaking his head.

With the bedraggled glider back at camp, laid out on the sand before the shed, the two brothers had another surprise: the damage was not so bad as it might have been. Throughout the whole framework there was a great deal of distortion, twisting, and loosening of fittings and wires, but actual breakage was limited to the right wing tips, both upper and lower. Here spars and ribs were cracked and the covering badly torn. Three or four days' work, Wilbur estimated happily, should make the machine as good as new. The next morning disassembly was begun.

As they worked, the two discussed what still seemed to them to be a problem in piloting. Not counting dozens of brief practice hops, they had now made perhaps fifty glides of some length. In most of them the lateral control—in half-turns and landings—had been wonderfully efficient and smooth. In only about ten instances had the control gotten out of hand. Both men were sure that the reason for this was their inexperience, though they differed on the exact cause. Orville was inclined to blame unexpected crosswinds suddenly hitting the machine and leaving the operator no time to think about corrections. Wilbur, on the other hand, "maintained that the trouble was just the reverse." Lateral tipping, he insisted, began with a loss of forward motion, on one side or the other, and it was this uneven slowing down that allowed the crosswinds to disrupt control.

It may have been in connection with this discussion that the two were seen by one of the men from the lifesaving station, arguing on the beach one day, waving arms and hands in emulation of one of nature's greatest flyers. "They would watch the gannets," the man wrote years afterwards, "and imitate the movements of the wings of those gannets; we thought they were crazy. But we just had to admire the way they could move their arms this way and that and bend their elbows and wrist bones up and down and every which a way, just like the gannets moved their wings." The gannets, however, were not ready to give up their secrets, and the two had to agree that there was only one way to gain the necessary skills in dealing with crosswinds. Keep flying.

Early on the morning of September 29 they were again at the big hill. Orville led off with three fine glides, the longest of which was 216 feet and the time in the air twelve seconds. When Wilbur's turn came the wind had died away almost entirely. Even hard running with the glider could not impart enough initial velocity, so the next hour was wasted as five starts were aborted. When the wind picked up a little, the best that Wilbur could do was 152 feet at about seven degrees angle of descent. When they quit for lunch they had made only a half-dozen glides of a hundred feet or more but this was not too disappointing since they were not trying primarily for distance.

On each flight the operator was interested mainly in control—banking, correcting lateral balance, gently sweeping into quarter-turns, learning the degree of negative or positive elevator needed to steer up or down—and waiting with nerves taut for the reappearance of that peculiar slipping or sidling motion that might signal the start of a spin. Only once or twice had some hint of this been felt and it had quickly passed off.

By afternoon the wind had blown up again, reaching eighteen miles an hour. This time Wilbur led off, repeatedly sailing out well beyond the hundred-foot mark. Then he decided to get more distance by launching from near the summit of the dune.

Passing 200 feet after ten seconds in the air, he went into a slight turn to the right, and immediately felt the glider take on a pronounced slide toward the low wing, at the same time starting a right-hand spin on its own vertical axis. Quickly he threw his hips to the left to bring up the low wing, and depressed the elevator for a landing. He had not acted soon enough. As the ground neared, the right tip was coming up to the level but it was still too low. The tip made contact with the sand, dug in, and pulled the machine around to a hard, bouncing touchdown, nearly throwing Wilbur off the wing. When Orville and Tate ran up, Wilbur, grim-faced, said he wanted to repeat the flight, this time from the summit.

Minutes later he was again in the air, descending at a steep angle, nearly ten degrees. At 200 feet he went into another half turn to the right, waiting tensely for the first indication of slipping or spinning. It came, a slight shivering dip toward the low wing, and a tremor at the rear. Immediately he shoved the hip cradle to the left its full distance, about six inches, and was relieved to feel the right wing begin to rise and the sideslipping diminish. He touched down with the wings only slightly tilted, and came to a smooth, sliding halt. In the back of his mind a theory had begun to form. With this successful pullout from a spin, it became clouded again.

Orville now climbed aboard. Starting from lower down on the slope, he made a steady, controlled glide of 180 feet at an angle of only a little more than six degrees. A second effort was shorter and shallower. Then he was launched a third time. Watching from the ground, Wilbur saw the glider's right wing lift high, saw his brother move to correct the balance, without success. After covering only about a hundred feet the machine slipped to the left, the high wing revolving around the low one. The left tip hit the sand, dragged along, and finally pulled the glider around in a tight circle, bouncing it to a flat stop. Though he was roughly jostled, Orville managed to hang on.

The wind dying, the brothers quit for the day, more than a little downcast at their inability to overcome the spinning tendency. The trouble in diagnosing the unwanted movement and thus in correcting it, they agreed, lay in its apparent random occurrence. Why should the machine one time proceed trimly through the air to a disciplined landing, then the next time, under what appeared to be similar conditions, suddenly be thrown into utter confusion, as if it had gone berserk? And why at the end of such a wild plunge did the tip of the low wing always seem to stab the ground, throwing the glider around it as on a pivot?

On the next two days the brothers were out with the glider again, seeking answers. Time after time, one or another of them would take his place on the lower wing, shout that he was ready, then be carried forward into the wind and released over a shelf of the dune to drop into the airstream. About forty glides were made on these two days, the brothers sharing them equally, each taking off five or six times in a row in order to build the experience of one flight directly on another. As before, the spinning and sliding occurred with about every third flight. Some of the landings were so rough that, as Wilbur said, "we often considered ourselves lucky to escape unhurt." Undaunted, if a little wary, the two men held doggedly to their purpose, deliberately "taking the chance over and over."

Exactly what day it was when the solution finally dawned on Wilbur it is hard to say with certainty; the evidence suggests it may have been the evening of September 30, or perhaps the next morning. The source of the trouble, he theorized, lay not in any lack of piloting skill or failure to cope with the crosswinds. It lay solely in the tail. As he pieced the puzzle together, it appeared that the fixed tail, instead of always equalizing the wing speeds, and thus warding off a spin, sometimes had just the opposite effect. Whenever the tilted glider, through loss of speed, went into a side-slip—the rate of this sideways descent "increasing in an accelerated ratio"—the tail actually increased its tendency to revolve on itself. The reason, as Wilbur saw it, was that in this sideways movement the fixed tail brought pressure to bear on the wrong side. From the diagnosis, the proper cure leapt immediately to mind. "We felt that if this were the true explanation," Wilbur wrote afterwards, "it would be necessary to make the vertical vane movable."

Though he is matter-of-fact in recording the genesis of the movable tail, the concept was totally new. Others who had specified a movable tail had meant to employ it in the direct action of steering, as with a ship. Wilbur's rudder, on the other hand, would be used only to maintain balance, while the tilt of the wings brought about the turning. It was in reality another brilliant concept, the simplicity again disguising the brilliance. Yet in another way it can be said that the true originality lay in Wilbur's spotting the theoretical flaw in the fixed tail. From awareness of that flaw the idea of making the tail movable must sooner or later have inevitably followed. If unwanted pressures were striking the wrong side of the tail, then why not swing it over to expose the other side? And since both sides would, at one time or another, be the wrong side, why not give the rudder the capability of swinging either way?

Having a theory in hand, Wilbur now felt it was necessary to submit it to further study, a thing hard to do without a further flirting with danger, since it meant more gliding. With Wilbur taking the lead, the two brothers spent the next few days making flights that gradually grew in distance and duration. On October 1 Wilbur three times exceeded 300 feet, Orville's efforts remaining under 200. This pattern was repeated the next day, with Wilbur consistently bettering 300 feet and then, in the afternoon suddenly —and a little surprisingly—soaring out to unprecedented distances. In successive flights he covered 506 feet, then 504 feet, concluding the day with a grand effort of 550 feet. All three were low, straight-line glides, occupying about twenty-five seconds each, with Wilbur in perfect control and no hint of the sliding effect. By the evening of October 2 he seems to have become convinced that his theory of a movable tail was the answer. Writing to his father, he reported that "we now believe that the flying problem is really nearing its solution."

Admittedly, it is somewhat difficult to fit Wilbur's 500-foot glides into the known pattern of events, since they apparently involved some unnecessary risk. Perhaps they indicate a desire to make sustained observations, perhaps they were prompted by an unaccustomed exuberance, a desire to put his growing skills to a real test. The last of them, in fact, was an unusual and rather breathtaking performance. It was made in a light wind, blowing about twelve miles, and this together with a fairly steep start built up the glider's ground speed to something like thirty miles an hour. As it neared the 250-foot mark it let down and appeared about to land. The machine's runners were just scraping lightly along the sand, when Wilbur threw the elevator to full positive and the glider bore rapidly upward again, high in the air, continuing to a smooth landing another 300 feet away.

Though he was now ready to alter the tail, to make it movable, one thing still bothered him: the complications that a third control would impose on the operator. Three controls, three possible maneuvers, when the operator often had only a second or two to make his decision, would tax even the most intuitive skills. No doubt with sufficient practice a man could learn to handle three controls at once, but not at first, and certainly not before anyone could even be sure that the new control would indeed do what it was supposed to do. Here again Wilbur was faced with the old problem, simultaneously inventing a mechanism and learning to use it, under conditions that left little margin for misjudgment or slow reaction. This time the answer was found not by Wilbur but by Orville.

On the evening of October 2 Orville sat up late talking aeronautics with George Spratt, who had arrived the day before, and with Lorin Wright, who had come to spend a vacation with his younger brothers. In bed, he found he couldn't sleep as the problem of the movable tail ran through his mind. Gradually he began to see that a definite relation existed between the warp and the rudder—so much bank to the right side, so much rudder pressure on the right, and the same to the left. Why not, then, make the movement of the rudder automatic, wiring it directly into the warping mechanism? That way the operator could forget entirely about rudder movements and give his full attention to elevator and warp. Wilbur, when Orville explained the idea to him the next morning, agreed that such a linkage would probably work, and the two set about making designs.

Unfortunately, the technical details by which they made their analysis have been lost or were never set down, but the problem certainly was not the uncomplicated one usually pictured. The central question—how much tail surface to expose in conjunction with what degree of warp—must have generated a good deal of discussion and may have led to experiments on the ground. However long they spent studying, they wasted little time in reaching a decision. The tail's two six-foot vanes were reduced to a single vane, five feet high by fourteen inches broad. Distance between the trailing edge of the wings and the leading edge of the vane remained about the same, three and a half feet. Operating wires led obliquely from either side of the vane and were attached to the warping wires on the wings.

By afternoon of October 4 alterations had begun. The next day,

Sunday, brought both a heavy rain and the arrival of Octave Chanute, with his assistant, Augustus Herring, and a small, multiwing
glider. The arrival of this group caused some interruption, but by
the next afternoon Wilbur was back at work on the tail and it was
completed that evening, after a total of only eight or nine hours'
work.

The first trials of the new tail took place on October 8, when in
the course of an hour and a half about twenty glides were made,
most of them by Wilbur, the longest just over 200 feet. It appears
that no turns were attempted, and probably these glides were intended only as a gingerly tryout. On the following day the winds
were too light for sustained flights. The time was again spent in
practice.

By the tenth, the brothers were eager to begin real gliding and
the winds this time did not disappoint them. "The day opened with
a calm," noted Orville in his diary, "which was followed about
seven o'clock, with a northeast wind that grew stronger and
stronger as the day advanced." They took the machine first to the
small hill, where some time was spent getting accustomed to the
high winds, blowing about eighteen miles an hour. Then they
moved over to the big hill.

Still cautious, Wilbur insisted on making the first few glides himself. None of these covered more than 300 feet but in two of them,
after picking up speed, he deliberately nosed up, came almost to a
dead stop high in the air, then turned and landed with the wind
blowing directly against the side of the machine. In another, he
banked right and left consecutively, taking the strong crosswinds
at a number of different angles, first one side and then the other,
all very smoothly. When it came his turn, Orville had some difficulty coordinating the controls, especially the elevator, but he soon
settled down and was able to make a number of long, shallow
flights in which the angle of descent barely exceeded six degrees,
even as he went into quarter- and half-turns.

It was an exhilarating day, with the two making perhaps thirty
flights without the least mishap and with no recurrence of the side-
slip or tailspin. The brothers had wrought with uncanny precision:
a thirty-degree pivot, approximately, of the rudder into the airstream on the low side had instantly and magically transformed a

fractious pair of wings into a docile flying machine, responsive to every command.

Successful powered flight was still fourteen months away; to accomplish it would require more ingenuity and daring. But it may be said that, in a way, the day on which man finally conquered the air was this day, Friday, October 10, 1902. For, as Wilbur had insisted from the start, the whole problem of human flight was the achievement of control, not the designing of light motors. An engine and propellers were, so to speak, merely more efficient substitutes for wind and gravity. There was no doubt that a glider which could, under all conditions, be controlled in a descent of a few hundred feet, could with modifications be made to fly on and on, to unpredictable distances, once it carried its own source of power.

The immediate need was for more practice. As Wilbur had said repeatedly, a pilot's primary requisite was to make his reactions as nearly automatic as possible. During the next two weeks the brothers took every opportunity to fly, sometimes from the small hill, and sometimes from the big dune, both from its summit and from the lower slopes. In an impressive feat of sustained energy, they cast off a total of nearly four hundred times, glided down, then trudged back up the hill lugging the glider, grateful to have the wind at their backs. During almost two hours of air time there was nothing resembling a real accident, though once Wilbur encountered a phenomenon he found hard to explain.

In one of his shorter glides, at a height of about ten feet, he heard a peculiar flapping noise, like little waves striking the bottom of a rowboat. Then, without any change in attitude, the machine suddenly dropped in a flat curve to the ground, Wilbur's body lifting off the wing until only his hands and feet were in contact. There was no damage, it was not even a particularly rough landing, and since it occurred only once it did not raise fears over a new control problem. Wilbur satisfied himself that it had been caused by some temporary vagary of the air itself, probably the wind gusting erratically. Actually, he had been accorded the honor of discovering what for many years was popularly called the "air pocket" (and which later research would reduce to what Wilbur suspected it was, a prosaic matter of sudden downdrafts and erratic turbulence). It was his nearness to the ground that had ended the flight; if he had been any higher, he would simply have lost altitude, then continued on his way.

On one day the two made a little experiment to determine the shallowest angle at which the glider could sustain itself. Two lines were drawn in the sand: one a short distance up the gently sloping foot of the dune, and another out on the flats. The distance between the lines was 156 feet and the angle of descent from one to the other was exactly five degrees. Four trials were made, the glider being released at the upper line. Twice it failed to cover the distance, the lift dissipating. The other two times it flew straight to the mark.

All the flights of this period were long ones, even from the start exceeding 300 feet. On October 20 both men managed to better 500 feet, Orville once and Wilbur four times. Then, three days later, the two seem to have gotten caught up in a friendly rivalry, trying to outdo each other in distance. Orville led off with 336 feet, Wilbur followed with 351, and Orville topped this with 426. Two more glides by each fell short of that mark, then Wilbur took off from the summit of the big hill and when he finally landed he had covered the longest distance of the season, 622 feet, staying up for the longest time, twenty-six seconds. Thus challenged, Orville warmed up with two 500-footers. At last he sailed past the 600-foot mark, only to land seven feet short of Wilbur's record.

On the weekend of October 25 the brothers stored the glider in the shed and made everything snug for the winter. In a cold, blustery drizzle they walked the four miles over the sand to Kitty Hawk and started home. Swarming in their heads were questions about engine output, weight-to-power ratios, and propeller thrust.

9

The Flyer Is Built

For once Wilbur had miscalculated. The motor and the propellers, he was dismayed to find soon after reaching home, were going to present far more difficulty than he had imagined.

All along he had assumed that a suitable motor could be purchased from the existing stock of some manufacturer. But inquiries to a dozen firms brought only the information that an eight-horsepower motor weighing under 200 pounds was not to be had. While such an engine was then entirely feasible, the routine needs of the day—cars, boats, industry—had not yet called for weight-to-power ratios in the narrow range desired by the Wrights.

Aerial propellers did not even exist at this time, of course, and each experimenter had to devise his own, according to whatever theory he favored. Wilbur had planned to draw on marine technology, taking over the propeller theories and formulas that he assumed had been worked out during decades of shipbuilding; the forces at work in a water medium, he felt, should be easily translatable to the action of air. The idea was legitimate but a few days of rummaging in Dayton libraries demonstrated the flaw in it: there existed *no* marine theory of propeller propulsion. Despite their long use of propellers, marine engineers had never reduced their observations and experiments to a formal statement of theory, being content with hit-or-miss methods that yielded screws of about fifty percent efficiency. This they could do, since even an inefficient propeller could still move a boat. In a flying machine, however, an inefficient propeller might be totally worthless, unable even to get the plane off the ground.

Thus, before 1902 was out, Wilbur's twin tasks had run into formidable complications, and of the two the propeller promised to be the most troublesome. Not only was there no generally accepted theory in existence, even the most fundamental facts had avoided scrutiny. "At the time the Wrights were endeavoring to master the problems of designing a propeller," points out one modern expert, "the forces in action on aerial propellers had never been correctly resolved or defined."

To Orville, Wilbur designated the lesser task, the designing and making of the engine, assigning Charles Taylor to do the actual machine work. He then plunged into a study of propellers, reading his way through all the technical works available. As with the wind tunnel, he quickly found himself once again in virgin territory, working with concepts that were, in many ways, more abstruse and quicksilverish than any he had yet encountered.

About three months were consumed in this pioneering effort and at its end Wilbur had produced (*conjured up,* one feels the urge to say) the first reliable airplane propeller theory. In this work, Orville, too, took a hand, making his most important theoretical contribution to the flying machine.

The remaining records of the Wrights' propeller studies, unfortunately, are meager, comprising only three small notebooks and some incidental remarks in letters and articles. Neither man ever supplied a full description of the steps followed, nor was the theory on which they finally constructed their propellers ever formally set down. A natural desire for secrecy kept them, in the early years, from making any revelation, and with Wilbur's death the subject disappeared from public notice.

Of the three notebooks, two of them—crammed with estimates, measurements, calculations, and performance data—were kept by Wilbur. The third, in Orville's hand, contains the various formulas and tables derived from the experiments. Analyzing these, Fred S. Howard, in an appendix to the Wright *Papers,* was able to unravel much of the technical aspect, but he had finally to admit that there was no way fully to reconstruct the actual stages of thought and theorizing by which the brothers slowly made their way. Enough remains of the outward circumstances, however, to afford a brief glimpse of the two as they wrestled with a problem they had never anticipated facing.

It was Orville who later described the elusive nature of the task at its outset. "It is hard to find even a point from which to make a start," he wrote, "for nothing about a propeller, or the medium in which it acts, stands still for a moment. The thrust depends upon the speed and the angle at which the blade strikes the air; the angle at which the blade strikes the air depends upon the speed at which the propeller is turning, the speed the machine is traveling forward, and the speed at which the air is slipping backward; the slip of the air backward depends upon the thrust exerted by the propeller and the amount of air acted upon. When any of these changes, it changes all the rest, as they are all interdependent upon one another. But these are only a few of the factors that must be considered . . ."

The brothers did have one advantage over earlier experimenters, one that they, again, provided for themselves. They had very soon come to see that a propeller had more than a marginal relation to aerodynamics, that in reality it was intimately linked to the same laws that governed the action of the wings themselves. In short, propellers were wings, except that instead of moving forward, they moved in a circular course. Their thrust, consequently, was not produced altogether by reaction against the medium behind, as with marine screws, but by acting on the air ahead. This being so, it seemed to follow that the forward surfaces of a propeller should be curved, or cambered, in the same way that the upper surfaces of wings were curved. Before the Wrights, so far as is known, no one had fully appreciated this, not Bell, not Maxim, not even Langley. It proved to be the key by which the Wrights would unlock the secrets of aerial propulsion.

While Orville with the close help of Taylor busied himself with the designing of the engine, Wilbur began his propeller experiments by observing the blades of a large fan in motion, at the same time making theoretical calculations based on a variety of hypotheses. His immediate goal was to acquire enough information to permit the making of an experimental propeller, bearing a camber derived from one of the wind tunnel model surfaces. With so many factors needing simultaneous evaluation, he frequently found his thinking painfully knotted, and at such times would turn to the quick, eager mind of his brother for a fresh viewpoint.

More and more, as the days went on, the two would drop into discussion of the propellers, one proposing, urging, the other evaluating, altering, adding, discarding, the talk frequently mounting to argument. Slumped on the sofa in the parlor at home, Wilbur would listen glumly to his brother loudly defending a point as he paced the floor, would then raise himself, announce his disagreement, and proceed to offer corrections, Orville stoutly resisting. For a period of six or seven weeks, whenever the two were together at home in the evenings and on weekends, they would begin talking quietly and would soon hit a point of dispute. In minutes, the talk would flare into heated disagreement, the shouts of the two resounding through the house, the rooms echoing to such unfamiliar words and phrases as pitch, slip, throwdown, blade angle, thrust, torque, gross speed, resultant velocity, all intertwined with sines, cosines, secants, cosecants, coefficients.

The hectic probing often continued during the day in the shop where Charles Taylor was a bemused spectator. "I don't think they really got mad," he recalled, "but they sure got awfully hot." As it happened, and as the two later freely admitted, now and then each would find himself defending a position he had earlier scornfully rejected, each having imperceptibly gone over to the other's side. Taylor remembered how "one morning following the worst argument I ever heard, Orv came in and said he guessed he'd been wrong and they ought to do it Will's way. A few minutes later Will came in and said he'd been thinking it over and perhaps Orv was right. First thing I knew they were arguing it all over again, only this time they had switched ideas." It is no coincidence that about this time Wilbur is heard confessing in a letter that he relished "the pleasure of a good scrap," and observing that "discussion brings out new ways of looking at things and helps to round off the corners."

Katharine Wright was not one to interfere with the progress of

science. At first she even found her brothers' battling rather stimulating. Then, after a few weeks, tired with changing the noise of
her classroom for the noise in her parlor, she requested some peace,
and went unheeded. Finally, as she herself recalled it, on one particular raucous night she exploded. "If you don't stop arguing," she
cried in total exasperation, "I'll leave home!" The brothers' pause
was only momentary.

Early in February Wilbur made his first experimental propeller.
From a long strip of wood, using a hatchet and drawknife, he
shaped a propeller whose length from tip to tip was about eight
feet. Its helicoidal surface had a camber derived from one of the
model aerofoils, the one with the most efficient lift/drag ratio for
the purpose. This propeller he tested in the shed behind the bicycle
shop, mounting it on the shop's two-cylinder motor.

Either at this time or earlier, he had begun to see something else
which had never been quite understood by others. "The thrust generated by a propeller when standing stationary," he noted, "was no
indication of the thrust when in motion." The air in front of a propeller when moving forward, he had discovered, was never at rest
when it met the blade, but was subject to acceleration *toward* the
blade because of suction. Both propeller and air, in other words,
were rushing to meet each other, but at different speeds. This overlooked fact introduced a new element into Wilbur's calculations
and the theorizing continued on its convoluted way.

It was March before he decided he had learned enough to permit
designing propellers that, hopefully, would fit the special needs of
the machine he had in mind, and it was another month before two
eight-and-a-half-foot propellers stood propped against the wall of
the shop, gleaming in coats of aluminum paint. Each of the slim,
glossy blades had a maximum width, near the tip, of seven inches,
tapering to the hub in precisely calipered curves and angles. Each
was made from three laminations of spruce, again shaped by Wilbur with hatchet and drawknife. The tips were covered with a thin
layer of light duck canvas, glued on, to prevent splitting.

Orville, especially, took delight in the accomplishment, though
not forgetting that their handiwork had yet to prove itself in action.
"We had been unable to find anything of value in any of the works
to which we had access," he wrote Spratt, "so we worked out a

theory of our own on the subject, and soon discovered, as we usually do, that all the propellers built heretofore are *all wrong*, and then built a pair . . . based on our theory, which are *all right!* (til we have a chance to test them down at Kitty Hawk and find out differently)." They were so unusual, he added, so removed from the theories of their predecessors, "that they will either have to be a good deal better, or a good deal worse." Better, is what the brothers confidently expected. Final calculations indicated that they had attained nearly seventy percent efficiency, in contrast to the uncertain forty or fifty percent that had satisfied earlier workers in the field.

The motor, in the meantime, had been successfully completed with only a minimum of difficulty. Actually finished within the short time of six weeks, at its first testing in February the aluminum casing had cracked (dripping gas had deprived the bearings of oil). Getting the local foundry to cast another required nearly two months. By May the motor again stood on the blocks in the shed back of the shop ready for its shakedown run.

Whether Charles Taylor had taken any direct hand in the designing is not recorded. Years later Orville was to say that the surprisingly fast production of the motor was largely due to Taylor's "enthusiastic and efficient services," but he seems to have been referring to the actual machining and construction, not the design. Still, the brothers must have had an unusual faith in their assistant and he himself seems to have possessed an accommodating nature, ready to tackle anything, even where he had to learn as he went along. Prior to this, as he later said, his experience with gas engines had been limited to "an attempt to repair one in an automobile in 1901."

The only metalworking machines in the shop were a lathe and a drill press, run by belts from the small, two-cylinder motor. On these Taylor did all his work. "We didn't make any drawings," he recalled. "One of us would sketch out the part we were talking about on a piece of scratch paper and I'd spike the sketch over my bench." It was the crankshaft, made from a slab of machine steel, that appears to have required the most time and effort. On the slab Taylor traced an outline, then drilled around it "until I could knock out the surplus pieces with a hammer and chisel. Then I put it in the lathe and turned it down to size and smoothness. It weighed nineteen pounds finished and she balanced up perfectly, too."

There were no spark plugs, the spark being provided by make-and-break contact points in the combustion chamber, fired by a magneto. The ignition control was an ordinary light switch "we bought at the hardware store."

The completed engine was a stripped-down version of an ordinary automobile motor,* a combination of aluminum, steel, and cast iron. Started by a dry battery, after each of its four cylinders had been primed with a few drops of raw gas, it had only one speed, at its best attaining just over a thousand revolutions per minute. Once running, it could be stopped only by cutting off the supply of gas that was gravity-fed from a small overhead container.

The aim had been to achieve at least twelve horsepower and at first the engine easily reached that level, though it was found that after a few minutes' run the valves became so hot that power dropped about twenty-five percent. Even so, as one expert later concluded, Orville and Taylor had done their work well: they had taken "the state of the art of their time and very competently adapted it to their special purpose."

It would be slighting the truth, however, not to record a further fact. This first Wright engine, judged solely as an engine and without regard to the "special work" for which it was intended, was far from being a triumph. As has more than once been observed, and as Orville himself later admitted, with only minor alterations in the design, and with more professional workmanship, its power could quite easily have been more than doubled. "Ignorant of what a motor this size ought to develop, we were greatly pleased with its performance," Orville said afterwards. "More experience showed us that we did not get one half the power we should have had."

It thus becomes an interesting question as to why Wilbur—remembering his usual great care and foresight—did not seek the help of an automotive engineer. The answer seems to be threefold. Neither of the brothers at that time knew much about the finer points of engine construction; in those days relatively few men did. Lacking this knowledge, and having succeeded in getting the power de-

* The actual car engine Orville used for a model appears to have been that in the Pope-Toledo, a make long since defunct.

sired, Wilbur never thought to question the motor's real efficiency. And so accustomed by now had the brothers become to doing everything for themselves, so convinced were they of their abilities, that there was little room for self-doubt. Lastly, there was Wilbur's growing desire for secrecy, which from this time on was to become a prime consideration.

The dimensions of the new machine—the Flyer, as the brothers had begun to call it, or the Whopper, as their nephew had christened it after seeing it partly assembled at the rear of the shop—had been settled on even before the completion of propellers and motor. Wingspan was to be a few inches over forty feet, the chord six and a half feet, thus preserving the aspect ratio—six—that had proved so effective in the 1902 glider. The wing ends were again given a decided droop, this time ten inches, imparting to them something of the seagull's graceful arch.

The camber was deepened to 1-in-20, from the 1-in-24 of the 1902 glider. This, while making the fore-and-aft control a little touchier, gave some added increase in lift. The gap between the wings—because of their enlargement and the need to accommodate motor and propeller assembly—was widened to over six feet. Both the elevator and the rudder were increased in area and given double instead of single surfaces. The total weight of the Flyer, with motor, propellers, and the operator aboard, was estimated at 750 pounds.

The motor was to be attached to the ribs of the lower wing, just to the right of center; the operator would take his place in the hip cradle beside it. Because the engine weighed about thirty pounds more than either of the brothers, Wilbur had made the wings unsymmetrical, providing four inches more span, and thus more lift, on the heavier side.

As had almost all other experimenters, he would use two pusher propellers in order to obtain as much thrust as possible. Driven by heavy-duty sprocket chains linked to the motor, the propellers rotated in opposite directions, neutralizing each other's torque and gyroscopic effect.* To obtain a counterrotation in one of them, the chain was simply turned over in a figure eight. Since, in motion, the

---

* A single propeller would tend to pull to one side (torque) and would offer resistance to turning in the opposite direction.

chains tended to slap, they were sheathed in a loose metal tubing. (These chains were not ordinary bicycle chains, as is often thought. They were specially made by an Indianapolis firm.)

When the motor and propellers were finished, early in June, construction of the machine itself was begun, with the brothers again doing all the work themselves, though this time Taylor made most of the metal fittings. Since they continued to incorporate many small refinements, such as hollow ribs and specially contoured spars, the machine took shape more slowly than had the earlier gliders.

They were still at the task in the middle of July when disconcerting news reached them. They were to have a challenger, it appeared, for the honor of being the first men to fly. Professor Samuel Langley had finally put together a full-size machine and was about to test it.

Langley had been unable to supply the army with a flying machine by the start of the Spanish-American War, and that conflict had lasted only four months. But the army's interest had remained high. Under official urging, Langley had worked on, still in secret, his efforts, however, being retarded by his other duties. Not until the beginning of 1903 was he satisfied that he was ready, and word had soon leaked out that he would probably make a test before the end of the year. This news reached the Wrights, through Chanute, probably as early as January, and it had urged them on—their impatience no doubt contributing to the violence of their well-remembered arguments over the propeller.

Originally, they had planned to return to Kitty Hawk with the Flyer by spring. The cracked motor casing and the riddle of the propellers had canceled that hope. In June, as everything at last rounded into shape, they were still looking toward a flight in late summer. Then newspaper accounts put an end to all Wilbur's thoughts of beating Langley to the first attempt. In mid-July it was reported that Langley's houseboat, its top fitted with a large, sophisticated catapult launching platform, had been anchored in the Potomac off Widewater, Virginia. As with the 1896 model, the experiments were to take place over open water. Inside the houseboat, ready for assembly, still enshrouded in secrecy, was the flying machine that it had taken the scientist seven years to evolve.

While dozens of reporters haunted the shores of the Potomac and bobbed precariously about the houseboat in rented skiffs, Langley gruffly refused to talk about his plans, or even to describe his machine in any detail. Some frustrated reporters managed to get hold of a few specifications, then filled out the picture from their own imaginations. Wilbur, reading these stories closely, was not misled. "It would be interesting," he observed to Chanute, "to attempt a possible computation of the performance of his machine in advance of its trial, but the data of the machine as given in the newspapers is so evidently erroneous that it seems hopeless to attempt it."

Not until August 8 did Langley make his first move and it turned out to be a surprise. A flying machine was hauled out and mounted on the launching catapult, sixty feet above the surface of the water, but it was not the full-size machine. To test his balancing theories, Langley had made another model, this time a quarter-size one, an exact duplicate of the big machine, which was to be flown unmanned. In a rather cruel headline, *The New York Times* reported the results of the first trial: "Airship as a Submarine—Defect in Steering Gear Sends It Below the Surface." Other papers were equally unsympathetic.

The model, instead of covering an expected three miles in a straight line, had curved through the air for thirty seconds, when the unidentified steering defect had sent it plunging into the water. A tugboat had immediately dragged for the wreck, lifting it from a depth of twenty feet. The reporters in their boats, converging on the spot, were denied a look at the mystery craft by a soldier who threw a canvas over the dripping model as it emerged, "so that it could not be seen by the spectators."

Despite the headlines, confusion lingered over the outcome. While the papers pronounced the flight a failure, Langley stoutly insisted, through a spokesman, that "all the data which the machine was designed to furnish were obtained." If so, then perhaps Langley was nearer to true flight than anyone suspected; of this even the Wrights could not be sure.

Nothing was said in the reports about when Langley might unveil the big machine. To the Wrights in Dayton, still putting their

Flyer together, this uncertainty, so galling to the newsmen, no longer mattered. Wilbur knew that he could not hope to have everything ready at Kitty Hawk for a trial in much less than three months. By then, surely, Langley would have taken to the air.

Confronted with a situation in which ingenuity could do nothing, Wilbur made the best of it. His rival might fail, of course, but even if Langley succeeded it would not be devastating. Wilbur would still have his own Flyer, would still have opened up a new life for himself. A first flight, while conferring immortality on whoever made it, was in reality nothing more than an initial step, tentative even at its best, leaving much to be done. What counted was the development of the flying machine thereafter; that was the challenge of the future. And for this Wilbur knew that he was as well equipped as Langley or anyone else. Resigned to the idea that he might at the eleventh hour be deprived of half his old dream, he went on building the Flyer and preparing for the move to Kitty Hawk.

His plans were carefully laid. Since a good deal of mechanical work would have to be done on the Banks, and since more room would be needed than was available in the old shed, he decided he would put up a second, larger shed to serve as workshop and hangar. Then he and his brother would assemble the Flyer and, before mounting the motor, would test it separately as a glider. This glide testing might consume perhaps a week of precious time but it was an obvious and necessary precaution. Putting a motor on untried wings, no matter how much faith the brothers had in their calculations, would be worse than foolhardy.

An important part of the program, also an irritating delay but necessary, was practice gliding on the old 1902 machine. The amount of time that each had spent gliding the previous year—hardly an hour for Orville, somewhat more for Wilbur—began to seem ridiculously inadequate in the face of the big, powerful machine they were now bringing to completion. There was, of course, no way to gain piloting experience on the Flyer before taking it up. They could only trust that what they had learned about control on the glider would hold true for powered flight.

In the first week of September they crated the disassembled Flyer, packed up tools and other equipment, and shipped everything to Kitty Hawk. Their own departure was set for later in the month. If all went well, then on some fair day near the end of October, with the sun shining and a light wind blowing, one of the two would make the first attempt. They had agreed to let the flip of a coin decide to whom the honor should fall.

10

High Noon at Kitty Hawk

During the first two weeks at Kitty Hawk the brothers were kept busy building the new shed and repairing the old one, which had again been shoved off its foundations by howling winter gales. They had also quickly resumed practice with the old glider, making about eighty glides from the big hill only three days after their arrival. Less concerned with distance than hovering, Wilbur in one of these glides managed to stay aloft for nearly half a minute while advancing only fifty-two feet; Orville did almost as well. The long layoff had not rusted their skills.

Several times in the following days, however, they were sharply reminded that the sky had not yet become man's natural habitat. On October 3, after Wilbur had raised his record to forty-three seconds, Orville barely escaped a bad accident. In quartering into the wind he hit some turbulence and was roughly jostled out of the shallow hip cradle unto the downsloping wing. He hung on and managed to crawl back just in time to bring the glider under control. Another day Wilbur, in making a very tight half-turn, allowed the left wing to get too high, when the machine was caught by a rising gust and thrown sideways. Before he could act, the right tip had hit the sand and ploughed a trench twenty feet long. In another glide when Orville lost control and swooped down to where his brother was running along the sand, a serious injury to Wilbur was averted only by inches as the tip of the left wing struck him a glancing blow on the head. The wing went on to hit the ground hard, breaking uprights at front and rear. Such incidents, though not frequent in the 200 or so glides made before the Flyer claimed the brothers' full attention, kept them from taking their skills for granted. Safety in the air, they saw, demanded constant attention and anticipation, as well as quick reaction.

Though fall had descended on the Banks, the weather at first was mild, with only light winds, clear skies, and a blessed absence of the driving rains that so often swept in from the sea. Constantly occupied, the two had been able to put into the background all thoughts of Langley's imminent flight. In these early weeks neither their letters nor the diary kept by Orville makes any reference to the scientist or his dragonfly-winged machine.

On October 7 the diary records the only work for the day, a modification of the old glider: "We made tail so as to operate directly from cradle" (the tail wires now linked directly to the cradle instead of to the warping wires). Over the lonely Banks that evening the weather suddenly changed, bringing unusually strong winds and a "cloudburst" of rain. The Wrights went to bed early to lie tossing in restless sleep, unaware that Langley, less than two hundred miles to the north on the Potomac River, without advance warning had made his first attempt and had failed—totally and ingloriously.

Most newspapers carried long, circumstantial accounts of Langley's sad defeat, not mincing words as to the utter foolishness of it all, many indulging in outright derision. Even the soberer papers found strong phrases for their headlines. "Flying Machine Fiasco," announced *The New York Times*. "Professor Langley's Airship Proves a Complete Failure."

Describing the launch from atop the houseboat, and the sudden descent, the *Times* explained how "the immense airship sped rapidly along its seventy-foot track, was carried by its momentum for a hundred yards, and then fell gradually into the Potomac River, whence it emerged a total wreck. . . . At no time was there any semblance of flight. The initial momentum, the lightness of the machine, and the sustaining surface of the wings furnishing the con-

ditions which account for the hundred-yard transit of the machine
from its sixty-foot elevation to the water."

At the controls was Langley's assistant, Charles Manly, who had
built the remarkable radial engine that powered the two propellers
(developing fifty-two horsepower and weighing only 125 pounds, it
was perhaps the best light engine then in existence). When the machine hit the water and went under, taking Manly with it, there
were fears for his life. The twisted mass soon bobbed up again and
Manly was quickly hauled into a rowboat. The machine itself—the
"Buzzard," as some papers irreverently dubbed it—was lifted from
the water by a big army derrick, its four broad wings "hanging limp
beside the frame."

The Wrights must have heard the news within a day or two.
Even while feeling a twinge of pity for their distinguished rival,
they could hardly have suppressed some stirrings of elation. The
only recorded remark of the two, however, occurs in a letter of
Wilbur's to Chanute. "I see that Langley has had his fling and
failed," he wrote matter-of-factly. "It seems to be our turn to throw
now and I wonder what our luck will be."

Assembly of the Flyer had not yet started, owing to the non-
arrival of some parts. These showed up on October 9, probably the
same day that brought the news of Langley, and the task was immediately begun. There was now no hurry. If Langley was to make
a second attempt, Wilbur felt, he certainly could not be ready before the end of the year. Even at a leisurely pace, putting the Flyer
together and testing it as a glider, he estimated, would take a
month at most. By the first week of November he should be ready
to "throw."

As assembly proceeded, parts of five days were given over to
practice on the old machine, with records being set for height—a
breathtaking sixty feet, perhaps not quite intentionally—and time in
the air, about a minute for each. The weather, after one violent
three-day period in which the winds reached seventy-five miles an
hour and tore away some of the large shed's roofing, settled back
into a pattern of calms followed by light winds. The rain, when it
came, was usually a light drizzle and soon over. But toward the end
of October another factor of life on the Banks made itself felt, the
penetrating cold. After trying to heat the shed by making a small

fire in a carbide can and nearly smoking themselves out, they improvised a stove, with a pipe going out the side, and soon found their living quarters quite comfortable.

In the meantime, George Spratt, eager to be present at the first attempt, had arrived. Chanute, who was having some difficulty with his many business interests and was uncertain whether he could attend, at last informed the brothers by letter on October 24 that he could, after all, get away. This letter the brothers received on Sunday, November 1. An enclosure in it—a newspaper clipping —suddenly and drastically altered their plans.

Professor Langley, while badly disappointed, had by no means been crushed by his initial failure. The trouble, he insisted, "lay with the launching mechanism, and not with the machine itself." The catapult, he meant, had, through some defect, caused the flight to abort before it had fairly gotten started. He had prevailed on the Army Board of Ordnance and Fortification, announced the clipping, to grant him a hearing to present his case for another test. The board was to meet on November 8. If Langley was persuasive —and a second test was only logical—he might very well, Wilbur concluded, be ready within days afterward. Very likely he had already been repairing the machine for probably a month. The specter of losing his renewed opportunity, in a heartbreaking irony of timing, once again rose up before Wilbur.

The wings of the Flyer, and the elevator, stood completed and ready. Still to be assembled and attached was the tail. After that, a few days, at least, must be given over to glide-testing the wings. Another week perhaps would be needed to mount and ground-test the motor and propellers. Under that program, even if nothing went wrong, it would be approaching November 15 before the Flyer was ready, and there would still be the takeoff track to prepare and set down.

This track was to be made up of four lengths of two-by-four lumber, each fifteen feet, set end to end and propped on edge, the top sheathed with an iron strip. The wheelless Flyer, its runners balanced on a wheeled cradle, would take off after the sixty-foot run along this rail. With so much to be done Wilbur had to admit there was no way to be sure that he would have his first throw before Langley had his second.

No direct evidence remains of the animated talk that must have gone round the stove in the old shed that Sunday evening, among the two Wrights and Spratt. Only from the events of the next few days does it become clear that there was a discussion, and that it was terminated by Wilbur when he made a decision that was at once the boldest and rashest of his life, a decision in which Orville concurred. Spratt, assuming a voice in the matter, strongly dissented.

The glide testing of the engineless Flyer was to be canceled. Early next morning, while the tail was being completed, they would start mounting the motor and propellers. If they worked around the clock, in three days, perhaps four, the Flyer would be mounted on the starting rail. Originally, they had planned to take off into a wind of about fifteen miles an hour. Now, when they were ready, on November 5 or 6, if there was any wind at all, even as little as five or six miles an hour, they would go.

On the face of it, this appears an impossible program, even irresponsible. That it was a calculated gamble, involving very real danger, the Wrights well knew. But to appreciate the real strength of their feelings, it is necessary to see that the danger was more than personal. A smashed Flyer, a broken engine, whether or not the pilot received injury, would put an end to that season's attempts, delaying another trial for many months. Surely, behind so desperate a decision, so quickly arrived at, can only have been Wilbur's old, urgent desire for "fame" as well as fortune, his hope that he might with one spectacular gesture wipe out the memory of that lost decade.

The brothers began their hectic schedule on the morning of November 2, by ensuring that they would have no unnecessary interruptions. Chanute had written that he would be arriving with a companion, an aeronautical visitor from England. Orville wired him that he and his friend would be welcome "after November fifth."

Brief entries in Orville's diary record the brothers' progress over the next few days.

November 2: "Began work of placing engine on machine, also uprights for screws. . . . Wind still light, probably 4 meters [about nine miles an hour]."

Astonishingly, the next evening he is able to write: "Have engine and screws nearly ready. Completed attachments for working tail." The first irritation also showed up on November 3: "Discovered that nuts for fastening on screws are missing."

Somewhere the nuts were found and by the next night Orville could note: "Have machine now within half day of completion. . . . Wind of 5 to 6 meters from south."

That same day Spratt, caught up in the excitement, had pitched in, laying the sixty-foot takeoff rail in the sand, a short distance west of the sheds, ready to be shifted round into the wind. The next afternoon, the brothers were confident, the Flyer would rise.

When the men awoke the following morning the winds were just right, about fifteen miles an hour from the southwest. If they held, conditions would be perfect. While Spratt swung the rail around, the brothers went to work hauling the Flyer out. But it was not to be. Orville's diary tells the story of how a defective part brought the eager preparations to a halt.

"We got the machine ready for testing engine and screws in the building preparatory to taking it out. We had much trouble in fastening the sprockets on tight, and found finally that the lock-nut screwed up against shaft without touching sprocket at all. This allowed the screws to play almost a half turn. After a number of trials to get the engine running properly, in which the screws vibrated on account of the irregularity of the engine resulting from missed explosions, the pieces to which the screws were fastened were jerked loose from both shafts, thus taking away all chance of a trial for ten days or so."

The play at the propeller hubs—unnoticed before because the completed propeller assembly had not been tested in Dayton—had been aggravated by the rough-running engine to the point where the vibrating propellers were ripped loose, in the process twisting the tubular shafts and damaging the wooden framework that held them. At bottom, the fault lay in the magneto which was misfiring and causing erratic vibration in the engine. About ten days would be required to have the shafts repaired by Taylor in Dayton and shipped down. Spratt, who had been in camp less than two weeks, now unexpectedly announced that he must return home. He volunteered to take the shafts as far as Norfolk from where they could be expressed to Dayton, along with a letter of instructions to Taylor. At four o'clock on the afternoon of November 5 he departed.

While waiting, the brothers kept busy repairing the magneto, tuning up the engine, bracing the Flyer's undercarriage, and testing its strength by hanging it on its wing tips. They also tested their starting track by using it to launch the old glider from a slight slope. It appeared to work perfectly and they could not help feeling some satisfaction when they compared its price—about four dollars —with the many thousands that Langley had spent on his own catapult platform.

In the meantime Octave Chanute had arrived and was disappointed to find that a flight could not be attempted until sometime after the middle of the month. He was also bothered by the weather, which had turned very cold and rainy, and by the rough life of the camp. The food supplies brought from home had run out and the brothers were now "living on pretty slim pickings," gathered from the Kitty Hawk villagers. Orders for groceries sent to the mainland were unreliable as to time of arrival, as well as completeness. When one expected shipment failed to arrive about this time, as Orville wrote his sister, "We had to come down to condensed milk and crackers for supper, with prospects for coffee and rice cakes for breakfast."

The sleeping arrangements were also not the most comfortable, the bitter nighttime cold often requiring, as Wilbur put it with only slight exaggeration, "5 blankets and two quilts. Next come 5 blankets, 2 quilts and fire; then 5, 2, fire and hot water jug. This is as far as we have got so far. Next comes the addition of sleeping without undressing, then shoes, hats, and finally overcoats."

These primitive conditions were too much for the sixty-six-year-old Chanute. He left camp to return home on November 12, after only a week's visit—and left knowing that another week or so might bring the one event of which he had been dreaming for forty years. His reasons for departing may have gone beyond the rough life of the camp, may have been connected with his business interests, and no doubt seemed adequate; the passage of time does have a way of obscuring such things. Yet the fact itself is stark enough to prompt wonder at the ways of men. On the afternoon of November 12 Octave Chanute, one of the pioneer apostles of aviation, made a decision not to be present at the Wrights' first flight. Assuredly, few other men with his background could have done the same thing.

Even during the week he spent in camp Chanute's attitude had been a little strange. While talking with the Wrights one day about what their plans might be if they succeeded, he suggested that they might, at his expense, take over and try to perfect his own gliders —might, in other words, become his assistants. "He doesn't seem to think our machines are so much superior," caustically remarked Orville in a letter, "as the manner in which we handle them. We are of just the reverse opinion."

Chanute also caused the brothers some unnecessary worry by casually inquiring, after an inspection of the Flyer, if they had allowed for the "usual" twenty-five percent loss of power in the chain transmission to the propellers. They had already tested for such a power loss and were satisfied that it did not exceed ten percent. But since the problem was a purely mechanical one, and since Chanute was a famous engineer, they felt it would be only sensible to make doubly sure of their calculations. After Chanute left they rigged a small but definitive test, using sandbags for weights, and found that their original estimates had been correct.

Eight days after Chanute's departure the rebuilt shafts arrived. By evening they were in place ready for testing, when another problem showed up. The sprocket plates affixed to the shafts could not be tightened sufficiently to prevent their working loose. "Day closes in deep gloom," noted Orville. Early the next morning, however, the gloom was dissipated, "thanks to Arnstein's hard cement, which will fix anything from a stopwatch to a thrashing machine." With shafts and sprockets heated, the melted glue was poured over the threads, the sprockets screwed up tight and allowed to stand. "I doubt whether they will ever come loose again," Orville jotted with satisfaction in the diary. Three more days were spent in careful adjusting and testing. By the afternoon of November 25 the brothers were ready for a flight—but further delays set in which, though frustrating, may actually have saved them from disaster.

On the twenty-fifth, just as they were about to move the Flyer out of the shed, rain began to fall, lightly, but enough so that the fabric wings would have been quickly soaked and loosened. The next day brought high winds and bitter cold, which continued into the twenty-seventh with the addition of some brief snow flurries. The morning of the twenty-eighth showed signs of clearing but as the Flyer was being readied a discovery was made: one of the propeller shafts had a hairline crack along its length. If the Flyer had been flown with the shaft in that condition, it might very well have shaken itself apart in the air.

With this, Wilbur must have conceded defeat in his race with Langley. Perhaps two weeks would be needed to get a new shaft from Dayton and ready the Flyer. If Langley was going to try again this year, he would certainly have done so before that. Moreover, by mid-December the Banks' winter would have firmly set in, bringing frequent high winds, fog, and freezing rain, not to mention the likelihood of hundred-mile-an-hour hurricanes. Doggedly determined, the brothers vowed that, in any case, they would not leave Kitty Hawk until they had accomplished at least one trial. It was agreed that Orville himself should return to Dayton to make the new shafts, this time of solid spring steel. He departed on Monday, November 30.

The secrecy about which Wilbur had been so careful had not yet been breached, the isolation and sparse settlement of Kitty Hawk putting it far outside the usual haunts of newsmen; nor would it be breached until Wilbur himself decided the time had come. But just now, with Wilbur alone in camp, an incident unrelated to the Wrights occurred that, ironically, focused the attention of the whole country on the Banks, at a spot just a few miles above Kitty Hawk, bringing a mob of spectators and reporters.

On December 3 a storm churned up the waters off the Banks, catching one of the U.S. Navy's most precious new vessels off guard. The *Moccasin,* one of the world's first fully practical submarines, had been proceeding south, under tow and unmanned, when the towline snapped. Driven by fierce winds and crashing waves, the sub drifted helplessly toward Currituck Beach, where it went aground still some distance out. The next day the story was front-page news and coverage continued for a week as navy tugs were rushed to the scene in an attempt to pull the *Moccasin* free. When the shallow water prevented the tugs from getting close enough, a sailor, Patrick Deering, became a national hero by swimming through raging surf to make a line fast on the stricken vessel. Eventually the sub was pulled off and the Outer Banks returned to their other-worldly isolation. But for more than a week there had been great excitement, and it is quite possible that Wilbur, with little to occupy him, traveled up the beach to view the proceedings, in the process rubbing elbows with the crowd of reporters, undetected.

When Orville arrived back at camp on December 11 he had with him a piece of news that was every bit as welcome as the new shafts. Two days before, Orville told his brother as soon as they met, Langley had tried again, and had again failed, in even more devastating fashion than before.

This time, on being launched, Langley's machine had scarcely cleared the edge of the platform when its wings collapsed. "On the signal to start," reported *The New York Times*, "the airplane glided smoothly along the launching tramway, until the end of the slide was reached. Then, left to itself, the aeroplane broke in two and turned completely over." Splashing mightily into the Potomac, up-side down, the sinking debris trapped the pilot, Manly. He was saved only by the quick action of another assistant who dove fully clothed off the houseboat into the icy waters and pulled the strug-gling aviator free.

Langley, who had been watching from the deck of a nearby barge, was described as "crestfallen." He defended his work by say-ing again that the catapult mechanism had fouled the takeoff. Few, if any, among the newspaper observers were inclined to agree with him and the accounts of the trial that appeared in papers across the country were even more savage in their ridicule than before. "Buz-zard a Wreck," headlined the Washington *Post*. "Aerodrome Did a Flipflop Then Turned Its Nose Up," said the New York *Sun*. "Slid into the water like a handful of mortar," reported another. Editorial writers cried out against this waste of the public money, cartoonists jeered in merciless fashion, congressmen rose in the House to pro-test any further government connection with so discredited an en-deavor as mechanical flight ("a professor wandering in his dreams," Langley was characterized by one legislator).

Langley was finished. His had been the most spectacular public failure in American scientific history. It broke his heart and his spirit and, many say, hastened his death, which occurred two years later. In his downfall he took with him much of whatever faith, public and private, had till then existed in the flying machine. After this, a great part of the nation, and of the world, was ready to concede, without trace of a smile, that perhaps the old saying was true, that men long ago would have sprouted wings if the Deity had meant them to fly.

The Wrights' new shafts were in place and the Flyer ready for a trial by late afternoon of Saturday, December 12. They had decided that if the winds were very light at their first trial they would use the assistance of a downhill takeoff, laying the starting rail on the wide-spreading skirts of the big hill. This, they knew, would lessen their achievement somewhat, since the Flyer would not be taking off solely under its own power. But at this point they were more anxious to test their machine's capability in the air, than they were to adhere to the technical niceties. If the Flyer would rise from a slight downslope run and sustain itself, there would then be no doubt that it could, with stronger winds, lift itself into flight from level ground by engine power alone.

The twelfth passed without an attempt, however, and Orville's diary entry tells why. "We did not have enough wind," he wrote, "for starting from flat and not enough time to go to the hill." The sun had been nearly down when the Flyer was ready and it would have been no quick or easy job to lug the 600-pound machine a quarter-mile over the sands, then fetch the track and set it up. The brothers wanted no murky light or shifting shadows to interfere with their judgment of distances, especially in landing.

They used the time, instead, to set the Flyer up on the rail beside the shed, shoving it back and forth to check their takeoff procedure. It was fortunate they did. At the start of one run the bottom of the low-slung tail frame caught the end of the track and was broken. Happening at the start of a powered flight, this could have been disastrous. To avoid a repetition they would have to start a little farther up.

December 13 dawned bright and perfect, with the wind just right at about fifteen miles per hour, and the air warm. No move was made to ready the Flyer as the two spent the day lolling about camp and reading. It was Sunday. Not even to make history's first flight would they go back on their word to their father that they would keep the Sabbath holy.

Monday also brought fair skies, though with weak winds of about
five miles an hour, and renewed cold. The morning had to be spent
repairing the tail frame. If the winds did not pick up by afternoon,
they decided, they would go to the hill to make the attempt.

Previously, they had arranged with the men of the Kitty Hawk
lifesaving station to fly a flag as a signal that they were about to
make a trial. Those who wished to be present would then have
ample time to walk down to the site. This was done only partially as
a courtesy to the men the brothers had come to know through four
seasons on the Banks. Primarily, the Wrights wanted to have reliable witnesses present. That these witnesses were unlettered, especially in things aeronautical, unable to relay technical descriptions
of the Flyer, gave Wilbur just the situation he wanted. At one thirty
on the afternoon of the fourteenth the signal was hoisted, and the
Wrights started with the Flyer for the big hill.

Getting the heavy machine over the sands was now fairly easy,
since someone had thought of the obvious method: mount it on the
sixty-foot takeoff rail, trundle it to the end, then take up the rails
behind and add them to the front. Even so, it needed nearly three-
quarters of an hour to make the trip. When they arrived at the hill
five spectators had caught up with them, all men from the Kitty
Hawk lifesaving station. Two young boys, spotting the odd procession, had also tagged along.

A gentle, smooth slope was found for the laying of the rail; measurement showed it to be a descent of nine degrees. The upper end
of the rail was fixed in the sand some 150 feet up the slope; thus
the start would be made at an elevation about twenty feet above the
flats. With everyone present lending a hand, the Flyer was carried
up the hill and preparations made to set it on the track.

First, a small "truck"—a short length of wood to which wheels
were attached at front and back, the wheels made of bicycle hubs—
was rested lengthwise on the metal-topped rail. Across this a plank
of wood about six feet long was balanced. The Flyer was placed
atop this plank, the sledlike runners that formed the Flyer's landing
gear straddling the plank from side to side, coming near both edges.
To keep the Flyer upright while at rest a small wooden bench supported one tip. To balance it on takeoff a man would run alongside
holding the end struts.

Wires from a coil box were hooked to the engine and the motor started, after which the coil wires were disconnected. The sudden, raucous blend of unfamiliar noises from crackling engine and whirring propellers that rent the quiet of the sandy wastes caused the spectators to jump a little, particularly the two boys. As Orville noted with amusement, the youngsters "made a hurried departure over the hill for home."

Though the propellers quickly reached their rated thousand revolutions per minute, the Flyer was held in place by a stout wire fastened to the track. When the pilot was ready, this wire could be slipped loose, releasing the machine. For a final few minutes the two brothers stood listening to the smooth rattle of the engine and making a last check of the propellers.

It was shortly after 3 P.M. when Wilbur took a coin from his pocket and turned to his brother. The coin was flipped, Orville called out his choice, and Wilbur came up the winner.

Pulling down the peak of his cap, he crawled aboard the lower wing and spent a few seconds adjusting himself in the hip cradle. At the right wing tip stood Orville; at the other was one of the spectators who had volunteered to assist. A shout came from Wilbur that he was ready, then he reached down in front to release the restraining wire, only to find that he could not work it free. The weight of the Flyer and the thrust of the propellers was exerting too great a pressure for manual release. Orville shouted for some of the men to take a hand at the tips and push the Flyer back a few inches to get some slack in the wire. This was done and the machine started forward, slowly at first but rapidly gaining speed. Orville, grasping the right end-struts, made long dashing strides to keep alongside. After about ten yards he gave up and came sliding to a breathless halt, the Flyer continuing to move ahead.

In Orville's hand was a stopwatch. His eyes glued to his brother's form—the dark clothes standing out as a thin black streak against the bright fabric of the wings—he waited tensely until he saw the Flyer, when about six feet from the rail's end, leap away from the ground. He snapped the watch, then gazed, fascinated, as the Flyer rose sharply, steadily, the propellers faintly smudging the blue of the sky with two shimmering blurs.

The hope of the brothers even on this first attempt had been, rather quixotically, to go as far as possible, to stay up as long as the small supply of fuel held out. The half gallon of gas in the cylinder, affixed near the top of one of the center struts, could actually have taken the Flyer about eight miles, but it is doubtful if they really meant to try for that distance. More likely they had their eyes set on the village of Kitty Hawk, some four miles away. Prudence, of course, might have dictated a few practice hops, with such sustained flights being attempted later, but there is no evidence that the Wrights ever considered any approach except that of getting up into the air and staying there until they had to come down. Their experience with gliding, perhaps, had misled them into a false confidence.

In any case, when Wilbur took off he fully intended to cruise at least to the village of Kitty Hawk, at an altitude of about fifteen feet above the sand. That his flight, instead, ended abruptly is another one of those fortunate circumstances that so repeatedly saved the two from disaster. If he had been able to continue there is no telling what variety of difficulties he might have met with, totally inexperienced as he was in the control and landing of a power machine.

The end of Wilbur's flight occurred less than four seconds after takeoff, and after covering only 105 feet. The reason for the quick termination, as Wilbur saw it, concerned only a bad start. The wind had been a little to one side, he said afterwards, and the starting rail had not been laid straight down the slope. The real fault, however, had been his own "error in judgment." After lifting off the track, in his anxiety to gain height he had used too much elevator, causing the machine to turn up too sharply. "As the machine had barely speed enough for support already, this slowed it down so much that before I could correct the error, the machine began to come down though turned up at a big angle."

At the top of its climb, some sixty feet out from the end of the track, the Flyer had reached a height of fifteen feet. From there it gradually sank to the ground, speeding up again to about twenty miles an hour at the last moment and giving Wilbur hope that he might continue. But he had descended too far to recover. As the Flyer came near the ground the left wing was low. It hit, without too great a shock, dragged the Flyer around in a thumping slide, scraping the front skids sideways in deep sand. They snapped under the strain and as the machine twisted to a halt the double-surfaced elevator crumpled out of shape. Wilbur was unhurt. All things considered, as he said, "it was a nice, easy landing."

Neither brother considered the trial of December 14 a legitimate flight. It had, of course, been gravity-aided, the landing point being about fifteen feet lower in altitude than the takeoff point. Also, it had been much too short, in both duration and distance. So briefly was the Flyer in the air that it had been impossible for the observers to decide whether it was sustaining itself, or was merely riding out its first impetus, as, for instance, would a glider (and as the Langley machine had at its first attempt).

Just how long a flight would be required to permit making such a judgment no one was quite prepared to say; naturally, there were no standards. But for those on the ground they weren't really needed. An attentive observer, measuring with the naked eye the trim bulk of the Flyer against the landscape, its speed and altitude, physically aware of the strength and direction of the wind, taking in at one moment the life-size feel of dimension and distance, would be able to tell, would know in his bones, just when the Flyer had passed the point at which the force of liftoff had been dissipated. If the Flyer was flying, an eyewitness would recognize the exhilarating fact beyond a doubt.

Yet, while the brothers did not consider they had made a proper flight, one that would satisfy all objections, they did believe that the capability of the Flyer had been amply demonstrated. To his father on the night of the fourteenth Wilbur wrote that if it had not been for his own inexperience with the controls, and the hillside launch, "the machine would undoubtedly have flown beautifully. There is now no question of final success."

Repairs to the undercarriage occupied the whole of the following day and most of the morning of the sixteenth. By afternoon the wind, at a weak seven miles an hour, was much too light for a start from the flat. However, just to be ready in case a stronger blow should come, the brothers set the starting track in the sand about fifty yards south of the sheds, heading west into the wind, poised the Flyer on it, and sat down to wait. If the wind did kick up they would hoist the signal flag and wait for the arrival of the men from

the lifesaving station. Two or three hours later they gave up and
took the machine in again, though not before a strolling stranger
had afforded them a quiet laugh.

Walking along the beach, a man had spotted the unusual scene,
had come up, introduced himself, and inquired as to the nature of
the big kite with all the machinery. It was a flying machine, Wilbur
told him briefly. Did they intend to fly it today? Yes, answered Wilbur, they were only waiting for favorable conditions, a suitable
wind. Casting a critical eye over the Flyer, the stranger made a
tour of appraisal then returned to where the brothers were sitting
beside the shed. "I should think that thing *would* fly," he agreed,
sounding more courteous than convinced, "when you get a suitable
wind." And with that he went off down the beach again, leaving
the brothers with the distinct impression that when he said "suitable wind" he meant about seventy-five miles an hour.

The brothers went to bed that night acutely aware that winter
had permanently settled its chilling grip on the Banks, giving little
promise of favorable days ahead. They were now nearly two
months behind the time they had originally planned for the first
flight.

The morning of Thursday, December 17, brought a sudden wors-
ening of weather, as the drab light from leaden skies mottled the
dull stretches of gray sand, glinting here and there on pools of
frozen rainwater. The air was almost empty of birds; only a few
gulls could be seen dipping low over the white-foamed surf that
boiled up the nearby beach in a continuous faint roar. Stepping
outside, Wilbur found a strong wind blowing, too strong for flying.
The anemometer showed it to be nearly twenty-seven miles an
hour. Again, they would have to wait, this time for the wind to die
down.

Two hours later the two were still huddled round the glowing
stove in the shed. Outside, the wind whistled round the corners of
the building, forcing sand through every tiny opening in the boards.
Which of the two first suggested they might try flying in such dangerous conditions has gone unrecorded. Probably it was not Wilbur.
Knowing the next turn belonged to Orville, he would hardly have
thought of sending his younger brother up in such a wild blow.
Perhaps Orville, impatient with all the delays, insisted that he was

ready to take the chance, pointing out that a strong wind would actually be a help in landing, since it would retard the Flyer's speed.

Though it has now long been forgotten, the hazard that Orville offered to face that day was a formidable one, requiring not only sheer courage, but also a certain degree of innocence, of blissful ignorance. A decade afterward he could still vividly recall the calculated gamble he took. "With all the knowledge and skill acquired in thousands of flights in the last ten years," he wrote, "I would hardly think today of making my first flight on a strange machine in a twenty-seven-mile wind, even if I knew that the machine had already been flown and was safe. After these years of experience, I look with amazement upon our audacity in attempting flights with a new and untried machine under such conditions." Compounding the danger, of course, though Orville did not mention it, was the fact that the Flyer had not been tried even as a glider.

At 10 A.M. the signal flag was run up and the two began laying the track in the sand about sixty yards to the west of the large shed, pointing due north. So cold was it that they had to return to the stove in the shed at intervals to warm their hands. Four men from the lifesaving station braved the cold to watch, and assist if needed. Two of them had been present on the fourteenth, John T. Daniels and W. S. Dough. Two others had been occasional visitors to the camp, A. D. Etheridge and W. C. Brinkley. With them came a seventeen-year-old who had stopped at the station to talk, Johnny Moore of Nags Head.

By ten thirty the Flyer stood poised on the takeoff rail, the engine sputtering in a warmup. Behind it and a few feet to the right, Orville had set up a tripod camera, aimed at a point near the end of the track, the point from which he expected the Flyer to rise. John Daniels volunteered to operate it; as the Flyer lifted he was to snap the shutter.

When all was ready Wilbur motioned to his brother and the two walked a little apart from the others, where they stood talking quietly for a few minutes. "After a while they shook hands," remembered Daniels, "and we couldn't help notice how they held on to each other's hand, sort o' like they hated to let go; like two folks parting who weren't sure they'd ever see each other again." The substance of this conversation was not recorded, though it probably included a reminder from Wilbur that Orville was to be careful not to let the Flyer get too high; between ten and fifteen feet was the height they had agreed on.

Orville climbed aboard and adjusted himself in the hip cradle. Wilbur, before taking his place at the right wing tip, walked over to the five spectators who were standing a short distance to the rear of the Flyer. He told them, as Daniels recalled, "not to look sad, but to laugh and hollo and clap our hands and try to cheer Orville up when he started." As Wilbur walked back to the Flyer the five set up a noisy demonstration.

Above the sound of motor and propellers rose Orville's shout of readiness. The restraining wire was slipped. The Flyer started forward, Wilbur's grasp on the right wing tip struts keeping it level. He had no trouble in staying with the machine since the strong wind kept the Flyer's ground speed under ten miles an hour. Just before reaching the end of the track Orville's left hand moved the elevator control, opening the two-surfaced elevator to nearly full positive. The Flyer lifted, tilting a little to the left. As it passed the end of the track the skids were less than three feet above the sand. Wilbur came to a halt, gazing apprehensively.

Leveled out, the Flyer continued to rise until it had reached a height of about ten feet, then it dipped sharply down to four or five feet, rose again, dipped again, came up again. At about one hundred feet from the end of the track it made a last downward dart, in which it covered another twenty feet, then the skids made contact with the sand. The Flyer's full weight came down on them, cracking one slightly as the machine came to a straight sliding halt. Orville reached over and turned off the gas supply. The engine died as the propellers slowed to circular blurs, to single blades, then stopped. Now the sound of the wind whistling through the wire bracing could be heard.

Wilbur and the others ran up, congratulating Orville. While the spectators were probably not overly impressed with the 120-foot flight (they had seen the Wrights' gliders go much farther) Wilbur knew that something significant had been accomplished. The Flyer had been in the air twelve seconds, had flown forty yards against a twenty-seven-mile-an-hour wind. If the speed of the retarding wind was added to the Flyer's true ground speed, then the airspeed came to something like thirty-five miles an hour. In a flight of twelve seconds this would be the equivalent of a distance of 600 feet or so. Technically, then, it could be said that Orville had flown the longer distance, surely enough to prove that the Flyer had stayed up by means of its own power.

And yet, of course, the Flyer had not really flown for 600 feet, nor could any amount of mathematical calculation substitute for actual performance, particularly where a first flight was concerned. To those watching, the laymen as well as the expert, a first flight could only mean a flight in which sufficient ground was actually covered, one in which human eyes could *see* a machine maintaining itself in the air, proceeding on and on until all doubts evaporated in the unarguable sight of the wondrous thing being *done*.

Although Orville's flight of 120 feet in twelve seconds is today universally accepted as the first flight in history, that is only another of the myths that managed to spring up during those long, silent decades following the death of Wilbur. It is based on a purely technical position, reached by a curious species of behindhand reasoning: since the Flyer later flew, then its first flight from level ground, when corrected mathematically, was the first flight. But at Kitty Hawk on December 17 neither brother accepted the first trial as, incontestably, a proper flight. It had simply been too short.*

With the help of the spectators, the Flyer was picked up and carried back to the starting rail. The cracked skid was soon spliced with strong cord and at that point the Wrights and their guests gave in to the cold. They had been outside for nearly an hour and were chilled to the bone; all retired to the shed to warm up.

His undulating progress, Orville explained to his brother, had been caused by control difficulties, not any basic deficiency in the Flyer. To begin with, it appeared that the elevator was not balanced adequately. The fulcrum was too near the center, so that the elevator "had a tendency to turn itself when started . . . too far on one side, and then too far on the other." This condition would have been promptly uncovered if the Flyer had been tested as a

---

* This fact can be appreciated even today by anyone who visits the Kitty Hawk site, where markers now stand at the takeoff spot and at the landing points. For further comment see the Notes.

glider, and there would have been time to correct it. Stopping now to make a structural change was out of the question.

Then, also, the brothers' experience on the glider had not prepared them for dealing with winds of such great strength, even if the elevator had been properly balanced. During the trial Orville had been nonplussed to find that a slight change in the elevator's attitude was enough to exert a powerful directional change on the machine, much more powerful than anything he had encountered when gliding in lighter winds. Wilbur, who would be making the next attempt, would have to use a subtler touch to compensate for both the skittish elevator and the wind.

At twenty minutes past eleven Wilbur took his place on the lower wing of the Flyer, Orville moving over to the right wing tip struts. The start and the takeoff were duplicates of the first effort, smooth and sure. At an altitude of about ten feet Wilbur leveled off but quickly found that his brother had not exaggerated the touchiness of the elevator. As the Flyer drove forward it alternately rose and fell exactly as it had done before, not once achieving straight flight. Passing over the spot at which Orville had landed, it went on for another fifty feet or so, then swooped low, touched down and came to an easy stop. Time in the air was thirteen seconds. History's first official flight had not yet taken place. The Flyer was lugged back to the rail and set up again.

At twenty minutes to twelve Orville took off. To those watching, it was immediately apparent that he had the machine under good control, with very little undulation in the attitude. The Flyer churned its way ahead, zooming over Wilbur's landing spot and appearing very much as if it would go on indefinitely. Then, abruptly, it jumped up to a height of more than fifteen feet as the right wing lifted, tilting in a manner alarming to those on the ground.

Orville had to make two hasty corrections, in two directions, simultaneously. He had to apply negative elevator to prevent the machine from rising any higher and in fact to bring it down to what the brothers had agreed was a safe altitude. He had also to apply warp to bring the right wing level. Not surprisingly, he overdid both controls. The Flyer came down fast, the wings leveling off so rapidly that the right tip, which had been climbing only a split second before, made first contact with the ground, though lightly. The machine slid to a halt about 200 feet from takeoff. Time in the air was only fifteen seconds.

At precisely twelve noon Wilbur began the fourth trial of the day. It did not start well. With Wilbur overcorrecting on the controls, the undulations immediately set in. Passing the 200-foot mark, the Flyer was dipping and rising fairly violently, once coming within a foot of the ground. But it kept going and at 300 feet the lifting and falling became less pronounced. By the time it had reached 400 feet the watchers back at the starting point could see that Wilbur had gotten it under much better control. About ten feet above the sand, it was boring straight into the wind, the mingled snarl of propellers and engine diminishing as the distance lengthened.

It was now, at approximately twenty seconds after twelve noon, with the Flyer calmed to level flight, that everyone knew, without need of stopwatches or measurement, that the machine was flying, was sustaining itself in steady progress through the air. On it flew: 500 feet, 600 feet, 700 feet, the bright spread of the wings growing smaller and smaller against the gray background of sand and sky. To those gazing happily after the shrinking Flyer it seemed that Wilbur was going to make good his intention of landing at the village of Kitty Hawk, nearly four miles away.

Aboard the Flyer, Wilbur, too, had his eyes set on the sprawling cluster of trees and houses directly ahead of him. Between lay only the open sands. Then, at about 800 feet, as he tried to rise a bit to clear a slight hummock, the machine began pitching again. This time he could not settle it down. Dipping low, it touched the sand. The skids dug in, tipping the Flyer forward and putting all the weight on the elevator's substructure. To the sound of cracking, twisting wood, the machine bounced to a halt as the surfaces of the elevator tilted brokenly out of line. The Wright luck still held, for if the descent had been a few degrees steeper the Flyer might have flipped over, certainly it would have been much more badly damaged.

Man's first flight was over. It had lasted a second less than one minute, covering 852 feet.

Not all great moments enter history accompanied by the rolling drum and the swelling chorus. This was one of those that didn't. When the Flyer came to a stop, sand kicking up from the ploughing elevator frame, Wilbur cut the engine and climbed off. What thoughts may have gone through his mind as he stood looking at the machine he never said—was there perhaps some fleeting memory of that young invalid of long ago who thought his life a ruin? For two or three minutes, before Orville and the others ran up, Wilbur stood there alone. Only the wind, still sweeping roughly over the solitary sands, sighing against Flyer and pilot, whispered its acceptance of man's new status as a denizen of the air.

It was a grudging acceptance, however, and the wind had one last petulant bit of mischief to perform. With the broken elevator removed, the Flyer was carried back to camp where it was temporarily set down in the open. Repairs would take a day or two, then it would be Orville's turn again. For a few minutes all stood in a little group talking about the successful flight. The wind had picked up and was now over thirty miles an hour.

Someone shouted and everyone turned to look. The wind had lifted the Flyer by its front edges and was throwing it over backwards. Wilbur rushed to the front, grabbed at a skid but couldn't hold on. Orville and John Daniels ran behind as the big wings tumbled "like an umbrella turned inside out and loose in the wind." The lower wing, weighted by the engine, came down heavily. Orville jumped clear but Daniels was caught between the wings, trapped by the wire bracing.

"I can't tell to save my life," he said later, "how it all happened, but I found myself caught up in them wires, and the machine flowing across the beach and heading for the ocean, landing first on one end and then the other, rolling over and over, and me getting more tangled up in it all the time." He had been caught near the center of the span and found himself repeatedly thrown against the motor and the propeller chains. "When the thing did stop for a second I nearly broke up every wire and upright getting out of it."

The others ran up to examine the badly frightened man. Aside from torn clothes, a good many bruises, scratches, and cuts, and wobbly legs, he was not badly hurt. Wilbur and Orville "pulled my legs and arms, felt of my ribs, and told me there were no bones broken." The Flyer, of course, was done for. The motor had been broken loose, the chain guides bent, struts and ribs broken. There could be no more flying that season.

The machine was stored away, the other men drifted back to their work, taking Daniels to be patched up. The brothers sat down to a well-earned lunch. About the middle of the afternoon they set out along the beach for the Kitty Hawk weather station, to send a telegram to their father.

11

The Story of the Century— Almost

Evening shadows had begun to fall around the Wright home in Dayton. In the darkening kitchen the cook, a girl in her twenties named Carrie Grumbach, struck a match and lit a gas lamp hanging over the table, then started preparing supper. Upstairs, Bishop Wright was resting in his room. Katharine had gone out for a while. A settled serenity, born of nearly thirty years' occupation by the Wright family, embraced the neat, quiet rooms. The time was a few minutes before six.

There came a rap on the front door knocker, the sharp echoes ringing through the silence. Carrie put down her pot, went through the hallway to the front door, took the proffered telegram, saw that it was for the Bishop, climbed the stairs to his room, then descended to the kitchen again. A few minutes later she heard him coming slowly downstairs and went to meet him.

Bishop Wright's manner was calm as always but across his bearded face was spread a smile of mingled pleasure and relief. Offering the telegram to Carrie, he said quietly, "Well, the boys have made a flight." The girl read: "Success four flights Thursday morning all against twenty one mile wind started from level with engine power alone average speed through air thirty one miles longest 57 seconds inform press home Christmas."*

At that moment the front door opened and Katharine came in. She read the telegram and joined in the expressions of delight at the news. The wire had said "inform press," so the elder Wright suggested that Katharine might take the wire over to Lorin's house, four blocks away. Lorin could take it down to the office of the Dayton *Journal*, supplying a brief statement with it.

Lorin was at his dinner when his sister entered and displayed his kinship to Wilbur by finishing his meal before leaving for the newspaper office. It was nearly seven o'clock when he stood at the desk of the *Journal*'s night editor explaining how his two brothers had flown in a flying machine, one flight lasting for fifty-seven seconds. The editor, an old-timer named Frank Tunison, kept on with his work. Without looking up, he said crustily, "Fifty-seven seconds? If it had been fifty-seven minutes then it *might* have been a news item." What rejoinder Lorin may have made, or what explanations he may have given, are unknown. In any case he did not succeed in convincing Tunison that his story should be printed, and he left the *Journal* office muttering at the thickheadedness of the press.

Tunison was never allowed to forget his blunder (the incident is prominently mentioned by Kelly, where the editor is pictured as "annoyed over being expected to accept such a tale") yet the full truth is far kinder to the newsman. It shows him to have been a victim of his times and, almost certainly, an inadequate explanation by Lorin.

Like most people then, including most newsmen, Tunison knew little of the difference between machines that were lighter than air and those that were classed as heavier then air, knew next to nothing of what was called "mechanical flight." On the general subject of balloons he was probably as well informed as the average person —many varieties of experimental balloons, he knew, carried engines and propellers, even a kind of winglike horizontal rudder. Listening to Lorin's description of what his two brothers had accomplished,

---

* "Twenty-one mile wind"—for the third and fourth flights the wind had lessened somewhat; the brothers were reporting a conservative figure, and meant each flight was against *at least* a twenty-one-mile wind. "Longest 57 seconds"—this was a Western Union error for 59 seconds.

Tunison received the impression, perhaps merely assumed it, that these local boys had managed to get up into the air with some sort of modified balloon, and had stayed there for nearly a minute. Well, that was nice, no doubt, but in 1903 a balloon ascent of only a minute, no matter what kind of contraption it was, simply did not amount to news.

Very likely it never even occurred to Tunison that his visitor was talking about the same sort of balloonless flight at which the great Langley had, nine days before, so stupendously failed. If some idea of that fact did momentarily nudge him, he may be excused for dismissing it as an impossibility. The famous Langley's preparations and experiments had taken seven years and when it came time for his full-scale trials all the world had known what he was up to. No one had heard of these Wrights, even in Dayton, until the moment Lorin entered the *Journal* office. (You say they have a small bicycle shop, Mr. Wright? Over on Third Street? West Third, I see. And where did you say this Kitty Hawk is?)

Of the two other daily papers in Dayton, Lorin seems to have visited neither. Evidently it had been decided that the news could wait until Wilbur and Orville had a chance to decide on a proper presentation. That would delay things only a few days, at the most a week. This decision, however, reckoned without the enterprising American newsman, for no sooner had the telegram been flashed from Norfolk to Dayton than two reporters were on the trail of the story. And it was through these two men that the world received its first hint that the age of flight had arrived. While it is true that much of the detail they supplied was grossly inaccurate, the deficiency was in no way their own fault. They were working in a technical vacuum and furthermore were faced by a barrier of deliberate silence.

In the whole Wright story there is no belief more persistent than that the nation's press failed utterly to grasp and report what the brothers had done, rejecting their claims to flight if not with a horselaugh still with a smile of pity, stupidly neglecting to give ear to one of the biggest stories of the century. That, too, is a myth. In reality, the press was avidly interested in running down the complete and exact truth. If given full information and pictures, and if allowed to see the Flyer in the air or even on the ground, American newspapers and magazines would quickly have spread the whole incredible story to the farthest parts of the world. But such full disclosure was precisely what Wilbur Wright did not want and the press failed in its duty only because Wilbur was largely able to work his will.

Even before the first flight, his instincts had led him to adopt a difficult policy of secrecy-with-publicity. For the *performance* of the Flyer on December 17 he wanted all the coverage possible, but over the details of its construction and capability he preferred to draw a veil of absolute secrecy. The five witnesses to the Flyer's successful trial had been asked not to talk about what they had seen, beyond admitting that there had been a flight. Chanute and Spratt had both received pointed requests not to give out any details of the machine's construction. Photographs of the Flyer, in the air and on the ground (about a dozen had been taken), were on no account to be allowed out of the Wrights' hands. Pictures of the earlier gliders were also to be kept from publication—Wilbur now regretted that he had supplied two or three views of them to illustrate the printing of his talks in the *Journal* of the Western Society of Engineers. Some of those pictures had already found their way into the pages of the *Scientific American.*

It is unclear just how far into the future Wilbur had, at this point, projected his plans, uncertain how long he meant to maintain secrecy. As it developed, however, it was to become a fixed policy stretching over more than four years, giving rise to some astonishing situations, and sowing confusion and doubt not only among newsmen but in the aeronautical circles of America and Europe as well. The first small step in Wilbur's program took place at Kitty Hawk—and it was also there that the first breach in the hoped-for secrecy occurred.

It was about three hours after the first flight that the brothers entered the Kitty Hawk weather station to send their telegram. This government wire was the only direct communication with Norfolk and thus was available for private use. The message would go to the weather station at Norfolk and from there across town to the offices of Western Union. No sooner had the Kitty Hawk operator finished sending the thirty-two-word message than the Norfolk operator flashed back a request that he be allowed to give the news to a reporter friend. The Wrights, lingering at the station, responded with a firm *no!* and the refusal was tapped out. They wanted the news to come from Dayton, the brothers explained, simply as a matter of legitimate home-town pride.

There was some truth in that, no doubt, but their real reason for refusing concerned the fact that they were still on the Banks and could not hope to get away for home in less than two or three days. Dismantling and crating the Flyer for shipment (in "two boxes and a barrel") and packing up would take at least that long. They did not relish the idea of local reporters rushing into camp, firing questions, nosing round the Flyer, and trying to get pictures, which they certainly would do even in the face of a prohibition. On the other hand, if a short item went out from Dayton, then the fact would be on record and it might very well be overlooked by local papers, at least for a few days. By then the brothers would be home, the Flyer safely tucked away.

That Lorin might encounter skepticism in the offices of the Dayton papers seems never to have occurred to either. Equally overlooked was the possibility that the telegraph operator in the Norfolk office might choose to disregard that emphatic *no*.

To his friend H. P. Moore, a cub reporter for the Norfolk *Virginian-Pilot* who covered the "marine" beat, the operator showed the Wrights' telegram. Moore in fact had already heard, through his contacts among the lifesaving crews, of the brothers' presence on the Banks. For some unknown length of time he had been keeping a casual eye on them. Now, galvanized, apparently never in doubt about the truth of the claim, he set about gathering data. Just how he did this, in the face of the distances, the isolation of the Banks, and under the pressures of a deadline for the next morning's paper, is not known. Certainly he kept various telegraph wires humming.

Almost at the same time that Moore began probing, another reporter for the *Virginian-Pilot,* a veteran named Ed Dean, also got wind of the story and he too began sounding his sources, also mainly by telegraph. It is probable that the lines of inquiry of the two crossed more than once; whether one knew the other was working on the story is not recorded. Some time that night Dean checked in at his paper's office. Together with the editor, Keville Glennan, he began shaping his story from the bits and pieces he had gleaned. A little later Moore checked in and added his store of notes to the pile.

Considering the difficulties under which the two had operated, the total information gathered was impressive, but there were obvious contradictions and important gaps. The three men, none of whom had any special competence in aeronautics, did their best to fit the pieces together. As they finished, copy was sent to the composing room and Glennan set to work on the headline.

Before they quit for the night, Moore and Dean prepared a shorter version of the story and telegraphed queries to twenty-one other papers, asking if they were interested. Five papers immediately replied in the affirmative, the others preferring to think it over or to wait for the Associated Press to pick the item up, thereby saving an extra fee and getting the blessings of the prestigious AP on a story that could not help raising doubts in hard-pressed editors—such "wildcat" claims from out-of-the-way corners of the country were by no means unusual. The condensed account was promptly teletyped to the five buyers and Moore and Dean then went home, each richer by nearly a full month's pay (the night's work eventually brought them a total of $170 in free-lance fees).

On the morning of December 18 readers of the *Virginian-Pilot* found a front-page banner headline stretching across the paper's seven columns, with additional one-column subheads leading into the text. Whether all readers fully grasped the implications of the words is unlikely. That the main headline contained two errors, in the form of exaggeration, probably would not have bothered any-one even if it had been known.

FLYING MACHINE SOARS 3 MILES IN TEETH OF HIGH WIND OVER SAND HILLS AND WAVES AT KITTY HAWK ON CAROLINA COAST

NO BALLOON ATTACHED TO AID IT

THREE YEARS OF HARD, SECRET WORK BY TWO OHIO BROTHERS CROWNED WITH SUCCESS

ACCOMPLISHED WHAT LANGLEY FAILED AT

WITH MAN AS PASSENGER HUGE MACHINE
FLEW LIKE BIRD UNDER
PERFECT CONTROL

Unerringly, the opening sentence went straight to the heart of the matter, expressing the leading fact in a way that would be most readily understood by readers. "The problem of aerial navigation without the use of a balloon," it announced succinctly, "has been solved." In much of its detail the remainder of the story is less accurate and though it is easy to smile now at the errors of Glennan, Dean, and Moore, they did their best to make sense out of fragmentary facts gathered at second, third, and perhaps even fourth hand.

Wilbur Wright was the pilot, stated the paper, identifying him as the "chief inventor." The machine took off from "a platform"— clearly an effort to make sense of the wooden track. It rose after a slight downhill run—just as clearly a confusion with the trial of December 14. Calling the Flyer "a big box"—it did of course resemble a box kite—the paper described how "the machine slowly began to go higher and higher until finally it soared sixty feet above the ground." This was more than three times the actual height attained but such exaggeration among eyewitnesses is common; probably the two reporters had brought back estimates of heights far greater than this and Glennan had chosen what seemed a sensible compromise.

Strangely, the speed of the Flyer over the ground was given almost exactly. "The forward speed of the huge affair," said the paper, "increased until a velocity of eight miles an hour was attained." The fact that there is no mention of other attempts may indicate that all four trials somehow became coalesced into one long flight of three miles.

The course of the flight was smooth, according to the paper, and the machine had been put through "all sorts of maneuvers." The source of this error obviously lay in the violent undulations that had plagued all four trials, probably also in the sudden loss of control Orville had encountered on the third attempt. The landing of a flying machine without wrecking it or injuring the pilot had always been thought of as one of the most serious difficulties in the way of powered flight. Since all four of the Wrights' landings had appeared easy and smooth, the paper made an effort to stress that fact, though it did go a bit too far. "He selected a suitable place to land," ran the account, "and gracefully circling, drew his invention slowly to earth, where it settled like some big bird, in the chosen spot."

Only in describing the Flyer did the paper go wildly awry. The two single propellers at the rear became two six-bladed propellers, one at the rear and one affixed underneath the lower wing, this "underwheel" supposedly providing additional lift.* The engine itself was supposedly "suspended just below the bottom plane." The pilot sat in an "operator's car." But perhaps, in light of all the circumstances, even these errors are understandable. There was only one really ludicrous touch and that concerned not the flight of the machine but Wilbur himself. The three newsmen evidently felt that so stupendous an achievement must have had, at least needed, a fittingly dramatic conclusion. After Wilbur landed and climbed off the machine, the paper explained, he did not just stand there. " 'Eureka,' he cried, as did the alchemist of old." The brothers were to chuckle over that line for a long time.

That same morning of December 18 only two of the five papers that had bought the shorter version used it: the Cincinnati *Enquirer*, which gave the story prominent page-one headlines, and the New York *American*, which tucked it discreetly away on an inside page. But the Associated Press in Norfolk immediately picked it up and flashed a condensed version around the country. Many afternoon papers on the eighteenth featured it, errors and all, including the three in Dayton. It appeared in Boston and Washington, and the Kansas City (Mo.) *Star* carried it on page one under a headline that proclaimed "A Machine That Flies."

* An "underwheel" was not really such a bad guess, after all, it seems. Octave Chanute, who had seen the Flyer with his own eyes, on encountering in the New York *Herald* a faked sketch of the machine, inquired of Wilbur: "This shows a horizontal propeller under the front of the apparatus. Is this correct?" Actually there was an underlying reason for Chanute's apparent ignorance. For a long time he suspected that the Wrights possessed some kind of "secret" which they had not revealed even to him.

By that evening reporters began calling at the Wright home looking for corroboration, details, additional background, and pictures
of both the brothers and the Flyer. Since the two were not yet
home, all the newsmen obtained were corrections of the wilder aspects of the original release, and these were promptly passed on.
The New York *Herald,* for instance, on December 19 devoted a full
column on its front page to the news illustrated by two photographs
of the 1901 glider (hastily obtained from the *Scientific American*).
The story led off with the Norfolk AP release, the errors uncor-
rected, but below was printed a later Dayton release in which the
true facts of the flight were stated and backed up by quotation of
the telegram. Obviously, deadline pressures had left no time to rec-
oncile the contradictions, even if there had been anyone in the paper's office qualified to make an assessment.

The brothers were identified by the *Herald* as "sons of a bishop,"
and characterized as "intelligent mechanics." This phrase, which
now sounds so patronizing, was evidently the best the paper could
do in explaining the brothers' lack of scientific background. Unfortunately, it was picked up and used repeatedly in the following
months and years, to the great chagrin of Wilbur and Orville. In a
subtle way it seemed to imply that the brothers' success was not a
triumph of original research, but was based on an ingenious selec-
tion from the work of other men. Later, this attitude was to come
into the open—led by certain rabid adherents of Langley—and survives even today among the uninformed.

A few publications, more enterprising, tried to make direct contact with the Wrights at Kitty Hawk. On the nineteenth both the
New York *World* and *Century Magazine* wired requests for exclusive rights to the first-person story, with pictures. The same day the
Scientific American and, rather unexpectedly, *Woman's Home Companion* both asked that photographs be rushed to New York. Pictures were the last thing the brothers wanted to have reach the
public, of course, and all four offers were declined. Unwilling to
give up, the *World* countered with an offer for a nonexclusive 600-
word account, to be sent by telegraph. This, too, was ignored.

During the five days between December 18 and 22, reporters
continued to call at the Wright home, waiting for the brothers to
arrive. In the meantime newspapers around the country printed

whatever bits of information could be gleaned in Dayton or else-where. Newsgathering in such a vacuum was aggravating but not, of course, impossible. On the twenty-second, for instance, while the brothers were speeding home by train, the New York *Herald* an-nounced that the two were "working upon plans to bring their ex-periments to a higher state of development," information probably based on some remark of Bishop Wright or Lorin. Adorning the story were studio portraits of Wilbur and Orville, side by side, topped by a drawing of an eagle with wings outspread (pictures that could have been obtained only from the family).

It was dark when the brothers finally arrived at Hawthorn Street on the evening of the twenty-third. Waiting outside the house they found a knot of reporters but the two refused to stop for questions (they "suppressed" the newsmen, Bishop Wright wrote in his di-ary). Reporters who called during the next few days found them equally uncommunicative, except to repeat the main facts of the flight. Probe and question as they might, the impatient newsmen could not pry loose even the smallest detail of the Flyer's construc-tion or the techniques and methods used for takeoff and control. Urgent requests for pictures of the Flyer continued to be refused. Not surprisingly, in a few papers there soon appeared faked state-ments, fraudulent interviews, and even gimmicked photographs of the machine, made by retouching photographs of the earlier gliders.

A few days after New Year's the brothers at last put out an offi-cial statement. Their ostensible purpose in this move was to correct the gross errors that had gained currency, but an equally important reason was a desire to put a stop to harassment by the press. The statement was a brief one, revealing nothing new or startling, ex-plaining such things as the sequence of the four trials and the strengths of the winds. It was in the last paragraph that the real point was made: "As all the experiments have been conducted at our own expense without assistance from any individual or institu-tion, we do not feel ready at present to give out any pictures or de-tailed description of the machine."

Released through the Associated Press, the statement was car-ried by many papers around the country. This firm announcement that the public was not, any time soon, to see or be told what the Flyer looked like, did its work. The parade of reporters to the

Wright front door stopped. Editors, no whit less anxious to get the full story, simply assumed that the Wrights meant what they said. And there was another factor operating to calm the usual insistent probing of the press: everyone, without exception, took for granted that if a flying machine had been invented, then it would not be long before it would be *seen* in the air by a multitude of witnesses. Unlike almost all other inventions, this one could not perform its natural function except in public. Let so marvelous a thing as an "aeroplane" rise off the ground, even in the secluded hinterlands of the country, and the fact would be common knowledge in no time. There was no need to pursue such a story. All reporters need do was wait until the Wrights began flying again and then the story would inevitably unfold itself, dramatically framed by the open sky, a clear object for cameras and racing pencils. You simply could not use an aeroplane, or experiment with it, in hiding.

But in the fertile mind of Wilbur Wright that was precisely the idea that had begun to take shape. Before the year 1904 was a few weeks old he had settled on a plan for doing the impossible. He would develop the machine to the stage of practical use at which it might be most readily and lucratively marketed, without showing it to the public or revealing any of its workings. The sale of the Flyer as a complete secret, he believed, would bring enough of an immediate return to make him and his family independent for life, "without exploiting the invention commercially or assuming any business responsibilities." Even the capability of the developing Flyer was to remain unknown—in other words, he preferred that the world should not know that a practical airplane had been achieved.

In or out of the history of invention, the scheme that Wilbur devised for accomplishing all this has had few equals for self-assured, almost nonchalant audacity.

12

The Goings-on
at Huffman's Pasture

On a day in late April 1904, an Interurban trolley, one of the electric cars that ran between the towns and cities of southern Ohio, came to a momentary stop at lonely Simms Station, about eight miles east of Dayton. Down from the trolley to the dusty road stepped Wilbur and Orville Wright. Around the two lay open farm country composed of large fields, most of them grassy and bordered by rows and clusters of tall, spreading trees. Here and there, widely separated, a house or a barn lifted a gray roof amid the lush greenery.

The brothers walked a short distance, then turned into one of the larger fields, climbing between strands of a barbed wire fence. They crossed the field to its southeast corner, treading in fairly deep grass dotted by six-inch hummocks, and entered a wooden shed that was a larger replica of the two rough buildings that still stood on the sands at Kitty Hawk. Doffing their coats, they began ripping open crates and laying out the materials for assembly of Flyer No. 2. At dusk, after working five or six hours, they returned home.

This trip was repeated every day except Sundays for a month, sometimes both brothers being present, sometimes Wilbur with Charles Taylor, sometimes Wilbur alone. By the middle of May the new Flyer was complete, though with elevator and rudder still to be attached, since the shed was too narrow to take the machine with these in place (a later arrangement allowed the rudder to be partially folded into the wings for storage). During the whole month the work of assembly had proceeded without intrusion. "So far we have not been subjected to the slightest annoyance from visitors or newspapers," Wilbur observed in a letter. "I think the reporters are not aware of what is going on."

The new Flyer was very much like the first one in its conformation and main dimensions, but there were some changes. The rudder had been enlarged slightly and reshaped to give more horizontal surface. The wing camber had been decreased to a shallower 1-in-25. The hollow ribs in the wing were now tapered toward the rear. Capacity of the gas cylinder had been increased and, most important, the elevator control was now located off-center, to the rear, to give easier handling. An entirely new and more efficient engine had been installed. Other changes imparted a greater structural strength overall. Total weight was increased by about a hundred pounds.

When assembly was completed, there followed a week of checking, rechecking, making final adjustments on fittings and wires, and test-running the new engine inside the shed. By May 25 the Flyer was ready to take to the air. It was a day the brothers had worked toward and planned for in meticulous detail for five long months. It was also a day on which Wilbur Wright would perpetrate a daring deception whose sole purpose was to mislead and befuddle the press, hopefully freeing his future experiments from the constant surveillance of reporters.

Choice of this particular field had been made only after a careful reconnoitering of the countryside. It had turned out to be part of a large dairy farm owned by the president of one of Dayton's banks, Torrance Huffman. When Wilbur approached the owner with an offer to rent, he had been given use of the field free of charge, provided he would be careful not to "run over" the small herd of cattle and the few horses usually grazing there. Huffman's pasture had been chosen not only because its approximately ninety level acres gave plenty of room in which to fly, but because it lay in the center of wide-spreading farm country which was very sparsely populated and little traveled, and because tall trees, forty or fifty feet high, screened it on two sides—the greatest altitude Wilbur calculated his machine would require was about twenty feet. In shape a rough rectangle, the field's southern boundary was its longest, stretching for nearly half a mile, the northern border somewhat less. The western and eastern ends both extended about a quarter mile.

It was the Interurban trolley itself that posed the only real threat to privacy. It skirted the northwest corner of the field, and its passengers, going to and from Dayton, would certainly spread tales about anything they might see floating in the air. But this difficulty had been easily solved by a glance at a timetable. The trolleys going in either direction were not frequent, passing at about half-hour intervals. Wilbur did not intend to stay in the air, on any one flight, for anything like a half hour. Besides learning to control the Flyer in maneuvering and circling, there was still much to be determined about takeoffs and landings. As much could be accomplished in repeated flights of a few minutes each, Wilbur had decided, as in longer ones. All he need do was time his ascents between trolleys. If by some miscalculation or change of schedule a trolley did come by while the Flyer was in the air, its passengers still would not have a clear or leisurely view of the machine. The trolley's tracks lay just beyond the field's western and northern boundaries, along which stood an obscuring line of trees, and the moving car would be in the vicinity perhaps less than a minute, including the halt at the station. Further, because of the clustering of the trees and the conformation of the field, at no time would the airborne Flyer be closer to the tracks than about two hundred feet. It would take an unusually alert passenger to get excited about a rather small, strange object intermittently visible behind that leafy screen.

Even brief, low flights, however, would certainly be seen by casual passersby and by the few locals, and reports from these sources were bound to filter back to the news offices in Dayton. It was in the hope of forestalling the inevitable effect of such reports that Wilbur had dreamed up his ingenious deception. Instead of trying to hide from the press, he would openly invite it to be present at the first trials, thus disarming any suspicion of furtiveness. Then if the Flyer, unaccountably, were to end up an ignominious failure before the gallery of assembled newsmen, many of whom would no doubt

The perfected 1902 glider, with Wilbur as pilot, is launched from the higher slopes of Kill Devil Hill by Orville (foreground) and Bill Tate. Controlled glides of over 600 feet were achieved by both brothers with the 1902 glider.

ABOVE: Launched from the West Hill, a smaller dune, the perfected 1902 glider with Wilbur as pilot sails smoothly toward big Kill Devil Hill. The warp of the right tip can be seen as Wilbur acts to bring the wings level.

BELOW: Orville (front) and Wilbur in the new workshed at Kitty Hawk as they begin to assemble the Flyer, early October 1903. The old shed, now used for living quarters, stood just to the right.

The Flyer perched on the starting track on the lower slopes of Kill Devil Hill ready for its first trial, December 14, 1903. The men are from the Kitty Hawk Lifesaving Station. At the first crackle and whir of motor and propellers the two boys, frightened, ran away over the hill.

After a short run along the track into a strong wind the Flyer lifts off the starting rail, with Orville piloting. To the right Wilbur comes to a halt after running along to steady the wings. This first of four trials on December 17, 1903, lasted for 12 seconds and covered 120 feet. History's true "first flight" took place about an hour later, on the fourth attempt.

be skeptics in any case, the hard-nosed gentlemen of the press
would be less ready to believe any rumors about short flights that
might later be spread. If these Wrights had invited reporters once,
and failed, then surely when and if they succeeded the invitation
would be renewed—such was the attitude Wilbur hoped to induce.

There would be only one prohibition, and that an absolute one:
no photographs of the Flyer, either on the ground or in the air. To
make sure of compliance, no cameras would be allowed on the
field. The machine, after all, was very simple in its structure and
Wilbur was well aware that all sorts of valuable information could
be derived from pictures by close analysis and measurement.

Producing a "failure" would be no trick at all, even right in front
of the closely peering eyes of the witnesses: nobody then was quite
sure how a flying machine was *supposed* to work. A light wind, reduced engine power, a little negative elevator, a too-short takeoff
run, and the hapless Flyer could be made to struggle up from the
starting track and then immediately bounce to a mournful stop.
After all the fanfare over the flights at Kitty Hawk five months before, the doubts that still nagged at the minds of many people
would be sure to surface in strength.

Admittedly, though it was by no means foolproof, it was not only
a clever plan but a reasonable one, involving some understanding
of mass psychology. Perhaps only such a self-possessed individual
as Wilbur could have conceived and carried it out. Years later when
he was faced with a similar problem, he looked back with satisfaction to his successful hoax at Huffman's pasture: he had cooked up
another plan, he wrote, "which we are sure will baffle such efforts
as neatly as we fooled the newspapers during the two seasons we
were experimenting at Simms."

On the afternoon of May 25, in response to written invitations
sent by the Wrights to all the papers in Dayton and Cincinnati,
some dozen reporters stood crowded around the closed doors of the
shed. Also present were about twenty others, including the Wright
family, their neighbors and friends. The starting track, set near the
shed, faced into the center of the open field. The hinged end of
the shed was lifted and propped up. The brothers then trundled the
Flyer out endwise and hoisted it into position on the track. The
crowd milled around staring, reporters' pencils busily making notes.

All was ready, announced Wilbur, except for the wind. It was blowing too hard for safety. They must wait for it to lessen. An hour passed. The wind fell but a light rain started. The Flyer was hurriedly pushed back inside. Another hour and the rain had ceased, the wind was light. The Flyer was pulled out and put on the track, and the engine started. The crowd stirred and moved back.

Wilbur climbed into the hip cradle, waved to Orville, and released the starting wire. The machine lurched forward, impressively picking up speed. At the track's end, instead of leaping grandly away from the ground, it hopped lamely onto the grass, slid a few yards, and came to a bumpy stop.

Engine trouble, Wilbur explained, not enough power. There was no use trying again that day. They'd have it fixed by tomorrow. Would the reporters come back? Most said yes, though the faces of a number of them plainly showed a loss of enthusiasm. It was a long trip from Cincinnati.

The next afternoon a smaller crowd was on hand, the number of reporters no more than a half dozen. The Flyer was brought out and Wilbur climbed aboard. The holding wire dropped away, the machine whirred forward. Three seconds later it was sitting on the grass about ten yards from the end of the track, with a couple of pieces in the landing skids cracked. It had risen no higher than seven or eight feet.

The engine still wasn't right, apologized Wilbur, and the winds were too light. He wasn't sure when they'd be ready to try again but reporters were always welcome.

The stories that appeared in Dayton and Cincinnati papers (and were copied in other cities) were brief, usually printed on inside pages, and not really unkind. Even though written by professionals, the accounts still mixed in a good deal of distortion and exaggeration. *The New York Times* report affords a good example of what, in general, was said: "The machine, after being propelled along a track for the distance of a hundred feet, rose 12 feet in the air, and flew a distance of 30 feet, when it dropped. This was due, the inventors say, to a derangement of the gasoline engine that furnishes the power. In the fall the propellers were broken and the test could not be repeated."

A flight of thirty feet that had ended in an accident? Even uninformed readers would have shaken their heads at that. Whatever these Wrights might have done at Kitty Hawk, the age of flight still had not quite dawned. Newspaper editors and reporters at Dayton and in surrounding cities mentally filed away the Wright story to await more positive developments—if any. Soon after, with almost boyish glee Wilbur recorded the success of his little hoax. "The newspapers are friendly," he wrote in his best tongue-in-cheek style, "and are not disposed to arouse prying curiosity in the community."

The task facing the brothers now was, in its way, nearly as formidable, and every bit as dangerous, as had been the original problem. The less than two minutes of air time they had gained in the short, straight-line flights at Kitty Hawk had taught them almost nothing about the control of a power machine. Still to be learned was the whole range of maneuvering technique, beginning with basic circles and figure eights, and continuing through what they expected would be dozens of other movements of still unguessed subtlety. And once again, the only way to achieve this pioneering knowledge was for each of the brothers to commit himself bodily to the air.

Nor did they delude themselves that they had no more to learn about the configuration of a flying machine. As they gained more understanding of the aerodynamic forces at work, they anticipated, there would be revealed additional elements to alter, strengthen, and refine. Naturally, this in turn would further complicate the pilot's role.

By June 10 the two were at work in earnest, traveling to Huffman's on the electric cars every day, leaving Charlie Taylor to mind the shop. Though it was an exhilarating time for them, it quickly became evident that their secluded testing ground did have one drawback, a wind uncertain in both strength and direction, made even more erratic by the multitude of obstructing trees in the area. Undependable winds not only increased the danger, they considerably slowed down the work. As a result, during the first two weeks only a dozen takeoffs had been accomplished, all by Wilbur, with the longest flight under 300 feet.

In order to gain flying speed within a reasonable distance it was necessary for the Flyer to rise into the teeth of the wind. Since the wind was unlikely to come from the same quarter for very long at a time, this often meant a hurried shifting round of the long track, and a repositioning of the Flyer, sometimes only to lose the opportunity as the wind changed again or died down. At first the track length was fully 240 feet and when this proved unmanageable it was tried at 160 feet, a length easier to handle but which did not always afford a long enough takeoff run. Minimum wind velocity needed was twelve miles an hour, and even this was not always to be expected.

Both takeoffs and landings were, at first, more than a little ragged, with frequent breakage of pieces in the landing skids and tail assembly. On one flight it appeared that Wilbur had gotten well aloft, but the start had been made with the barbed-wire fence only 350 feet distant. Nearing the fence Wilbur realized he lacked sufficient speed to make a sure turn and, not wanting to fly beyond the field, had to come down. The next day he rose in what again appeared to be a successful attempt. He was too low, and in a sudden dip, at about twenty miles an hour, the elevator framework hit the ground a glancing blow and was shattered as the machine bounced heavily to a tilting stop, sustaining further damage to the right wing tip and the bracing wires.

The machine's center of gravity, Wilbur concluded, was too far forward. While making repairs he also moved the engine and hip cradle a little to the rear, no easy job since it meant altering many of the supporting pieces. There was some comfort in the fact that the new engine, at least, was performing well; with satisfaction Wilbur noted that it "met every requirement."

Through August the trials continued, gradually becoming longer though still in a straight line, with no more than four flights being made on any one day. Much heavy labor was required, and time consumed, by the simple act of getting the Flyer, which now weighed over 700 pounds, back to the track and mounted again. A small wheeled dolly was worked under the skids for the return across the field.

On August 6 Wilbur flew for 600 feet, about ten feet off the ground, Orville following with his first attempt of the year, making

200 feet. At last, on the thirteenth, Wilbur exceeded the best Kitty Hawk distance, cruising for more than a thousand feet across the center of the field and coming down near the trees on the western side. Time in the air, however, was only forty seconds.

On three occasions in the following week both brothers equaled or slightly bettered this distance, but it had become clear to Wilbur that he must find some more dependable means of launching the Flyer. The amount of effort they were putting into the struggle was out of proportion to the results. And the frequent wobbly take-offs were not only robbing them of the chance to improve their piloting skills, they were leading to some very bad landings. At various times breakage had been sustained in the rudder, the elevator, the wing tips, and the propellers themselves. Orville, after a short flight on August 24, had experienced a real crash in which the elevator frame collapsed and the Flyer tipped up and stood on its front edges, throwing Orville to the ground. Luckily, only his hand was bruised but he was "sore all over."

Plans for "a starting device that will render us independent of wind," in strength and largely in direction, now took definite shape and the result was a simple catapult, powered by a falling weight. A pyramidal tower ("derrick," Wilbur again called it) formed of four thirty-foot poles was erected at one end of the starting track. Inside the tower a heavy weight was lifted to its top and linked to the Flyer by a series of pulleys and ropes that ran alongside the track to the front end then doubled back to the machine. After experiment, a single weight of 1600 pounds was settled on. Falling some sixteen feet, this weight exerted a forward pull on the Flyer equal to 350 pounds, enough to get it into the air with a run of only fifty feet, even in a dead calm. It was tried first on September 7, with Wilbur as pilot, and promptly produced a flight of nearly 1400 feet in a very light wind.

While starting was now no longer a problem, Wilbur saw that the catapult, with its sudden, strong tug on the Flyer, introduced a disturbing factor into the handling of the machine. As he had done at Kitty Hawk in gliding, rather than let Orville take any undue risk he decided to make a series of flights himself to ensure the device's safety. In the succeeding week he flew at least a dozen times, taking off without mishap except in one instance when the tail made sharp contact with the rail as the front lifted, breaking a wooden brace. None of these flights exceeded about a half-minute in the air but all proceeded so smoothly that Wilbur was encouraged to take the next step, an attempt to turn a full circle.

On September 15, after flying a curving half-mile—toward the northern boundary, then sweeping left as he neared the barbed-wire fence—he was forced to land to avoid entering among the trees. A second effort the same day also failed after covering about the same course and distance, though the second landing was not so good, cracking the landing skids. The two half-circles, while failures, had given him some feel of the amount of bank needed, and an increased awareness of the behavior of the Flyer in a sustained tilt—for one thing, lessening his fear that the machine might simply go on revolving laterally and flop completely over. One bothersome new development was what seemed a tendency of the Flyer to respond to centrifugal force and slide sideways, to the outside of the circle, as it turned.

During the first three months of experiment there had been only two recorded spectators of the flights, aside from Charles Taylor, who was often on hand to help with measurements and timing. On the first day of the catapult's use, September 7, Katharine Wright and a friend, Melba Silliman, were at the field and saw Wilbur in a flight of a quarter-mile (these two were not the first women to see an airplane flying; that honor probably belongs to the wife of a farmer who lived just down the road, a Mrs. Beard, who brought over some liniment on the day of Orville's crash). In addition, the families of two or three farmers in the area had no doubt glimpsed the Flyer in the air from afar, and undoubtedly some passersby had also encountered the puzzling sight. Now, however, there came officially on the scene an outsider, a gentleman by the name of A. I. Root, who was destined to have a historic if minor role in aeronautics: it was Root who would write and publish the first eye-witness account of a flying machine in action. By a remarkable stroke of fortune the story would also concern the turning of the first circle.

Root, a resident of Medina, Ohio, located some 200 miles northeast of Dayton, was owner of a prosperous two-way business that sold supplies to beekeepers and honey to the public. For this trade

he also published a small magazine, *Gleanings in Bee Culture*. As
he said later, when he read in January of the Kitty Hawk flights his
enthusiasm had immediately been fired. He determined to meet the
Wrights and, hopefully, witness a flight. Just what happened next
—whether he wrote the brothers and received an invitation or simply set out on his own—is not known. In any case, by September 19
he was ensconced as a boarder at the Beard farm and intermittently
for more than a month was allowed free access to Huffman's pasture. As it happened, the very day after Root's arrival Wilbur succeeded in turning a circle, with the beeman as an entranced spectator.*

The day began dismally, with dark clouds hanging low in a
leaden sky. Despite the threat of rain Wilbur was anxious to proceed and the brothers, with Taylor, arrived at the field about mid-
morning. Though the wind was from the northwest, the takeoff
track was headed directly north in order to leave the whole center
of the field for making the left-handed circle.

Wilbur settled in the hip cradle, the engine crackled, and the
weight was dropped. The Flyer shot forward, rising easily and
leveling out at about fifteen feet. Some twenty seconds later, after
covering a thousand feet due north, and when about a hundred
feet short of the fence, Wilbur gently dipped his left wing, the right
one rising. The Flyer veered left, meeting the wind head-on and
circling widely round a forty-foot honey locust tree that stood as a
solitary obstacle near the field's center. It appeared for a moment
he would be able to close the circle, but he leveled out suddenly
and dipped his right wing. The Flyer reversed its path, slithered into
an S-turn and headed straight for the massed trees at the western
boundary. Quickly, he brought the Flyer down. He had flown for
a half-mile and for the first time had been in the air longer than the
fifty-nine seconds at Kitty Hawk: one minute five seconds.

His turn had been too wide, he explained, and he had not been
able to hold the banked position—he wasn't sure why. The machine
had again seemed to slide outward and the tail had also begun to

---

* I am inclined to think that there was some prearrangement between Root and the
Wrights, Wilbur wanting to have the historic first circle witnessed by a disinterested
party, one who could, moreover, record the fact in an unlikely, out-of-the-way publication. See the Notes.

fight against him in an unexpected manner, bringing on a feeling of instability. With his brother he analyzed the phenomenon, coming up with a number of theories but no conclusive answers, and again Wilbur knew that the only place a solution could be found was in the air. But now the rain began to come down heavily and the machine was hastily trundled back into the shed. It was afternoon before the downpour stopped.

The wind, at ten miles an hour, had shifted round to the northeast, which meant Wilbur on takeoff would receive a crosswind from the right and would have it on his tail at the first turn, not a particularly difficult situation yet the opposite to the conditions of his first attempt.

The Flyer was positioned on the track, was yanked forward, smoothly lifted, and went sailing noisily toward the north line. As before, when just short of the fence Wilbur put it into a bank and it eased toward the left. In a wide circle it again passed the obstacle of the solitary tree and to the delight of Orville and the others watching from near the shed, it continued turning, veering finally along the field's south boundary.

Root, gazing directly at the machine as it came toward him perhaps ten feet off the grass, fully understood the importance of the event and was transfixed. Orville called to him to move back out of the way in case the machine should come down suddenly but he scarcely heard. "When it first turned that circle," Root wrote later, "and came near the starting point, I was right in front of it; and I said then, and I believe still, it was one of the grandest sights, if not the grandest sight of my life. . . . I tell you, friends, the sensation that one feels in such a crisis is something hard to describe." By the time Root published his account in his own magazine he had finally found the only description that to him was adequate: the marvel he had witnessed, he said, "outrivals the Arabian Nights." He could find no comparison for the sight among familiar things so he offered his readers a picture that now appears clumsy, yet that must have made a graphic impression in that innocent era. "Imagine a locomotive that has left its track and is climbing up in the air right toward you," Root enthused, "a locomotive without any wheels, we will say, but with white wings instead . . . coming right toward you with a tremendous flap of its propellers, and you will have something like what I saw."

Wilbur brought the Flyer past the shed, making sure to cross his takeoff point exactly, then landed without mishap. He had flown some three-quarters of a mile, round a circle with a diameter of some four hundred yards. He had stayed up for more than a minute and a half and knew that, if he had wanted to, he could have remained in the air till the gas ran dry.

The accomplishment had not been without its difficulties, however, especially in a tendency of the Flyer to increase its tilt the longer it was held on a curving path. Wilbur had managed to correct this by a slight shift of the cradle to the right, sufficient to counter the exaggerated dipping, yet not enough to restore the Flyer to the level. It was a movement, as he reported to Orville, that demanded a fine sense of touch and balance.

The difficulty had been produced in the first place, he reasoned, because the outside wing in turning a circle would necessarily have more distance to cover than the inside wing, and would therefore be traveling faster. Its greater speed had set up increased resistance, lifting it even higher, while the inner wing's slower speed allowed it to decline. The other problem, the pull of centrifugal force, still remained to be solved but for some reason it had not given much trouble on this flight. Perhaps it would come seriously into play, thought the brothers, only under certain conditions.

Now came Orville's chance to learn the use of the catapult and fly a circle. Day after day he rose into the air only to have each flight for one reason or another aborted. On October 1 he twice flew smoothly curving half-miles, in the second of which he appeared to be well on his way. At the critical moment as he turned toward the south boundary he saw directly ahead of him some cows that had browsed their way unnoticed out from under the trees. His altitude was scarcely ten feet. Easing the elevator into positive, he climbed a little, zoomed over the startled animals, then came down again—too much. The Flyer tilted crazily and the right wing tip scraped along the grass. Orville hurriedly righted the machine then flopped to a hard landing, smashing skids and elevator frame.

Finally, on October 14, after some dozen tries, about the same number as his brother, he succeeded in closing the circle, a much wider one than that flown by Wilbur. He immediately went up again, flew a tighter turn, and missed a second circle by only a few yards. An hour later Wilbur climbed aboard and flew round the field for more than a mile, twice passing over bunches of straying cows.

The two returned home that evening happily convinced that their flying machine was very near to the stage of usefulness at which it could be marketed. They would inaugurate that important step perhaps in January, after they had flown a bit more and had safely stored the Flyer away. The very next day, however, they were taught a hard lesson, involving something that their steady march from success to success had obscured: they had not yet really become qualified pilots. The capricious air still had a few surprises to show them.

Orville, after getting off to a good start on the morning of October 15, went into a turn only to discover that the Flyer's bank was sharper than he had expected. When he tried to correct it he found that the machine would not respond, and a strong crosswind was hitting under the raised right wing. Unable to restore the balance, he could not stop turning and the Flyer was wheeling round in smaller and smaller arcs. To escape this alarming condition he dropped to a hard landing. The impact smashed the skids and kicked up the front of the hurtling machine so that both whirling propellers made churning contact with the ground, the blades splintering and snapping off. Bouncing and slewing in a cloud of dust and dirt, the Flyer finally came to rest after taking some engine damage. Orville was roughly jostled but held on.

Once or twice before, in shorter flights, the two had met some hint of this inability to right the machine and stop the turning. It appeared to derive from a problem in piloting technique but they couldn't be sure that it wasn't something simple and temporary, such as an alteration in wind conditions. In any case, it was now obvious that they would need a lot more practice, especially if they expected to teach others, a necessity in offering the Flyer for sale.

Aside from members of the Wright family and Root, and two local businessmen who had wandered into the field one day (the Flyer was in the air at the time and the two were treated to a quar-

ter-mile flight), so far there had been no close-up spectators. None
of the newsmen originally invited had ever returned, nor had there
appeared any reporters from the half-dozen small-town weeklies
published in the surrounding countryside.* Wilbur now began to
wonder just how long this could go on. "Intelligence of what we are
doing is gradually spreading through the neighborhood," he admitted to Chanute, "and we are fearful that we will soon have to
discontinue experiments." Briefly he thought about shifting the
work to some other, more secluded spot, perhaps going back to
Kitty Hawk. In the end he decided to stay where he was and take
the chance that he could complete the season before the press woke
up to the brazen manner in which they had been hoodwinked.

Through November the brothers flew at every chance, gradually
extending their average time in the air. On the ninth Wilbur stayed
up for just over five minutes, flying four times around the field for
a total distance of more than three miles and coming down only
because the engine overheated. This flight, he found unexpectedly,
had tired him much more than the shorter ones. "The strain upon
the human system of a single individual involved in the navigation
of an aeroplane," he told an acquaintance, "was excessively great.
Control of the equilibrium, the vertical steering, the horizontal
steering . . . kept the mind and body under continuous stress."
But this cost in fatigue, he felt, would lessen as his reactions became
more automatic.

It was during the five-minute flight that one of the Interurban
trolleys first caught the machine in the air. A car lumbered into
sight on its way to Dayton and instead of proceeding to Simms station for its regular stop it halted beside the field. Two men stepped
down and walked up to the shed, gazing open-mouthed at the Flyer
buzzing round the perimeter. They introduced themselves to Orville as Mr. Brown and Mr. Reed, officials of the trolley company

* Fred Kelly, the Wrights' biographer, was a cub reporter at this time, working on a
paper in Xenia, a small city some ten miles east of Huffman's pasture. He heard
something about the unusual goings-on at Huffman's but didn't bother to investigate.
The reason for this professional laxity, as Kelly himself expressed it, helps make clear
why many people ignored the rumors that had begun to spread. Kelly felt sure that
the talk must be nonsense because if it were true "surely it would be in the Dayton
papers." Behind this attitude, of course, was the assumption that a flying machine
simply *couldn't* be flown without the fact being detected and blazoned to the world.

making a special inspection run. There were no passengers on the car so the two men were allowed to remain, though they were admonished not to talk about what they were seeing. They agreed and, amazingly, kept their word.

Wilbur's five-minute flight was matched by Orville on December 1, and nine days later, as winter settled down, the experiments were terminated. Dismantled, the Flyer was stored away in the shed. It had taken six long months, more than a hundred takeoffs resulting in about fifty actual flights, something near an hour's total air time, repeated breakage and repair, a dozen close calls, half a dozen crash landings, a goodly portion of simple courage, and some extraordinary luck, but as 1905 arrived Wilbur and Orville Wright were in possession of the world's first practical airplane.

And the world didn't even know it.

13

Flying Machine for Sale

Honorable Robert M. Nevin, Republican representative from Dayton to the United States Congress, was at home for the Christmas 1904 holidays. A fifty-three-year-old lawyer whose political career had just begun to accelerate after a long halt, Nevin was in his third year as a congressman, one of twenty-four from the state of Ohio. His star, along with that of other Republicans, led from the White House by the irrepressible Teddy Roosevelt, was on the rise. It seemed that all Nevin needed to lift him into prominence was a stroke of fortune, some issue with significance beyond his state's borders. On the evening of January 3, 1905, just the opportunity he needed literally came knocking on his door. One of his constituents, Wilbur Wright, called at his home to enlist his aid in approaching the government about the purchase of a flying machine.

During the interview, as later correspondence makes clear, Wilbur explained how he and his brother had been experimenting in aeronautics for five years and had finally produced a power machine "fitted for practical use." They had just concluded work at their "experimenting station" in Huffman's pasture and wished Nevin to find out whether "this is a subject of interest" to the United States. They were making plans for the future and would appreciate a prompt answer.

Neither the Wrights nor Nevin left any detailed record of this meeting so it is not known what the immediate reaction of the congressman may have been to this bolt from the blue. Certainly he must have wondered how all this aerial experimenting could have taken place, over a period of six months, within eight miles of where he was sitting, without some word reaching him even in Washington. No doubt he posed some searching questions and perhaps Wilbur explained about all the precautions he had taken to ensure secrecy.

Probably also Wilbur showed Nevin one or more of the half-dozen photographs that had been taken of the Flyer in the air at Huffman's field. These, of course, while impressive, were not absolute proof of flight since, as Nevin would have realized, pictures can be faked. Even if authentic, a photograph of a machine in the air told nothing about how long the machine had been airborne. Obviously, a hop of a few seconds would have sufficed. And of the six pictures only one was really arresting, showing the Flyer stark against the sky at a height of about twenty feet, with the field's border of tall trees dwarfed in the background. In the other five photos the machine was scarcely six feet above the earth.

Whatever his first reaction, whether or not he was fully convinced, Nevin encouraged Wilbur to believe that there would certainly be definite interest on the part of the government. He was returning to Washington in a few days, he said, and suggested that all pertinent information be included in a letter to be sent to him there. He would personally take the letter to the Secretary of War, William Howard Taft, and arrange for the Wrights to visit Washington for a conference as soon as possible.

When Wilbur left Nevin's house that evening it must have seemed that the flying machine was within a matter of weeks of its debut on the world's stage, and the Wrights themselves close to reaping the inevitable great wealth. That it did not work out that way at all, that it actually took—astonishing to say—over three and a half years for the great event to come to pass, and involved tedious negotiations with England, France, and Germany as well, is a part of the story that deserves more explanation than it has so far received.

To understand how this delay could have happened it is necessary to begin with one fact long obscured: It was due not to the shortsightedness of governments or individuals, but directly and solely to the inflexible will of one man, Wilbur Wright. He had determined that in order to sell his invention as a complete and total secret he would not, under any circumstances, permit the Flyer to be seen by any prospective purchaser, not in the air, not even on the ground, until he had in his hands a signed contingency contract. In such an agreement the terms of sale would be automatically activated after certain proving flights by the brothers, bringing them an assured and immediate financial reward.

This attitude of Wilbur's was based on his belief that the Flyer was such a simple contrivance that, once revealed, it would be easy to duplicate, especially if close-up photographs of it were to get into circulation. It would be equally detrimental, he felt, if even a general impression of the machine's simplicity were to gain currency. The protection of patents would not avail against the mob of copyists, imitators, and improvers that was bound to spring up, freely infringing in the hope of somehow muddling through the legal tangles. The attempt to fight against such an onslaught could tie up progress and profits for years.*

With almost any other invention this position might have been tenable. With the airplane it was an entirely different matter. Since everyone assumed that a flying machine could not be developed in hiding, the claim that it *had* been put an enormous strain on human credence. Mingled with the wish to believe, the hope that the claim might be true, were the unavoidable doubts and fears that perhaps the whole thing was some monumental hoax.

As time went on it was to be generally admitted that the Wrights did have *some* kind of machine, perhaps had made *some* kind of flight. The question became whether the two unknowns possessed a practical machine, whether they had indeed flown as they claimed in the isolated precincts of Huffman's pasture. One short flight before competent observers would have settled all doubts in sensational fashion and there were to be many requests for such a demonstration, but this Wilbur would not chance in the absence of a contract.

---

* The Wrights' basic patent, covering their control devices, was still pending at this time, having been filed for in March 1903. It was granted in May 1906.

As the months passed he and his brother held to their view against the anxious urging of family and friends, and even in the face of threatened competition from European aeronauts. Looking at the outcome it is hard to avoid the conclusion that in this crucial instance Wilbur's usual good sense had at last played him false.

Naturally, this unwillingness to show the Flyer played its part in the difficulties that now developed with the United States War Department. And in these negotiations there was an additional factor operating, one that shows a side of Wilbur little realized or remembered, his "canny" side.

The letter to Nevin was sent on January 18. About three weeks later a reply from Nevin arrived at the Wright home. It contained the army's answer, signed by Gen. G. L. Gillespie of the General Staff. Instead of the eager inquiry that might have been expected, and an invitation to meet forthwith, Gillespie informed the Wrights that the army was no longer interested in *financing* aeronautical experiments but would be interested in hearing about a machine that had been "brought to the stage of practical operation." From the Wrights' letter, Gillespie went on, it appeared that their machine had not yet reached this stage. The army would be glad to hear from the two again "as soon" as the machine was perfected.

The Wrights, especially Wilbur, supposedly were so incensed at this unexpectedly cool response that they did not renew contact with the army for eight months. Indignantly, they saw the military's attitude as a "flat turndown," even an insult. Having given "a good clear knock on the War Department door," as Wilbur insisted, the brothers now felt free to take their invention to some more enlightened foreign government. With untroubled consciences, they turned to England.

What had gone wrong? Were the army's leaders really so devoid of vision, so old-fogyish, as history has ever since represented them? Did that single letter the brothers sent to Nevin really represent "a good clear knock"? Once again the prevailing tradition proves largely untrue. The army would have been overjoyed to receive the Wright invention if Wilbur had only taken pains to acquaint them with the real facts. That he did not take pains was no accident.

The letter sent to Nevin on January 18, and passed on by him to the army's Board of Ordnance and Fortification, when read in the full light of today's aeronautical knowledge appears to be adequate to its task. Yet when read in the dimmer light of its own day, and considering all the circumstances, it can be seen that it was almost perfectly calculated to lead to confusion.

The puzzled army board found itself reading a letter that had appeared almost literally from nowhere claiming to offer "a flying machine of a type fitted for practical use." This machine, stated the letter, was the result of five years' experiment and had already made over a hundred flights "in straight lines, in circles, over S-shaped courses, in calms and in winds." There is no explanation in the letter of why no one seemed to have heard of, or witnessed, these hundred flights, why the newspapers failed to report such phenomenal prog-ress. The Board's generals no doubt recalled the Wright name from the publicity it had received the year before, but that was hardly enough to prompt belief in so many wonderful phantom flights. Similar letters regularly reached the board from all over the coun-try, at the rate of two or three a month.

The Wrights' letter further proudly stated that the best of these flights had lasted for a period of five minutes. There was no hint that the machine could stay up longer—could in fact fly for a dis-tance of fifty miles or more, and a good deal further with fuel ca-pacity modifications (a pertinent bit of information that Wilbur did not fail to include in his later negotiations with the British). A flight of five minutes, over a distance of three miles—if this was the ma-chine's limit of performance, it could hardly be called practical. Of course, to knowledgeable men, a flight of five minutes should in it-self have been cause for excitement, if they believed it. But it is all too evident that like many others they did not believe it. A legiti-mate conclusion, particularly in the absence of proof, would be that the machine was indeed still in the experimental stage.

Conspicuously, there was no invitation in the letter for the army to send someone to observe the machine in flight. Instead, it con-cluded with an offer to get right to business. The Wrights were ready to provide "machines of agreed specification, at a contract price, or of furnishing all the practical and scientific information we have accumulated."*

Faced with such a perplexing communication, in which so many

* The complete letter may be read in the Notes.

questions were left unanswered, and still extremely wary of the
whole subject because of their public involvement with Langley's
failure, the assembled generals decided on a temporizing response.
Without committing themselves, yet not shutting the door, they left
it up to the Wrights to come back with some proof that they really
had been cavorting about the skies, unseen, within a short distance
of a large city; that they really had a practical machine.

The hurt reaction of the brothers to the army's reply was a
strange one. For Wilbur, especially, it seems entirely out of character. Such a rebuff, they must have realized, was not really a turndown but arose from a misunderstanding. Some additional correspondence, an exchange of visits, some frank discussion, a display of
photos, perhaps a questioning of the few persons who had witnessed flights, and some kind of decisive action must have followed.
Yet Wilbur made no effort at clarification and immediately went in
search of another buyer. The truth is that he was in no hurry to
make a sale to his own government and was perfectly satisfied with
the tepid reply. His one abiding concern was that the United States
Army might be so impressed by the military potential of the flying
machine that the government would be led to expropriate it whole,
to confiscate it, with all the formulations and scientific data on
which it was based, and to forbid sales to other governments. In
that event, Wilbur felt, he and his brother would have no guarantee
about a proper financial settlement, and would moreover lose the
rich rewards awaiting them in the European market. To avoid such
a devastating finale to his five years of effort, he wanted time to
make arrangements of some kind in Europe before tying himself
irrevocably to the United States.

Ideally, what Wilbur wanted was simultaneous contracts with
America and some European country, preferably England. This
would allow him to make simultaneous disclosure of the Flyer in
both hemispheres and thus, at one stroke, to capture the attention
and imagination of the whole world, opening up an unlimited market. It was, to put it mildly, no small-scale dream.

Wilbur saw nothing unpatriotic in all this, nothing disloyal. The
possibility that his flying machine might someday evolve into an
awesome, globe-girdling weapon of destruction was an idea incon-
ceivable in those days by anyone. Europe was far on the other side

of an immense ocean barrier; the Flyer in the hands of some Old World power could never be a threat to his own country. He was fully convinced, in any case, that within a very short time most of the countries of the world would possess flying machines.

A letter sent to the War Office in London brought, after about three weeks, a guarded expression of interest and a request for terms.* In no hurry, Wilbur did not respond until March 1, in the meantime settling with his brother the enjoyable question of how much to charge and on what basis. To hindsight, the offer on which the two finally decided seems surprisingly conservative and unnecessarily hedged about with conditions. Yet to the people of the time who had no means of knowing what the airplane was to become, it may have seemed high. The unusual thing about it was that the ultimate price depended on performance.

For one flying machine and lessons in piloting, the brothers asked $2,500 for each mile flown in the longest trial. From some later comments, it is clear that they were confident they could, in one continuous circling flight, easily cover anywhere from fifty to a hundred miles. They would therefore receive at least $125,000, perhaps as much as a quarter million. Beyond that, a flight of two, three, or even five hundred miles was not improbable, though at these distances there was more chance that something might go wrong. Distance depended mainly on fuel capacity and Wilbur had already computed that a flight of 500 miles would require a load of fuel equal to only about twenty percent of the machine's total weight. It was the stunning if uncertain possibility of earning a sum reaching toward a round million dollars that had prompted him to base payment on performance. And this was for only a single machine. It did not include purchase of any of the "secret formulas," as Wilbur now started calling the mass of experimental data. He was willing to make this immensely valuable material available to the British also, he said, price to be negotiated (the price he had in mind was an added $100,000).

It was the beginning of May before the British answer arrived:

---

* The Wrights' letter to England was sent on January 10, 1905, after the visit to Nevin but *a week before* dispatch of the letter requested by the congressman. Obviously, this was done in the hope of arousing simultaneous interest in the two countries.

they were still interested and would like to send a man to observe the machine in flight. Their military attaché in Washington, a Colonel Foster, would soon be in touch to make arrangements.

If it appeared to the brothers that the British reaction was much more enlightened than the American one, they would find that this, too, was an illusion. Wilbur had refrained in his initial letter from mentioning the one condition he considered paramount—the ban on demonstration flights until a contract had been signed.

14

A Sensation
of Perfect Peace

In late summer 1905 the brothers resumed flying at Huffman's pasture, not without some uneasiness. They too had begun to marvel at their success in maintaining secrecy and wondered how much longer it could go on. Probably they would not have renewed the risks of detection had they not felt there were still one or two improvements to be made on the Flyer, and at least one piloting problem to be resolved. They had really been a bit premature, they saw, in offering their machine for sale.

In addition, if they were going to keep to their policy of no-contract, no-flight, they would need to offer potential buyers some sort of interim proof that the machine really had been in the air. For this they had determined to invite as eyewitnesses some of the more solid citizens of Dayton, respected businessmen who could, when asked, swear to the truth of the Wrights' claims. Also, they would prepare a new set of photographs with the Flyer at greater heights and appearing in more dramatic attitudes.

The primary change that Wilbur wanted to make in the machine concerned the automatic link between wing warp and rudder. These had been hooked together initially to simplify the machine's operation, but experience gained in the flights of 1904 had shown that separate control of each would allow more flexible adjustment to the infinite variety of air pressures encountered in flight, giving the pilot more precise control. In Flyer No. 3, which the two had been busily building all spring, the wing warp would still be activated by the hip cradle, while the rudder control wires would run to a lever set at the pilot's right hand. The elevator would still be worked by the left hand. The brothers were now confident they could learn to master three, instead of two, control decisions.

To afford some degree of automatic correction for sideslip, two small semicircular vanes were set into the elevator, between its two surfaces, one on each side. These vanes, or "blinkers" as the brothers called them after the eye shields used on horses, were intended to hold the machine's front from slewing sideways, especially in turning. Various other improvements were also to be tried: larger and differently shaped surfaces in both elevator and rudder, as well as propellers of different sizes and shapes.

At the end of June they began flying. This time, in contrast to the six months' operation of the previous year, they expected that four or five weeks would be sufficient, provided the weather held good. By August the Flyer should again be safely stored away from prying eyes. But that hope proved to be far too optimistic, as the two found themselves once again facing frustration and near disaster.

The very first takeoff, with Orville aboard, ended badly when the machine failed to gain flying speed, and came down in a tilt to the left. The wing tip hit hard, cracking four ribs. The next day proved to be a bad one all around, beginning with a freak near-accident. The Flyer, resting on the track with the catapult weight raised and the engine running in a warm-up, almost took off by itself as the anchor stake slowly pulled from the ground. Orville, standing nearby, saw the machine start forward. He ran to the front and threw himself headlong onto the center of the lower wing, grasping for the elevator handle. With Orville riding backwards, the bucking Flyer ran all the way to the end of the track, where it slid off harmlessly onto the ground.

The day's bad luck continued as first Wilbur, then Orville, then Wilbur again failed to become airborne. On Orville's attempt, the Flyer tilted to the right while still on the track, the wing tip scrap-

ing along the ground as the machine shot forward. At the last moment he decided not to try for a takeoff. On Wilbur's second try the
Flyer rose into the air but at eight or nine feet it suddenly banked
to the left, smacking the wing tip hard against the rushing ground
and bringing the machine down roughly. The left tip was reduced
to a crumpled mass of splintered ribs and torn cloth.

A week later, with the machine repaired, the two were set to try
again. Suspicion as to the reason for the difficulties had settled on
the blinkers and these had been removed. Even so, the troubles
continued. In four attempts the longest distance covered was just
over 700 feet, all of the flights being aborted because of the pilot's
confusion at the controls. On the fourth try Wilbur, in working the
rudder lever, brushed the engine's shut-off valve, cutting the power.
In his confusion he neglected the elevator. The Flyer suddenly
nosed up, came almost to a dead stop at a height of ten feet, then
dropped rapidly to the ground. The impact broke two of the engine
legs loose from their mooring on the ribs, and smashed skids, spars,
and uprights. Wilbur climbed off unhurt but shaken and disgusted.

Repairs took only a few days but then the weather broke, the
rains coming in a flood that left Huffman's field awash. It was July
14 before the waters had drained off sufficiently to permit flying,
and immediately there was another accident, one that came within
a hair of causing serious injury to Orville.

He was in the air speeding along at about forty miles an hour in
what appeared to be the first good flight of the season. Preparing to
make a turn, his attention was on the warp mechanism and the
rudder lever when the Flyer began to undulate in its progress, then
nosed down strongly. Orville's hasty grab at the elevator handle
was too late. The machine hit the ground, elevator first, at a sharp
angle. The elevator framework collapsed backward and the skids
gave way, dropping the wings down to hard contact with the earth.
As they hit, still speeding forward, they bounced once, then twice,
spars and ribs cracking, cloth tearing as the machine sliced against
the numerous grassy hummocks. At last it came to an abrupt stop,
tilting over on its front edges. The momentum lifted Orville violently from his perch in the hip cradle, and flung him bodily against
the underside of the top wing. Crashing right through the loosened

cloth and the cracked ribs, he landed amid the remains of the elevator, crumpled in a heap. It was with no little amazement that Wilbur wrote in his day's diary entry that his brother had "suffered no injury at all."

Repairs and renewed rains delayed operations for more than a month. Finally, however, the brothers' determination began to reap its reward. On August 28 Wilbur flew the first circle of the season, handling the three controls with assurance. After that, the two went up regularly, two or three times a day, both of them circling the field in flights of up to five minutes, and gradually increasing their altitude until the Flyer was frequently at thirty or forty feet. There were a few rough landings and once Orville, in attempting a figure eight, was forced down hard, breaking the skids and one of the propellers, but there was nothing resembling a serious accident.

Competence at the controls came to both men at about the same time, their mastery growing with the feeling of confidence instilled by each successive flight. By the close of September Wilbur was ready for his first sustained effort. If all went well he would shortly begin inviting selected friends from Dayton to be witnesses.

Late in the afternoon of the twenty-sixth, with Bishop Wright watching from a seat near the shed, Wilbur took off toward the field's north boundary. He circled left at a thirty-foot altitude, came around toward the south side, flew past the front of the shed, and started again for the north fence. Round he went, again and again, the engine and propellers settling into a rattling drone. Five minutes went by, then seven, then eight. As he completed his tenth circle he had been up about eleven minutes and gave no sign of stopping.

Charlie Taylor, keeping track of the time, now called out to Orville and Bishop Wright that the Flyer had been up for fifteen minutes. As the machine droned on Taylor admitted he had lost count of the circles. It was fourteen or fifteen, he thought.

Not all the circles took the same course round the field. Some were more nearly squares, with the Flyer leveled out on the 200-yard straightaways and banking into a turn only at the corners. Others described actual circles, some small, some larger, with the

Flyer held in a continuous bank. Wilbur stayed up for another three minutes and when the engine began to sputter as the gas cylinder emptied he slid to an easy landing near the shed. He had flown eleven miles in just over eighteen minutes at an average speed of about thirty-five miles an hour.

In many of the shorter flights of September the two had deliberately held the Flyer in very tight circles, trying to duplicate the conditions that had, the previous year, occasionally sent the machine into something like a spin. Two or three times this inability to right the machine and stop turning had indeed reappeared, forcing the Flyer down. The brothers had agreed that the trouble must arise from the extra load exerted by centrifugal force. Since the engine did not have sufficient power to compensate for this increase, the Flyer slowed more and more, the inner wing soon losing flying speed. In this "stalled" condition the inside wing's warping mechanism was quickly deprived of its effectiveness.

Reasoning to this solution had not been difficult. The very feel of the machine under the body and hands of the pilot had told its own story. What did present a problem was finding the appropriate correction. While a more powerful engine would help in this particular machine, both men felt that an aerodynamic answer must also be found, a technique that could become part of a pilot's repertoire. Up to September 28 no hint of a solution had presented itself, by which time nearly forty flights had been made. On that day the answer came, largely by accident—or more precisely, in the effort to avert an accident.

Orville had taken the Flyer up to try and better his brother's long flight of two days before. The gas cylinder contained enough fuel for a flight of half an hour, and after nine minutes Orville appeared to be well on his way toward outdoing his brother. Eight times he had rounded the field, raising his altitude a little on each round until he was buzzing along near the tops of the tallest trees, about fifty feet. On the western segment of each circle, he had been hauling the Flyer round fairly sharply, using the solitary, forty-foot locust tree as a turning pylon. Now suddenly, as he was heading round the tree for the ninth time, the machine increased its degree

of bank—the left wing dropping, the right rising—and Orville found
that the inside wing would not answer the warp. The Flyer was
spiraling straight down into the thick spreading branches of the
tree, each limb bearing a multitude of long, sharp thorns. A forced
landing was his only way out, though this would mean violent contact and some breakage, perhaps even a crash. Yet even that was
preferable to a head-on encounter with a thorn tree. At the last moment Orville moved his left hand, jamming the elevator into full
negative.

With a jerk the Flyer dipped at the front, still in a tilt to the left.
Orville had acted a fraction too late and as the machine sped down
around the tree the left wing tip sliced against the end of a protruding branch, snapping it off and carrying it away embedded in
the cloth. But then, as the ground neared, Orville found that the
Flyer was leveling out—the lowered left wing had, seemingly on its
own, answered the warp. There was still enough room to avoid a
forced landing. Swinging the elevator to positive, he felt the Flyer
come up, just as the skids had begun to cut through the grass. Holding the machine steady as it sped east, about two feet from the
earth, he took a deep breath, thankful for his escape. Directly in
front of the shed he came to an easy stop.

The brothers appear to have simultaneously recognized the real
significance of the close call. The remedy for a stall was amazingly
simple: the Flyer need only be put into a brief dive. This restored
to the stalled wing the necessary speed, increasing its lift and
strengthening the effect of the warp. The technique had never
occurred to either of them before, partly because it seemed unnat-
ural, even against common sense, to further lower the nose when
the Flyer was already losing altitude. Also, they had seldom flown
at a height that would allow the time or room for such a maneuver.
Once having experienced the trick, it had all become instantly
clear.

Wilbur was now ready for the final stage of his season's plan, long
flights before carefully chosen witnesses. During the following
week a total of thirty people, friends and acquaintances of the
Wrights, all of them established, longtime residents of Dayton,
were invited to Huffman's field. Pledged to secrecy, they had agreed

that at the proper time they would provide a truthful description of what they had seen, barring only the details of the Flyer itself.

On most of these witnessed flights Orville was the pilot, Wilbur preferring to remain on the ground with the spectators to ensure that no interloper gained entrance with a camera. At a steady altitude of about sixty feet, Orville first flew twelve miles around the field in twenty-one minutes. The next day he covered ten miles in seventeen minutes, the next fifteen miles in twenty-six minutes. Finally he exceeded a half-hour in the air when on October 4 he covered fully twenty miles in thirty-three minutes. All were flawless flights, if exhausting for the pilot because of the prone position. It is no wonder that Orville complained later that as a result of the continual strain on head and shoulders he felt at times "as if my neck were broken."

In the course of Orville's last flight Wilbur had taken a dozen photographs, all of them showing the Flyer high in the air and each shot from a different angle. These pictures, along with the properly impressed witnesses, should have brought the season's operations to a close. There was some danger, in fact, of a general public disclosure of what was transpiring at Huffman's, since in the course of Orville's fifteen-minute flight two Interurban trolleys had passed, crowded with passengers, many of whom had exclaimed at the sight of the Flyer cruising above the treetops. Yet Wilbur, for all his detachment, was human, and instead of hurriedly packing the Flyer away, he decided to make one last flight himself. This he did on the afternoon of October 5, before fifteen witnesses.

Thirty times Wilbur went round the field, now at twenty feet, now climbing to sixty, sweeping through large circles, then banking sharply into tighter turns. At the end of a half hour he was still going strong, with fifteen pairs of hypnotized eyes riveted on his progress, fifteen pairs of ears attuned to the rattling hum of engine and propellers. Then the engine sputtered, signaling the emptying of the gas cylinder. The Flyer dropped smoothly to a landing near the crowd, sliding some distance on the grass before coming to a standstill. Wilbur had covered twenty-four miles in thirty-eight minutes and when he climbed down and stretched his cramped muscles he too felt as if his neck were fractured.

These long flights, in addition to documenting the Flyer's capability, also afforded the brothers the opportunity to reduce their piloting technique to the beginnings of a system. "Our most acute sensations are during the first minutes of flight," Wilbur explained later, "while we are soaring into the air and gaining the level at which we wish to sail. Then for the next five minutes our concentration is fixed on the levers to see that everything is working all right. But after that the management of the Flyer becomes almost automatic."

It was during this latter period, when the Flyer had settled into an easy cruise, that both brothers had first had the chance to feel the aesthetic side of flight, becoming deeply aware of the almost mystical new dimension they had added to human experience. "When you know, after the first few minutes, that the whole mechanism is working perfectly," said Wilbur, "the sensation is so keenly delightful as to be almost beyond description. . . . More than anything else the sensation is one of perfect peace, mingled with an excitement that strains every nerve to the utmost, if you can conceive of such a combination."

That observation stands as the first such description ever published about the miracle of powered flight. It can still be echoed today, with perfect fitness, by every neophyte pilot the world over.

The Flyer itself had now reached the final stage of perfection, its proportions, conformation, and workmanship imparting to it an uncluttered grace and cleanness of line that seemed in truth to make it a worthy relative of the bird. The elevator, its surfaces slightly enlarged, now stretched twelve feet in front of the wings, the added distance slowing down the machine's reactions. The rudder too had been increased in size and set further back. Span, chord, and camber all remained nearly the same as in the 1903 machine, but the total weight without operator had been increased to 710 pounds. Overall length of the machine, from the leading edge of the elevator to the trailing edge of the rudder, was twenty-eight feet. The height, from skids to upper wing, was just over nine feet. Throughout, many other small modifications had been made, such as giving the propeller tips a backward lean to eliminate a tendency to twist out of shape under pressure. The slight wing droop was gone. Now both bright surfaces ran rigid and straight from tip to tip.

Some idea of what it was like, at this time, to ride the Flyer was later provided by Orville in the brothers' first official description of powered flight, an interesting vignette, if all too brief. After the Flyer has lifted off the track, Orville wrote,

> the ground under you is at first a perfect blur, but as you rise the objects become clearer. At a height of one hundred feet you feel hardly any motion at all, except for the wind which strikes your face. If you did not take the precaution to fasten your hat before starting, you have probably lost it by this time.
>
> The operator moves a lever: the right wing rises, and the machine swings about to the left. You make a very short turn, yet you do not feel the sensation of being thrown from your seat, so often experienced in automobile and railway travel. You find yourself facing toward the point from which you started. The objects on the ground now seem to be moving at much higher speed, though you perceive no change in the pressure of the wind on your face. You know then that you are traveling with the wind.
>
> When you near the starting point, the operator stops the motor while still high in the air. The machine coasts down at an oblique angle to the ground, and after sliding fifty or a hundred feet comes to rest. Although the machine often lands when traveling at a speed of a mile a minute, you feel no shock whatever, and cannot, in fact, tell the exact moment at which it first touched the ground.
>
> The motor close beside you kept up an almost deafening roar during the whole flight, yet in your excitement you did not notice it until it stopped!

The evening of Wilbur's last flight the machine was taken apart and put away in a small shed behind the Hawthorn Street house. The brothers might have gone on flying in an effort to raise the record for time in the air over one hour, as Wilbur hoped to do, but the inevitable had happened. Some of the trolley riders who had goggled at the sight of the Flyer in the air had gone excitedly to the offices of the Dayton *Daily News*. Checking these reports, the paper had picked up rumors about all the people who had been the Wrights' favored guests. One of these, William Fouts, a Dayton druggist, could not contain himself when being questioned by a reporter. On October 5 the *Daily News* carried a brief story telling of "sensational flights" being made every day at Huffman's pasture. A Cincinnati paper reprinted the story the next day, bringing a small crowd out to Huffman's—where all was quiet again, the domain only of horses and cows.

15

The Troubles of Selling a Secret

All through the summer of 1905 the Wrights had been waiting to hear again from the British and to welcome their representative to Dayton. No one had shown up nor had there been any word of explanation about the delay. Wilbur, busy with the flights, made no further inquiry. "We are waiting for them to move," he calmly told Chanute as late as mid-September.

Meanwhile, he had decided to renew his contact with the United States War Department—cautiously. Not to be in touch with the officials of his own country, while talking with foreigners, created a confusing situation. Certainly the British must have wondered whether their own interest in the Wrights was known to the Americans, and whether that interest might be viewed as interference. On their part, the brothers were concerned over what the British reaction might be if it were to become known that their claims had failed to impress the American government. Better to be at least in touch with their own army, rather than admit that doors had been closed on them.

On October 9 a letter was sent to Secretary of War Taft, who turned it over to the army's Board of Ordnance and Fortification without comment. Once again the letter proved to be a strangely inept communication, very brief and even less informative than had been the first one eight months before. Nothing was said about the long flights just concluded, nor about flights of any kind. There was no attempt to explain how it was that the machine had been developed in secret, no real effort to be convincing. Instead, it abruptly offered to furnish a machine "on contract to be accepted only after trial trips in which the conditions of the contract have been fulfilled; the machine to carry an operator and supplies of fuel, etc., sufficient for a flight of one hundred miles." Minimum speed was to be thirty miles an hour. The price, as with the British, was to be determined by performance, though no base rate was specified. "We do not wish to take this invention abroad," the letter warned, "unless we find it necessary to do so." No mention was made of the British officer shortly expected in Dayton.

The army board's answer arrived ten days later. Predictably, since no proof of the flights had appeared in the meantime, it was no more enthusiastic than before, though it did carry a new note. The army, it explained, still was not interested in financing experiments. Then:

> Before the question of making a contract with you for the furnishing of a flying machine is considered it will be necessary for you to furnish this Board with the approximate cost of the completed machine, the date upon which it would be delivered, and with such drawings and descriptions thereof as are necessary to enable its construction to be understood and a definite conclusion as to its practicability to be arrived at.

This suggestion must have seemed more than reasonable to the board. These Wrights supposedly had a practical flying machine, though no one seemed to have seen it flying, and now not even the United States War Department would be allowed to see it until a contract had been signed. Very well, then, let the Wrights supply drawings, blueprints, and whatever other materials they had that would help in reaching some sort of understanding. This was not (as Orville later claimed) a ludicrous attempt to judge if a machine could fly by study of its plans. Quite legitimately, the board wanted to see if the machine, *provided it could fly,* could be adapted to military use. For all anyone knew, the Wright machine might be some weird agglomeration of fragile parts, unusable in rough circumstances, unable to stand up to continuous operation.

In contrast to their action eight months before, when they had simply dropped the whole matter, the brothers this time sent a second letter to the board. They were not asking for assistance: "We propose to sell the results of experiments finished at our own expense"—a confusing sentence, which could mean either "experiments we *have* finished," or "experiments we *will have* finished." Surprisingly, the Wrights insisted that they were the ones who needed more information, guidance as to the kind of machine the army wanted. "We cannot well fix a price nor a time for delivery," urged the letter, "till we have your ideas of the qualifications necessary to such a machine." Since no one in the army had the least idea what a flying machine *could* do, it was hard to say with any certainty what it *should* do.

Then, for the first time, Wilbur came to the point that was really troubling him: "We ought also to know whether you would wish to reserve a monopoly on the use of the invention, or whether you would permit us to accept orders for similar machines from other governments." The letter closed with a cryptic assurance to the board that "proof of our ability" to fulfill the contract was available. This meant, of course, both the photographs and signed affidavits from the eyewitnesses. Yet neither item was referred to in the letter.

It is not surprising that the board gave this reply scant attention, regarded it in fact with some impatience. Already the board had given the Wrights more attention than it had to any other of the numerous flying machine applicants. "The Board does not care to formulate any requirements for the performance of a flying machine," ran the answer, "or to take any further action on the subject until a machine is produced which by actual operation is shown to be able to produce horizontal flight and to carry an operator." And with that the Wrights once again lapsed into silence, supposedly resentful of the cavalier treatment.

The truth, of course, is that the army board in 1905 was ready to be convinced, had invited the Wrights to make an effort in that direction—something besides airy talk of contracts—and it was the brothers themselves who had chosen to call a halt. They would not, in any case, have released blueprints or drawings to the army, even if they possessed such formal professional trappings, which they did not.* Still, they need not have broken off after such a brief exchange and it is all too evident that they were once more content to leave a deal with the army in abeyance. Nothing demonstrates this better than the fact that, a few weeks afterward, they declined an offer from Chanute to bring the whole matter directly to the attention of President Roosevelt. This, Chanute could have easily done through his numerous contacts in the scientific circles of Washington, but Wilbur gave the offer not a moment's thought. "We do not think there would be any advantage in bringing the matter to the attention of the President or Secretary of War," he demurred flatly, adding with lopsided logic, "unless they were previously *fully convinced* of the practicality of the machine." Subsequently Chanute renewed his offer only to have it again refused. Two more years were to pass before Wilbur and the army board were finally to come face to face in the same room.

Directly on the heels of this unfruitful exchange with the United States, the British negotiations also failed, and for much the same reason. A series of letters between the Wrights and Colonel Foster in Washington brought out the fact that Foster was not authorized to discuss contracts but only to observe a flight. This, the Wrights returned, they were not yet ready to provide. If Foster came to Dayton, however, they would introduce him to a number of persons who had witnessed flights. Somewhat wearily, Foster replied that the War Office files were full of supposed eyewitness descriptions of flying machines. Finally in December the brothers were informed that the British were no longer in the market.

Disappointed, yet feeling no doubt about the ultimate correctness of his course, Wilbur next turned to the French, pursuing a contact initiated some time before by Captain Ferdinand Ferber of the French Army.

An avid experimenter with both gliders and tethered power ma-

---

* The army, accustomed to the elaborate plans that Langley had supplied to his builders, would have been further puzzled to hear that the Wrights had never felt the need to reduce their designs to blueprints, and had moreover built everything themselves.

chines, Ferber was a longtime acquaintance of Chanute, and thus readier to accept the truth of the Wrights' claims. As early as 1903 Ferber had inquired about the possibility of purchasing a glider from them and later had asked if a power machine was for sale, probably, as Wilbur thought, on behalf of the French War Ministry.

Results this time were quicker. After an exchange of letters, Ferber informed the Wrights that a representative of his, a civilian named Arnold Fordyce, would be arriving in Dayton in December with full powers to offer a contract. While Fordyce's affiliation was not specified, the brothers took it for granted that his ultimate authority derived from the military. It did, though with typical French convolution. Money for purchase of the Flyer was to be provided by a syndicate of wealthy businessmen, mainly from newspaper circles. Anxious to bring aviation to France, they were equally anxious to garner for themselves some prestigious decorations for service to their country.

Fordyce arrived in Dayton three days after Christmas 1905. In heady contrast to the hesitation of the British and Americans, after only a few days of talking and interviewing witnesses, a contract was prepared and signed.

For some reason the brothers' ideas on financial terms had undergone a change. They were no longer willing to let the price depend on the Flyer's performance. Instead they now specified a fixed sum—to include one machine, flying lessons, and all the secret data —a tidy one million francs, or $200,000. Again, while the sum may now seem comparatively small, it was a very large one for the time. In addition, Wilbur had in mind the galvanizing effect a sale to France would have on other countries. As soon as it became known that France was building an air arm, he was sure, then at least five other countries—England, Germany, Italy, Russia, and the United States—would all descend on Dayton in a rush, waving checks in similar amounts for a similar arrangement. If all went well, before the year 1906 was out the brothers would possess a fortune exceeding one million dollars, with a great deal more to come from their own commercial exploitation of the patents.

The French contract called for a number of demonstration flights, at least one of which had to cover a distance of thirty miles in a time of no more than one hour. In other flights the Flyer must be able to maintain a certain height and speed. The trials were to take place in secret, in Europe or America as the Wrights desired. As a binder, the French were to place in escrow in a New York bank the initial sum of $5,000 by February 5, 1906, with the rest of the million francs due in escrow two months later. The time between the contract date and April 5 was to constitute an option period, during which the Wrights were prohibited from dealing with any other party. If for any reason the French failed to make the second deposit, then the $5,000 would revert to the Wrights.

An important provision, one the Wrights granted with reluctance, gave the French exclusive use of the invention and all its secrets for a period of three months after acceptance, the United States alone excepted.

The binder money was duly deposited and once more it appeared that the airplane was about to be born into the world—and once again the bubble burst. No sooner had the contract been studied by the French military chiefs in Paris than they began to ask for changes, such things as a greater minimum speed, increased carrying capacity, a longer period of exclusive use, and a greater minimum altitude—no less than a thousand feet, a height the brothers had not yet thought of attempting.

To discuss these new arrangements a commission of French officers was dispatched to Dayton. They arrived, incognito, in late March, put up at an unpretentious hotel, and for two weeks filled the Wright parlor with firm if polite argument. Their basic concern really touched only two things: the thousand-foot altitude (anything less, they explained, would make the Flyer an easy target for ground fire) and an extension of the exclusive period to no less than one year. Both of these demands the Wrights refused. They had already agreed to conditions that left little margin for failure, and a failure for any reason, in any one of numerous conditions, would invalidate the contract. If that should happen the brothers would have revealed their machine to no purpose.

As the deadline of April 5 neared, Wilbur in desperation called on Octave Chanute to lend to the negotiations his urbane presence and his familiarity with the French mind. Chanute gladly responded, reaching Dayton on April 2 and immediately closeting himself with the brothers and their guests. It was all in vain. April 5 passed without deposit of the remaining monies. The contract was dead and the fact that the original $5,000 now belonged to the brothers was bare comfort.*

The French failure to close with the Wrights seems on its surface a sad mistake. Certainly, the price asked, considering the unique merchandise being offered, was not excessive, and the brothers had shown a willingness to be bound by some rather stringent conditions. In reality, neither the price nor the conditions account for the French reluctance, nor were they ever in serious doubt about the Wrights' ability to fulfill the bargain. Actually the French were hoping, and had good reason to believe, that human flight might at no distant time be achieved in their own country.

By the spring of 1906 there had been underway in France for a full three years, a feverish experimenting, first with gliders and then with various kinds of tethered motors. It had been a new awakening for the French, an aeronautical boom. It was sparked not by any original insights of the French, but by news of the brothers' Kitty Hawk success, coupled with information made available by Octave Chanute.

In April 1903 Chanute had visited France, had talked and lectured widely of the Wrights' glider work, and had written for the magazine L'Aerophile a lengthy article in which the Wright 1902 glider was both described and pictured in schematic drawings. A number of other magazines picked up detailed reports of his lectures, making available both the secret of wing warping and the true use of the rudder. Using this information and carefully sifting all that the brothers themselves had said and written, at least a dozen Frenchmen, some in rivalry, some working together, had built "Wright-type" gliders. Most did not adhere closely to the designs, however, or simply did not understand them, and this, coupled with haste, inadequate workmanship, and disregard of the need for practice, had greatly retarded French progress. Still, by early 1906 there had arisen a general air of optimism. In three

* When this sum was actually collected, a few months later, it more than repaid the brothers for all they had expended on their experiments since 1899, including construction of the various Flyers and even travel expenses.

months or six months, it was felt, surely within the year, powered flight would be attained in France. While nothing startling had yet occurred to support that belief it was pervasive.

Wilbur was aware through Chanute of all this sustained activity, knew that it was largely based on the principles discovered by him, yet he felt no great disquiet, no real apprehension that the French would achieve flight anytime soon. What did now begin to concern him was his realization that total secrecy could be a severe handicap in selling the Flyer. Some sort of solid news must be allowed to reach the public, he saw, just enough to create an atmosphere in which his claims to buyers would not seem entirely outlandish. "After thinking the matter over," he had written Chanute as early as November 1905, "we have decided that it will be best to absolve our friends from their obligation to keep secret the results of the season's experiments. . . . The strict repression of authentic news may be harmful with widespread rumors in circulation."

After the failure of the British negotiations he went further, writing a detailed account of the 1905 flights to the newly formed Aero Club of America, supplying also the names of seventeen eyewitnesses. The list was at once turned over to the *Scientific American,* the leading publication in its field, which promptly conducted an investigation by mail. In its issue of April 7, 1906 (just too late to impress the French), the magazine devoted a full page to the results, supporting the truth of the Wrights' claims. All of this, while it stirred many people, left others in even worse perplexity than before as they tried to imagine how such phenomenal things could possibly have been done in hiding.

The publicity generated by these disclosures caused a brief renewal of contact with the United States Army, which the Wrights promptly squelched. It came about through Godfrey Cabot and his kinsman, United States Senator Henry Cabot Lodge of Massachusetts. Urged by Lodge to send a man to Dayton to observe a flight, the army board informed the Wrights by mail that they were ready to do so. Wilbur responded with his usual offer to supply "convincing proof." Nothing was said about making flights. The board again lost interest.

Chanute, more anxious than Wilbur over the growing threat of competition from abroad, pressed the point on the brothers, sug-

gesting at the same time that their price was too high. This brought
from Wilbur a reply that demonstrates not only his unruffled confidence but the calculating side of his nature, noted by more than
one acquaintance:

> Our friends do not seem to exactly understand our position in the
> matter of supposed delay. We are not delaying an instant more than
> we consider necessary. We merely refuse to let our hand be forced.
> . . . If it were indeed true that others will be flying within a year
> or two, there would be reason in selling at any price but we are con-
> vinced that no one will be able to develop a practical flyer within
> five years. This opinion is based upon cold calculation. It takes into
> consideration practical and scientific difficulties whose existence is
> unknown to all but ourselves. Even you, Mr. Chanute, have little
> idea how difficult the flying problem really is. When we see men
> laboring year after year on points we overcame in a few weeks,
> without ever getting far enough along to meet the worse points be-
> yond, we know that their rivalry and competition are not to be
> feared . . .

Chanute, stung by that off-hand reference to his own lack of
comprehension, replied a little more frankly than was his custom.
Humbly agreeing that the flying problem was beyond him, he
asked somewhat testily, "Are you not too cocksure that yours is
the only secret worth knowing and that others may not hit upon a
solution in less than . . . five years? It took you much less than
that and there are a few (very few) other able inventors in the
world." This drew from Wilbur some measured observations in support of his position which also, to anyone knowing his personal
story, ring with hidden implications. He was not so foolish as to
claim that his success was the result of superior talent, he insists.
Men like Maxim, Lilienthal, Langley, and Chanute himself were as
fully endowed with inventive genius, and certainly there would be
others to follow of equal ability:

> To me, it seems that a thousand other factors, each rather insignifi-
> cant in itself, in the aggregate influence the event ten times more
> than mere mental ability or inventiveness. . . . If the wheels of
> time could be turned back six years, it is not at all probable that we
> would do again what we have done. The one thing that impresses
> me as remarkable is the shortness of time within which our work

was done. It was due to peculiar combinations of circumstances which might never occur again. How do you explain the lapse of more than 50 years between Newcomen and Watt? Was the world wanting in smart men during those years? Surely not! The world was full of Watts but a thousand and one trifles kept them from undertaking and completing the task. . . . We look upon the present question in an entirely impersonal way. It is not chiefly a question of relative ability but of mathematical probability. . . . Is it not wise to let the results of the season's experiments in Europe and elsewhere demonstrate that a really practical flyer is not the work of months but of years?

Of course, the chief of those "peculiar circumstances" of which he speaks was that seeming tragedy of his youth, which had wrenched him from the paths of normal life. He had at last begun to appreciate, in some wonderment, how it had preserved him from the thousand and one cares that usually beset and hamper and finally kill the desire to follow untrodden ways. He saw now how his lost decade had really been a time of preparation, endowing him with both singlemindedness and an untrammeled spirit.

Wilbur's insistence in the exchange with Chanute, it should be noted, was on the development of a fully practical machine, not a mere lifting into the air in short, straight-line hops. No one knew so well as he the bumpy road to be traversed between the two stages, and as usual the outcome would prove him largely right. In his patient reasoning, however, there existed a subtle flaw, one serious enough to wipe out his advantage and force him into action.

While *he* was aware of the hardships to be surmounted between a first flight and a practical machine, the rest of the world was not.

16

Competition

Near the end of October 1906 sensational news flashed out of France. The air had at last been "conquered," human flight had been achieved, this time beyond a doubt. A wealthy young Brazilian residing in Paris, Alberto Santos-Dumont, already famous for his exploits with dirigibles, in a strange-looking machine with wings made up of box-kite cells, had managed a flight of almost 200 feet. He had performed in public before a large crowd. His brief liftoff and sudden landing had been accompanied by roars of amazement and shouts of joy, even tears. The exhilarating news sped round the world, changing much of the old attitude toward human flight from one of derision to at least guarded belief.

In Dayton, the Wrights remained unmoved. Reading the accounts, they saw that there had taken place only a longer hop than usual, and on a windless day. The shortness of the flight and the construction of the machine—all the papers had carried pictures of it—were sufficient to assure them that serious competition had not arisen.

Then a month later, after making some changes in the machine and mounting a more powerful motor, Santos-Dumont tried again. With men shouting, women screaming, crying, and even fainting, he soared a distance of over 700 feet, awkwardly and very near the ground, yet there could be no doubt that his twenty-one seconds in the air had been a true if tentative flight. This time the Wrights listened. That glorious period during which only they among all mankind possessed the secret of flight had come to an end. Their unique monopoly had been broken.

The possibility that Santos-Dumont might quickly produce a practical flyer did not disturb them. His machine was an aerodynamic freak, they judged, incapable of further development. True, it could become airborne, but only briefly, on windless days and in a straight line. Its lack of proper controls and its weird configuration deprived it of stability and would obviously prevent turns or circles or maneuvers of any kind. What did concern the brothers was the notion, spreading fast even among knowledgeable people, that what the Brazilian had done others could improve on, that practical human flight was just around the corner. Such rampant faith, unjustified though it was, the Wrights now realized was enough to alter their situation radically. "The real disturbing element is the general *belief* that they will accomplish wonders shortly," wrote Wilbur. "As a hindrance to business this is almost as bad as reality." He and his brother could no longer wait for the world to come to them.

The Brazilian's feat, in the meantime, had once more focused the spotlight on Dayton. Loudly and persistently, the flamboyant Santos-Dumont began proclaiming that he was the first man to fly, a claim that was supported by a large portion of the European press. What of the Wrights? he was asked. They were nothing, Santos-Dumont replied brusquely, no one in France believed that they had done anything. This attitude, naturally, prompted a reaction in the American press. Hoping that the Wrights thus challenged would at last open up, editors rushed reporters to Dayton, but all came away more or less disappointed. The brothers would do no more than consent to interviews in which they only repeated what they had said before: Long flights had been made, the Flyer was practical, they were only waiting for the right deal.

One reporter, Sherman Morse of the New York *Herald,* was under orders not to return until he had something definite. Welcomed to the Wright parlor, he pressed the brothers to give their reasons for such inhuman reticence. "We will make no exhibition test of our flying machine," frankly replied Wilbur, "nor will we permit an examination of it . . . our only market must be a powerful government and publicity would only defeat our purpose to make such a sale." When Morse found that he would get nowhere asking for pictures or a description of the Flyer, he countered with a suggestion of his own. Would the Wrights agree to fly, in secret, before a select committee "made up of men with no practical knowledge of mechanics"? They would not. Well, then, would they agree to fly, in secret, before a single witness, respected in some other field but with no knowledge of mechanics, stationed at a distance and forbidden to use a camera? They would not.

Appeals by Morse on the basis of patriotism, the upholding of the country's honor, equally failed to make an impression, as did the suggestion that the brothers were letting slip the great personal glory that could be theirs. Wilbur's reply to that sally was unusually harsh, revealing his annoyance at the hint of disloyalty: "We shall receive our reward in something more necessary to us than glory or the plaudits of the world." Unlike many of the other reporters, Morse acted on Wilbur's invitation to talk to some of the people who had witnessed the 1905 flights. Trudging around Dayton, he called at offices, homes, stores, finding and interviewing about twenty of the men who had been present at Huffman's pasture. All eagerly corroborated the Wrights, some in their excitement forgetting their promise and describing the Flyer, though with the usual eyewitness distortions (a wingspan of thirty feet instead of forty; propellers three or four feet instead of eight; a rudder "at the front" which was used for turning). Morse's story, published in the *Herald* late in November, was widely quoted and reprinted in both this country and Europe.

Another writer a few months later was more resourceful if not quite as honest. *McClure's* magazine sent G. K. Turner to obtain a first-person story from the brothers, but a day spent prodding them earned little new information. Wilbur bid good-by to Turner satisfied that "he would write nothing." It took Turner some time to put together his offering, then in the magazine's February 1908 issue the brothers were amazed to find themselves explaining at great length all about the Flyer, their work, and their future plans. Turner had mined everything written by or about the Wrights and had dexterously woven the results into a first-person presentation, as if the brothers had answered all his questions exhaustively. Wilbur was incensed at this journalistic hocus-pocus, calling it "a gross fraud."

Despite their answers to Morse, the Wrights must have considered whether the altered situation called for a change in policy, whether indeed they ought to provide some sort of convincing demonstration. Their habit of caution was still too strong, however, and they decided to continue seeking a contract first. At the same time, they did concede that matters in Europe must somehow be speeded up, a way found to break through the wall of suspicion and disbelief that their own secrecy had erected. What they needed was some means of gaining direct entrance to the inner councils of European governments and for this it seemed they would need professional help. Before the year 1906 ended they were in touch with the Flint Company, a New York-based firm of international financiers and promoters.

Charles R. Flint, a wealthy, free-wheeling industrialist, had already earned the title Father of Trusts, and was perhaps the leading international private arms middleman. Once, on behalf of an emerging South American country Flint had bought, equipped, and manned a small fleet, serving up a ready-made navy. At other times he had bought warships for Russia, helped build the United States Navy in the Spanish-American War, had introduced Simon Lake's submarine to Europe, and had been deeply involved in the early merchandising of the automobile. His success was built on discretion, imagination, and personal acquaintance—his or his associates' —with most of the leaders of Europe's governments, as well as active association with the Rothschilds and J. P. Morgan. Among United States senators and congressmen his contacts were wide and he enjoyed some degree of personal friendship with Theodore Roosevelt. He was also acquainted with Octave Chanute. For the Wrights' purpose, it appeared, the Flint company was ideal.

At a series of meetings in New York the Wrights made it clear that they wanted help only in Europe, American negotiations were to be left to them. The Flint representative agreed and surprised the brothers by suggesting that his company might itself want to purchase all the European rights to the Flyer. The sum of a half million dollars, outright, was mentioned. Attracted, the Wrights weighed this quick wealth, and its avoidance of business entanglements, against the probability of the many millions that were to be made in Europe. Then, for reasons unspecified, the Flint company withdrew the offer. Final arrangements named the Flint company as the brothers' European agents at a commission of twenty percent, the Wrights to draw on Flint for their expenses, up to $10,000. By January 1907 Flint's men were at work preparing the ground at high levels.

Flint soon persuaded Wilbur to make two basic changes in his policy. Instead of selling the Flyer in single units and giving an option to obtain the formulas, the machine was to be sold in quantity, allowing a purchasing country to obtain a complete air arm at one stroke. Various offers were to be tried: ten machines of fifty-mile range for a half million dollars; twenty machines of 200-mile range for a million dollars; fifty machines of 200-mile range at two and a half million. Flint himself began negotiations with England, writing in code to a friend in London, who passed the messages on to Lord Haldane. In France, the Flint representative, Hart Berg, opened communication with the same group of men who had, the year before, failed to sustain the contract. The main effort, at first, was to be made in France.

The second change concerned the production of a sensation, a dramatic, semipublic flight that would stun the world and, Flint hoped, blow the seals off government coffers in country after country. The perfect opportunity for such a display was conveniently at hand. In April 1907 there would be celebrated the 300th anniversary of the founding of Jamestown, Virginia. As part of the festivities there was to be a grand naval review with dozens of ships, lead by the mighty dreadnaughts, steaming slowly through Hampton Roads. President Roosevelt and all the top officers of the army and navy would be on hand to take the salute. If the Flyer could suddenly appear in the skies at Hampton Roads, circle over the line of battleships, then fly off again, the effect on the spectators would, to say the least, be devastating. Flint did not have to spell out for the brothers the disturbing vision that would arise in the minds of the naval men present: bombs falling on the unprotected decks of their invincible armada.

Caution was to be observed, however. Final plans called for a takeoff from Kitty Hawk, a flight north over Currituck Sound, then overland to Hampton Roads, about sixty miles away. Most of the trip would be at very low altitudes, perhaps no more than fifty feet, and Wilbur feared that this might give opportunity for someone to take pictures. To make analysis of any such accidental photography doubly difficult, he decided to paint the whole machine a uniform silver. This would blend the parts, perhaps produce a blurring glare in the pictures. Secondly, he would take no risk of a forced landing in the water. Pontoons were to be fitted to the Flyer and both take-off and landing would be made from the surface of Albemarle Sound.

It is disappointing to record that this flight never took place. It would surely have been the single most spectacular day in world science, certainly would today be looked on as the moment in which the modern era began. It would have atoned for the brothers' long secrecy and been the end of all their difficulties. But it was not to be, and for a reason the brothers should have foreseen. The designing of pontoons for a water takeoff seemed at first a simple matter. That it was by no means so simple the two found after only a week or two of experimenting and by the end of March, a month before the Jamestown celebration, they were forced to reconsider their plans. They would perhaps have made the attempt without pontoons, operating from the land, but time was to run out on them. Down the waters of Hampton Roads, on April 26, 1907, steamed the battlewagons of the United States Navy, their commanders unaware of just how memorable that day might have been.

Affairs in France, meanwhile, had reached a promising stage. In May, Flint judged that the brothers might go abroad, where they could assist with the negotiations and be ready to make demonstration flights as soon as contracts were signed. As it happened, at this same time the United States War Department had once again been stirred to interest in the Wrights, this time by Congressman Herbert Parsons of New York.

The flights of Santos-Dumont as well as the experiments that were now taking place in many countries had quickened official interest in the flying machine. To President Roosevelt, Parsons sent some of the magazine and newspaper reports of the Wrights' 1905 flights, suggesting they be investigated. Roosevelt forwarded this material to the War Department with an endorsement. Taft endorsed it over to the army Board of Ordnance and Fortification. In a letter sent to the Wrights in May, the board explained that it had several propositions before it from other flying machine inventors: "If you desire to take any action in the matter, we will be glad to hear from you."

This was a little awkward, a bit premature, for the Wrights. They still hoped to make simultaneous demonstrations in Europe and America and while Flint was optimistic about the French business, they could not be sure that the two strands could be pulled together at the same time. Yet, since a French contract might well materialize in short order, they could not let slip this contact with the board. It was a tricky situation, impossible to handle with nice regularity. After an exchange of correspondence—in which the brothers said they were willing to talk, with the board requesting terms and conditions—a price was named: $100,000 for one Flyer and lessons, trials to be held after granting of a contract. The board inquired if they would be given a period of exclusive use, and if they could at least inspect the Flyer on the ground before signing a contract. Neither of these things was possible, answered the Wrights. The board retired to mull over the price, the conditions, and the sheer, unprecedented perplexity of it all.

Meantime, the brothers departed for France, Wilbur first, then Orville two months later with the disassembled and crated Flyer.

If it is possible to argue with the restrictive methods used by the Wrights in their efforts to market the Flyer in 1905–6, then fuel is piled on that argument by the six incredible months they wasted in Europe in the latter half of 1907, first in France, then England and Germany.

The magic of Flint's name and organization proved of little avail as the two endured endless meetings, wading through a morass of bureaucratic maneuvering, suspicion, unexpected demands, jealousy, and even corruption. The dreary spectacle of the two brothers, sole possessors of a practical embodiment of man's oldest dream, cooling their heels in hotel rooms, patiently answering the imperious calls of petty officials, writing and rewriting lengthy contracts, calmly accepting the abuse of an unfriendly press ("bluffers" was the word most frequently used), patiently defending their asking price—all this is enough to make anyone wish passionately that they had been able to throw caution to the winds and make just one electrifying public flight. Wilbur at one point confessed that he might have to do just that. "We doubt whether an agreement will be reached," he wrote Katharine, "before we have really made some demonstrations somewhere and stirred up some excitement."

Most of the time was spent in Paris, where the possibility of selling to the government alternated with the desirability of first setting up a commercial organization. The price to the government was the same $200,000, for a single Flyer, that had been specified in the Fordyce contract the year before—it had fast become apparent that Flint's wholesale approach would not work. Arrangements for commercial use would have netted about the same amount, along with a controlling interest in whatever company was set up.

During five months of negotiations no conclusion was reached along either line, as first the army hesitated and then the commercial interests fell to bickering. Once it seemed that a sale to the French Army was imminent. It collapsed when a demand was issued that the Flyer conduct its trials in winds impossibly strong, as high as those that could be tolerated by a captive balloon, and that there be included an exclusive period of no less than three years. Another time, when the military was again on the brink of a contract, a bald demand for a bribe was made. A high official suggested that all would go smoother if $50,000 were added to the price and the extra monies delivered to him. Calm despite his anger, Wilbur after thinking for a moment agreed—he would only require that the name of the man to receive the payment be entered in the contract and his services specified.

Twice Wilbur gave ultimatums to his intermediaries. If some progress was not forthcoming, he warned, he would pack up and go home ("rather warm heart-to-heart talk with Berg," he noted in his diary). Always the Flint men or others were able to convince him that a breakthrough was only days away. Finally, in November, he did call a halt, sailing for home and leaving the business in the hands of the Flint company. Orville stayed a few weeks longer in order to arrange for the building of two or three extra motors at the Paris firm of Barriquand and Marre. The Flyer, still securely stored away in a warehouse in Le Havre, was left behind to be available for a return on short notice.

Two events during the interminably frustrating months in France gave Wilbur some saving sense of accomplishment. The first was a balloon trip in which he soared over the French countryside for more than three hours, rising to a height of 3,000 feet. Looking down on the drifting clouds he was able to gain some idea of the wind conditions at higher altitudes—someday, he knew, his own machine would inhabit these regions of the sky and he was glad of a chance to inspect them at a leisurely pace.

The second event was more important, at least to the Wrights' peace of mind. Experimentation with flying machines had been accelerating in France all during the time of the brothers' visit and out of the crowd of dedicated aeronauts two or three names had emerged to join that of Santos-Dumont: as designer and builder, Gabriel Voisin, and as pilots, Henry Farman and Léon Delagrange. While no one had yet equaled the Santos-Dumont flight of the previous year, they were coming close. Then, on November 5, a week before Wilbur's planned departure for home, Delagrange flew 1,500 feet, creating a sensation. When it was announced that Farman would fly in public on November 9, near Paris, Wilbur arranged to be on hand.

In the eyes of the large crowd that witnessed them, Farman's flights were a huge success. In his best effort he covered more than a half mile in just over one minute. "It was the most wonderful flight ever made in such a contrivance," trumpeted a French paper. To the self-contained, derby-hatted young American standing silently in the crowd, however, the sight of Farman's ungainly machine lumbering straight ahead through the windless air, six or seven feet off the ground, revealed something far different.

While French progress in aviation might amaze the uninformed, the French machines in reality were not even in the same class as the original Kitty Hawk Flyer. The construction of Farman's plane, its mere workmanship, was surprisingly amateurish when compared with what the brothers, unaided, had done. Its makeshift propel-

ler, looking something like a canoe paddle, was woefully inefficient. Its aerodynamic design was a polyglot of ideas, some good,
some defective. For lateral balance it possessed only a dihedral angle in the wings, the old flat V shape. Turns—when Farman got
around to trying them—were to be effected by movement of a big
box-kite rudder at the rear, without putting the machine into a
bank, the same idea that Henson had contemplated sixty years before. The Wrights left France more convinced than ever that they
had nothing to fear in the way of actual competition. Wilbur's five-
year estimate in fact began to seem conservative.

In contrast to their months of fruitless work in Europe, the brothers found on returning home that the United States Army was now
willing, even eager, to reach an understanding. The flights of Santos-Dumont, Farman, Delagrange, and others in Europe had received enormous publicity and, short as they were, had established
human flight as a reality, its future practical use not to be seriously
doubted. In this receptive atmosphere a contingency contract with
the Wrights, considering all that had been said and written about
them, no longer seemed unreasonable. In two December meetings
in Washington, Wilbur and the army board reached an agreement
on terms, and on a time for the official trials—September of 1908.*

The intervening months were to be used in improving the engine
(it was now up to thirty-five horsepower) and in preparing the
Flyer, especially in converting it to use by two men, sitting upright. This meant that a new arrangement for the control levers had
to be devised and installed. Seats for pilot and passenger, on the
front edge of the lower wing, at its middle, had also to be incorporated. Never relaxing the care they had used every step of the way,
the brothers then wanted time to test the results in the air and to
familiarize themselves with the carrying of a passenger. This they
planned to do in a brief secret session of a week or two at Kitty
Hawk in the spring.

The price to the United States, for one Flyer and lessons, had
been radically reduced. At least so far as public expectations were
concerned, the Wrights were now in a competitive market, and in
addition they themselves were anxious to consummate a sale to the

* Much governmental red tape, unrelated to the main narrative, had to be unwound
in reaching the agreement. For some details see the Notes.

United States. Further orders would quickly follow a first sale, they
knew, and the total of such government business could far exceed
the sum they had originally named for a single Flyer. If the machine passed the tests in September they would receive a payment
of $25,000 in cash, provided the Flyer maintained a speed aver-
aging forty miles an hour. Some incentive was added by another
clause which stated that for each mile they attained above the
average they would receive an extra $2,500 (but that was balanced
—even here the watchdog of the public purse was at work—by another clause which said that for each mile below the average,
$2,500 would be deducted). If the average speed fell below thirty-
six miles an hour the government was not obligated to honor the
contract.

While this provision may now seem ridiculous—imagine refusing
to make use of the world's first practical airplane simply because it
flew no faster than thirty-five miles an hour—in the atmosphere of
the time it made perfectly good sense. The army board had no way
of anticipating whether the Wright Flyer would in fact prove superior to the machines being flown in France. Farman had already
touched fifty miles an hour, and in January 1908 he had at last negotiated a complete circle, staying up for nearly two minutes and
winning a $10,000 prize. (Newspaper accounts of Farman's circle
were glowing, but they told the Wrights that the Frenchman was
still far from having a practical machine. The turning had been accomplished by a nervous series of sliding quarter-turns in which
the angled rudder kicked the machine's tail sideways, the machine
itself skidding and jumping flatly.)

Early in February 1908 the Wrights' contract with the United
States was signed. Then, some three weeks later, Flint at last managed to make some sense of the French negotiations, putting together a syndicate for commercial manufacture and sale of the
Flyer. The contract with this syndicate, signed in March, called for
a cash payment to the brothers of $100,000 after trials, along with
a royalty on each machine and a third of the stock, as well as an additional $16,000 for four demonstration machines. The trials were
to be held in France in early fall.

Somehow it had all come out just as Wilbur wanted. He would
unveil his invention, simultaneously, on two continents.

The brief practice session at Kitty Hawk proved to be anything but secret as a number of newsmen managed to spy on the operations.

A young reporter for the Norfolk *Landmark*, D. Bruce Salley, was the first to spot their presence on the Outer Banks, late in April 1908, having heard about it from his contacts among the Kitty Hawk lifesaving crew. Approaching warily, every day for a week he reconnoitered the Wright camp from the safety of a straggly patch of scrub pine along the inland side of the Banks, patiently gazing for hours through a telescope at the brothers' preparations. Each evening he would return south along the shore and cross in a small boat to the village of Manteo on Roanoke Island, where he would spend the night. On the afternoon of May 6 this diligence was rewarded.

Through his telescope Salley saw the big doors of the nearest shed thrown open and the long white wings of the Flyer slowly emerge. At some distance west of the shed, in full sight of the young newsman, the machine was lifted onto the track. Moments later Salley's shaking hands were trying to hold the glass steady on the rising Flyer.

Salley was also associated with several New York papers, including the *Times* and *Herald*. On the morning of May 7 the *Times* carried a page-one headline: "The Wrights Fly 1,000 Feet." Two days later another page-one *Times* headline announced "Aeroplane's Ten Flights." One of these had covered nearly two miles, the story read, the machine circling between and around some small dunes and landing some distance south of the big hill.

With that, a small mob of reporters from eastern papers converged on the Banks. They were not there, as was later mistakenly said, to obtain proof that man could fly. That had already been well established in Europe, and Léon Delagrange in France now held the record, six minutes for a flight of more than two miles. Even in America a rival to the Wrights had arisen. A group organized by Alexander Graham Bell, called the Aerial Experiment Association—it included famed Glenn Curtiss, motorcycle racer and builder of engines—had already built a machine that had managed to get off the ground. It had flown only a hundred feet and lacked adequate controls, but it was only a matter of time until the AEC should hit upon the right combination of elements available to it from the work of both the Wrights and the Europeans.

The reporters who now cautiously infiltrated the Kitty Hawk environs were there to satisfy the public's curiosity about the brothers, and if possible to determine, once and for all, whether America was in fact the leader in world aviation. (A subhead to one subsequent story gave the facts as witnessed "by an Uninvited and Impartial Jury Representing the World at Large.")

These newsmen knew better than to rush down upon the Wrights, though one or two did saunter into camp—and quickly departed when they found that in their presence no flights would be made. One had donned the rough dress of the Outer Bankers as a disguise but had been instantly spotted. The more successful of the intruding journalists were five men who formed themselves into an "attacking party," as they called it, persuading Salley to act as scout and guide. They not only repeatedly observed the Flyer in the air, they also obtained the first photographs of the machine ever published (incidentally proving that Wilbur's old fears about the prying camera had been well founded).

On May 13, 1908, just as a merky dawn was breaking over the Banks, the attacking party made its way by boat from Roanoke to the sloping inland shore south of Kill Devil Hill. Then came nearly two hours of trudging through swampy vegetation, crawling under brush and among scrub pine, hiking up loose slopes with the wind blowing sand in their faces, and dodging past open spaces. At last they reached the furthest point of cover provided by the brush and stumpy trees. Here they crouched down, slapping at ticks, mosquitoes, and flies, scarcely a mile distant from the Wright camp. "There were dazzling white sand dunes, almost mountains, to the right," later wrote one of the party, "and to the left in the distance more sand dunes and a glimpse of the sea, and the Carolina sun, pouring down out of a clear sky, immersed everything in shimmer and glare."

Near the shed, moving around something on the sand, were "two black dots." The object on the sand took the shape of "a rectangle of hazy gray lines" topped by an oblong streak of white. The six newsmen patiently studied the activity through field glasses for an hour or more. Then suddenly there was noise and movement:

> Two whirling circles appeared and across the quiet distance came a sound like that of a reaper working in a distant field. The circles flashed and whirled, faster and faster, then the white streak tilted, moved forward, and rose. Across the flat, straight for the ambush it swept, as fast as an express train. It grew into shape as it approached, the planes, rudders, the operator amidships—swerved and tilted slightly, righted itself, dipped and rose, now close to the ground, now thirty or forty feet above it.

As the distance between the oncoming Flyer and the hidden newsmen shortened to a hundred yards or so, the machine banked right and slowly swerved north. James Hare, a photographer for *Collier's Weekly*, leaped excitedly to his feet and rushed into the open, aiming his camera. "Don't shoot till you see the whites of their eyes!" shouted a companion in all seriousness. As the machine came around broadside to Hare he clicked the shutter, then clicked again. With the Flyer receding in the north he stood there gazing, his heart pumping, happily aware that he was the first news photographer to get a picture of the mysterious Wright machine in the air.

The attacking party observed four flights on the thirteenth, the longest lasting for nearly three minutes. All were so excited by the spectacle that they felt like running up to the "two plucky young men" and congratulating them. They returned to Manteo that evening bedraggled and sunburned, but tired as they were, the next morning bright and early they were again crouched in the underbrush.

So far the Flyer had carried only one man, the pilot. Now at eight o'clock on the morning of the fourteenth the huddled reporters gazing through binoculars and telescopes saw a second man climb onto the wing and take a seat at the pilot's right elbow. The Flyer rose easily, veered west, leveled out, continued for a couple of hundred yards, then landed.* Shortly after, the Flyer rose once more,

---

* Wilbur was the pilot. The time was twenty-eight seconds, distance 600 feet. The passenger was Charles Furnas, a Dayton mechanic hired to help in the trials. Some six weeks prior to this Farman and Delagrange had attempted the first passenger flight together, managing a hop of about 300 feet.

again with two men aboard. In the face of a stiff wind it cruised toward the West Hill, rounded it, turned north past the little hill, then skirted the West Hill again on its return to the shed. "There was something weird, almost uncanny, about the whole thing," wrote another of the newsmen. "Here on this lonely beach was being performed the greatest act of the ages, but there were no spectators and no applause save the booming of the surf and the startled cries of the sea birds. . . . Flocks of gulls and crows, screaming and chattering, darted and circled about the machine."

In the afternoon the reporters saw only one man get aboard. It took off, rounded the West Hill and the Little Hill, headed west where it passed almost over the heads of the watchers in the brush, veered south along the shore, lifted itself over a sand ridge as it turned east toward the ocean, then banked north again along the beach. Checking their watches as the machine disappeared from sight behind the Big Hill, the reporters noted that the machine had already been in the air more than seven minutes. With their glasses trained on the spot at which they expected the Flyer to reappear, they waited. Then the clatter of the propellers suddenly stopped and three men from the shed were running across the sand.

At this, two or three of the reporters decided they had seen enough that day and started on the return to Manteo, eager to file their stories: the seven minutes in the air, they calculated, had broken Delagrange's record, though it would not count since it had not been officially witnessed. Salley and the others remained and were glad they did. After nearly an hour had passed, through their glasses they caught sight of a small cart being pulled slowly across the sand to the sheds. Laid across the cart was the lower wing of the Flyer, with the engine in place. Behind it was the other wing, crushed and twisted, with the propellers and various parts piled atop it. Evidently there had been an accident behind the big dune. Still, it did not appear as if anyone had been hurt. All four figures were busy pushing and pulling the cart.

The next day the newsmen, two of whom boldly entered the Wright camp and announced themselves as reporters, found that there had indeed been an accident, very nearly a serious one. Wilbur had been the pilot. When he disappeared behind the big dune he had been traveling at over forty miles an hour, some fifty feet off the ground. Hit by a sudden wind gust he had momentarily become confused over the new controls and the machine had nosed sharply down. He had gotten it leveled a bit when it crashed into the sand at an angle, blasting up a heavy spray as it ploughed forward. Stopping hard, it tipped violently over onto the smashed elevator framing. Wilbur was thrown hard against the underside of the tilted top wing and came to rest in a tangle of wires. When the others extricated him it was found that his nose was cut and there were bruises and cuts on both shoulders as well as on his arms and hands. Nothing was broken, however, and the only after-effect, as he admitted to the two reporters, was a general stiffness through his whole body.

But the tests were over, Wilbur added. While he would be glad of the chance for a little more practice, repairs to the Flyer would take too long and there was barely time now to prepare for the official trials in France and America. He was sure that the newsmen would be glad to hear that, he finished with a smile, considering how they had been suffering such sleepless discomfort to spy on the flights from the brush.

All twenty-two flights made during the eight days of operations had been duly chronicled in the papers, stirring much public interest. Yet the fervent response that might have been expected for these first eyewitness reports was lacking. There was no swelling of national pride, no exulting chorus of approval for the Wrights. It was too late for that. In both Europe and the United States daring men were making progressively longer and longer flights, and were doing so in public where thousands of casual spectators were able to share in the thrill of discovery. Some of these aviators had begun to understand the value of the Wrights' wing warping for lateral balance, and had translated the principle into "ailerons," small movable surfaces set into the wing tips, or between them. These gave vastly improved balance control and, though their use still was not thoroughly understood, quickly led to longer and longer flights.*

* The Wrights had foreseen that their principle of wing tip angle variance would have more than one mechanical application, and their patent proved adequate to cover these "ailerons" (a French word meaning "little wings").

On May 21, at Hammondsport, New York, Glenn Curtiss flew more than a thousand feet, making quarter-turns to left and right.

On May 30, at Milan, Italy, Léon Delagrange stayed in the air for fifteen minutes, covering seven miles. Three weeks later he raised his record to nineteen minutes for ten miles.

On June 25 Glenn Curtiss twice flew for a half-mile. Then on July 4 he extended his time in the air to nearly two minutes as he covered a mile over an S-shaped course, winning a trophy put up by the *Scientific American.*

On July 6, at Issy-les-Molineaux, France, a relative newcomer named Louis Blériot, piloting the first single-wing craft, flew six miles in eight minutes. The same day, on the same field, Henry Farman recovered the leadership from Delagrange by circling for just over twenty minutes.

In the light of such a continuing public spectacle, giving promise of greater things to come, the Wrights and Kitty Hawk grew dim indeed.

17

Wilbur Wright's Triumph

Wilbur Wright left the Hotel Meyerbeer on the Champs-Elysées about nine o'clock on the evening of June 16, 1908, and climbed into a carriage hailed by the doorman. He gave the name of one of the Paris railway stations and settled back in the seat. Simply dressed in a gray suit and a black derby hat, his long, lined face showed only his usual alert composure. But he was not a happy man.

Since his arrival in France three weeks before, he had been constantly abused and derided by the French press, which refused to take seriously American accounts of the recent Kitty Hawk flights. So hostile were these journals in defending the priority, and even superiority, of French aeronauts, that an English magazine felt compelled to come to Wilbur's defense. "Mr. Wright deserves better than that," urged London's *Automotor Journal,* "even if he has defied the press and evinced a shocking intolerance of the ubiquitous snapshotter. After all, the Wrights are perfectly entitled to behave as seems proper to them with a view to maintaining the market value of their research."

As background to this paper clamor, lending it a semblance of justice, and adding to Wilbur's depression, were the public flights of Farman, Delagrange, and Blériot. Their continuing success had become a real source of worry to Wilbur as it seemed they might soon be able to match or surpass the thirty miles he had agreed to perform for the syndicate. Already he had heard some rustle of doubt from among the syndicate's wealthy backers. "However, we must take things as we find them," he wrote resignedly to his brother, "and do the best we can."

There was also his nagging worry about Orville, who had been left behind to conduct the tests for the army, to be held on the open parade ground at Fort Myer, Washington, D.C. Wilbur knew that his younger brother did not possess the same unswervable attention to detail, the fierce concentration, that characterized his own work, and Orville would have a thousand distractions to contend with, from the military, the press, and the public, consuming his time and draining him physically. More than once Wilbur had been on the point of postponing the French tests to go home and take charge of the American trials.

Then it developed that the extra engines built to the Wrights' specifications by Barriquand and Marre were not performing as expected. "They are such idiots!" he burst out in a letter, "and fool with things that should be left alone. I get very angry every time I go down there." As it turned out, the engine difficulties were not entirely the manufacturer's fault. Impatient to get into the air, Wilbur for once was feeling the pressure.

At the railway station he boarded a train for Le Mans, a small town 125 miles southeast of Paris. Just outside of Le Mans was a large racecourse whose infield was relatively flat and clear of trees. Here he would make the flights. The place had been suggested to him by a friend of Berg's, an automobile manufacturer named Léon Bollée, who had also offered the facilities of his nearby factory for the assembling of the Flyer. The machine, still in the crate in which it had arrived in France the year before, had already been delivered to the factory. It was midnight when Wilbur's train slid quietly into the sleeping town where he was met by Bollée and taken to a hotel.

Instead of the sense of release that Wilbur expected to gain with the start of work the next morning, he found only more irritation. A large room had been set aside for him by Bollée and here he began opening the large packing crates that contained the Flyer. As the first lid came off he saw that the materials were in chaos. A hurried look through the jumble of wood and metal disclosed many broken ribs, the cloth wing-covering torn and dirtied, the radiator, magneto, coils, seat, propeller axles and tubes either smashed, broken, bent, or dented. Also, many of the parts were not in the finished state he had expected.

A single glance at the devastation was sufficient to tell him that he would need to add many days of work to his schedule and his pent-up wrath erupted against Orville, who had done the packing. "I opened the boxes yesterday and have been puzzled ever since," he wrote his brother scornfully, "to know how you could have wasted two whole days packing them. I am sure that with a scoop shovel I could have put things in within two or three minutes and made fully as good a job of it. I never saw such evidences of idiocy in my life." The crates, he instructed, should have been packed and reinforced in such a way that they could be safely dropped ten times from a height of five feet, "once on each side and the other times on the corners." When he found afterwards that much of the damage had been caused by the curious and not too careful hands of the French customs inspectors, he apologized.

Clad in the same type of overalls used by Bollée's factory workers, Wilbur set to work, keeping the same ten-hour day as the others and eating his lunch with them, out of his own pail, when the noon whistle sounded. To the workmen this casual behavior was extraordinary, so unlike the glamorized picture of an inventor-aeronaut that had been fostered by men like Santos-Dumont, who did little work with his own hands and mixed only with his colleagues. This however, was only the first taste that Frenchmen were to get of the unusual Wilbur Wright personality. In time he would be talked about almost as much for his manner and his way of doing things as for his flying, and it is not too much to say that early European ideas of the typical American character took much of their final coloring at this time from the silent man of Dayton.

Two weeks of work brought the various components of the Flyer barely to the point where assembly could begin, all except the water-cooled engine, which still needed tuning. By the end of June, Wilbur's anxious calculations indicated that he should be ready to fly in another two weeks or so. The first flights would be short ones, of course, merely for practice. At the same time, he knew that even

Huffman's pasture, Dayton, 1905. Piloted by Orville, the Flyer is just taking off to the left. Running after the machine is Wilbur. Standing at the right end of the takeoff rail is Charles Taylor. Behind him rises the catapult framework. At the rear is the brothers' shed-hangar.

ABOVE: Huffman's pasture, Dayton, 1904. Wilbur Wright gazes at the Flyer as it makes a bad landing just after takeoff, tipping over on its forward edges and throwing Orville against the upper wing. In the foreground is the takeoff rail.

BELOW: At a height of about 60 feet Orville Wright guides the Flyer in circles around Huffm'an's pasture, September 1905. This was an unusual height for the secret flights at the isolated field just outside Dayton. Most of them, during 1904–5, rose no higher than 15 or 20 feet.

The third day of Wilbur Wright's triumph in France, August 11, 1908. Before a delirious crowd of three thousand people at a racecourse in Le Mans, he flew for four minutes, performing breathtaking maneuvers. His flight of August 8, on the same field, had been a revelation to the world, the first public flight of the first practical airplane.

Wilbur Wright, dressed in his flying togs, greets King Alfonso of Spain on the field at Pau, France, 1909. At this time Wilbur, who was making almost daily flights as well as teaching other men to fly for the French Wright company, was the most sought after, most talked about personality in Europe.

Photo: Brown Brothers

Fort Myer, September 17, 1908: Orville Wright at the controls ready to go up with a passenger, Lt. Thomas Selfridge, during the Army trials (ABOVE). About five minutes later, the machine developed rudder trouble and crashed (BELOW) from a height of some 100 feet. Orville was badly injured. Lt. Selfridge died an hour later, the first fatality of powered flight.

Wilbur Wright on the return leg of his daring and memorable twenty-mile flight up the Hudson River and back to Governor's Island, October 4, 1909. Undertaken during New York's Hudson-Fulton Celebration for a fee of $15,000, it was his last public flight.

short flights would be seen by many people, would set to rest the persistent sniping by the French press and, he hoped, would place him firmly back at the center of world aviation. His frustrations at last seemed over. But they weren't.

On the afternoon of Saturday, July 4, in his room at the Bollée factory he was running the engine in a speed test. It was turning over at 1500 rpm with Wilbur standing just in front of it at a distance of about three feet, his sleeves rolled up above the elbow. Without warning, a water hose broke loose and jerked forward, releasing a wavering jet of furiously boiling water. It hit Wilbur on the left arm and chest. Léon Bollée, as it happened, was in the room at the time. He caught the staggering Wilbur, eased him to the floor, and called for help, then ran to his own office for a bottle of picric acid. For two or three minutes Wilbur's pain was intense. It began to subside only as Bollée applied the salve.

A few days later, writing to his father, Wilbur explained that his arm, being bare, had suffered the most and now carried a blister about a foot long that extended all the way round the arm. The blister on his chest was smaller, about six inches across. "The scald over my heart," he added, "had more dangerous possibilities," a remark that shows how his old fear had never quite left him. (It is too easy to forget that through all the strenuous dangers he had courted while perfecting the Flyer he was accompanied by, and had to make an effort to subdue, the whispered apprehension of a defective heart.)

The accident was immediately reported in the papers, though Wilbur himself would say nothing beyond admitting that it had happened and would delay his preparations. Reporters' requests to see the wound were shrugged off. Inevitably, this prompted several papers to wonder openly whether the accident had been real, whether this might not be just one more Wright stratagem to avoid a showdown. The word "coward" even made an appearance in the columns of the more rabid journals.

Wilbur rested in his hotel during Sunday, July 5, then the next morning, though the bandaged arm was still very sore and stiff and could not be bent, he was back at the factory tinkering with the defective hose. Necessarily the work now went much more slowly, but exactly a month later the Flyer stood ready—an anxious, nerv-

ous month in which the wounds on arm and chest did not completely heal and in which Farman, Delagrange, and Blériot continued to hypnotize large crowds with their aerial feats. Then came
another surprise. Henry Farman announced that he was departing
for the United States to fly exhibitions in various cities, starting
with New York. American promoters, envisioning the fortune to be
made from the hordes of people who would pay to see an airplane
in flight, had offered Farman a $25,000 guarantee.

By early August Wilbur was desperate to get into the air, though
his instincts warned him that he should wait until his arm was more
reliable. Since the Flyer's controls were now arranged handy to a
seated pilot, and since he had very little practice with the new arrangement, it seemed folly to attempt flying until he was physically
whole. Reaction time in flight, particularly when doing forty miles
an hour at low altitudes, was measured in seconds and split seconds. He waited a day or two and when the arm did not apprecia-
bly improve he decided to go.

Previously, when renting the racecourse for the flights, he had
also arranged for the building of a shed hangar at the track. After
darkness had fallen on the night of August 4, the Flyer was moved
amid much secrecy from the factory to the shed, towed on a cart
behind Bollée's automobile. Trailing along were a few reporters
who had been keeping watch. They tried to get a closer look at the
machine but in the darkness could only make out its general features, such as the chain drive on the propellers, and this was reported in the next day's papers as a major discovery. In one corner
of the shed Wilbur had set up living quarters for himself—a cot,
chair, and wash basin, and a small gas stove handy for making
meals. Here he bedded down for the night within a few feet of the
stored Flyer. For the next five months he would not often sleep
apart from his machine.

Talking to reporters the next morning, he announced that he was
now ready and everything depended on the weather. Pressed to be
more exact, he explained that he couldn't, since the condition of his
arm complicated things. It still pained him when he bent it. A voice
piped out of the crowd asking for a look at the arm and after a moment's hesitation Wilbur rolled up his sleeve. "His arm is really
bad," wrote one reporter. "He showed me the healing wound this

morning and certainly no man who could avoid doing so would undertake hard work with that important limb in such a condition. Mr. Wright made light of the matter though he had to confess that the healing process was taking far longer than he had expected."

When still urged by the newsmen to pinpoint a day so that they might inform the public, Wilbur ended the interview with typical dispatch. He had told them he was ready, he repeated, "it is up to you now to find out when I fly. I don't know myself, but you can be sure I will not wait because there are no spectators." The next day, August 6, there were high winds and the dark skies threatened rain. The next morning was a little better but the arm flared up with pain.

His impatience was growing by the hour, especially since reports had come from America that Farman's flights had begun and were drawing thousands of people to a field at Brighton Beach, Long Island, to gape at a series of short, straight-line hops. Farman, announced the papers, was searching for a larger field to make an all-out assault on the records. Wilbur decided to wait no longer. On August 7 he announced to the newsmen who daily gathered round the shed that he would definitely fly the next day, if the weather held good.

At 7 A.M. on August 8 Wilbur climbed out of his cot, donned overalls, brewed some coffee, then for the hundredth time began a systematic check of the Flyer. The few early-rising reporters waiting outside the shed could hear him "whistling and hammering." An hour later workmen started setting up the catapult at one end of the oval field. Many papers that morning had carried the news that "Wilbur Wright May Fly Today," and people began drifting into the enclosure early. By ten o'clock the small wooden stands were filled and the crowd spread out along the sidelines. Most came prepared to spend the day, bringing supplies of food, and since no admission had been charged they remained patient even when noontime passed with no sign of the Flyer on the field.

About one o'clock Hart Berg informed the audience over a loudspeaker that photographs would not be permitted. Afterward he strolled around to make sure that the prohibition was observed. At two o'clock a stir went through the crowd as the big doors of the shed were thrown open and the brightly painted Flyer was trundled out, its white wings gleaming in the intense rays of the sun. The tail, which had been collapsed inward for storage, was now extracted to its full ten-foot distance and fixed in place.

As the Flyer was moved across the field to the catapult, balanced on a small wheeled cart, an annoying mishap occurred. The man steadying the right wing tips allowed them to dip when the machine was lifted over a shallow ditch. The underside of the right wing hit a pointed stump, the cloth receiving a tear about six inches wide. Wilbur inspected the damage, pulled from his bulging pocket a patch, needle, thread, and a container of glue, and crawled under the wing. With the crowd of reporters, helpers, and hangers-on pushing around the machine, fascinated, he painstakingly sewed the patch in place and swabbed on the glue.

At the catapult the Flyer was lifted onto the rail and hooked up to the weight. Then Wilbur walked back and disappeared into the shed, to emerge moments later attired in a gray suit, collar and tie, and a cap which was turned backwards. No aviator of that time would have thought of flying an exhibition dressed in mechanics togs (later he would be one of the first to set aside such formality, in the cold weather donning rough trousers and a leather jacket).

It was after five when Wilbur started the engine for a warm-up run. Then for another hour he tinkered, poked, and probed, at one point discovering a short in a wire. At about six thirty, when he stepped over the wooden slats that braced the elevator and climbed into the pilot's seat, a murmur went up from the stands. But he still wasn't ready. After listening to the rattling hum of the engine for a few minutes, as an eyewitness recalled it, "he called to one of his mechanics who was standing at the back of the machine asking him whether some quite small last-minute adjustment had been made on the motor. The man replied promptly that it had. At which Wilbur sat silent for a moment. Then, slowly leaving his pilot's seat, he walked around the machine just to make sure, with his own eyes, that this particular adjustment had, without the slightest shadow of a doubt, been well and truly made."

Seated aboard again, Wilbur remained immobile for a few more seconds, fingering the control sticks at either side of his knees. What happened next took place with such unexpected swiftness and breathtaking grace that the spectators were left stunned, not quite sure of what they had seen. It was a reporter for the *Herald* who best captured the moment in two short sentences: "In a flash the catapult has acted. Mr. Wright has shot into the air, while the spectators gasp in astonishment."

The Flyer had leaped up after a short run on the rail. Quickly it rose to a height of thirty feet. Such a sure ascent had not been seen in Europe before, where takeoffs were uncertain operations, managed only after a long run across a field and not always at a first try. When the crowd had recovered from its surprise it sent up a thunderous roar of approval.

Seconds later the Flyer's left wing dropped sharply as the machine banked left for a tight turn. At this totally unanticipated movement a renewed roar went up. Men shouted that the machine was falling. Women screamed and covered their eyes at the "terrifying" tilt of the wings, something else no one in Europe had ever seen before, or thought to see. Those who had flown or had seen flights or read about them, had come to accept the flat, wide, lumbering, level-winged circle as the proper mode of turning a flying machine. But here before their astonished eyes was Wilbur Wright zooming on radiant wings in the topsy-turvy manner of a bird, with all a bird's swift grace and confidence.

Wilbur guided the Flyer smoothly round in a circle whose diameter was barely sixty yards, droning past the clamoring grandstand. On around the field he went a second time, again coming before the grandstand, in which the frightened cries had turned to wild cheering as it appeared that the plane was not going to fall or turn over.

This first trial was meant merely for getting the feel of the machine and the grounds. After nearly two minutes in the air Wilbur came down, landing gently near the catapult. Even before he came to a stop a wave of spectators flooded from the stands and across the field.

Around the machine pushed hundreds of noisy, excited people, waving arms and hats, shouting congratulations, reaching to shake the hand of the man who only the day before had been the object of derision and who now "while looking pleased, remained cool and collected." One reporter shoved his way to Wilbur's side and asked if he was fully satisfied with his performance. "Not altogether," replied Wilbur. "While in the air I made no less than ten mistakes owing to the fact that I have been laying off so long, but I corrected them all rapidly so I don't suppose anyone watching really knew I had made mistakes at all." Ten mistakes in less than two minutes, all instantly corrected so that they were not apparent to observers—not a bad performance considering that it had been nearly three months since his last flight, which had ended in a crash, and that he had had little experience with the new controls to start with.

Two or three of the French aviators had managed to be on hand, including Louis Blériot. Now, lost in the milling crowd, he had a stunned look on his face. Buttonholed by a reporter, he was asked for his expert reactions to the flight. Trying to gather his racing thoughts, Blériot stared at his questioner. "I consider that for us in France and everywhere," he murmured, "a new era of mechanical flight has commenced." He hesitated, groping for some means of expressing the implications of what he had just witnessed. Finally he confessed: "I am not sufficiently calm after the event to thoroughly express my opinion."

Another aviator in the crowd, René Gasnier, who less than a year before had switched to flying machines from balloons, was also asked to comment. "Compared with the Wrights," he replied with a shake of the head, "we are as children."

The disappearing sun brought shadows lengthening across the racecourse, making it too late for another flight, though many implored Wilbur to go up again. Then as the crowd thinned, the Flyer was rolled back and stored in the shed. Waiting for Wilbur to accompany them into Le Mans were Bollée, Berg, Blériot, Gasnier, and a dozen others, including reporters, all in a mood to celebrate. Wilbur quietly said no, he'd rather not. He wanted to check the Flyer over again before renewing his practice on Monday, and he couldn't do the work the next day since it was Sunday. "In spite of all persuasion Mr. Wright refused to go into town," wrote a reporter later that night, "and is now sleeping peacefully by the side of his creation." As Wilbur slept a hundred toasts were offered to his name in the crowded cafés and restaurants of the little town.

A single trial of less than two minutes had sufficed to demonstrate the thrilling nature of true flight and to obliterate much of the fame of Farman, Delagrange, and their compatriots. The next day's papers, in page-one headlines, all lamented their former unpleasantness, agreeing that Wilbur Wright had revolutionized aeronautics, achieving "not merely a success but a triumph." The more perceptive writers also admitted that all the machines flown in Europe were but poor copies, stumbling imitations, of the magnificent Wright designs.

The evening of the flight the heady news was sped to the United States by cable and the next morning Americans, too, found page-one headlines hailing the Wright name. Most of the stories were careful to point out for uninformed readers that it was not the length of the flight that impressed. What was so "startling" was the fabulous control and the way the machine "turned corners" at the dizzying speed of about forty miles an hour.

At 11 A.M. on Monday, August 10, Wilbur was ready for another flight, the Flyer poised on the rail before the catapult. Overflowing from the packed stands were some two thousand spectators, among them Léon Delagrange, who had hurried back from his own exhibitions in Italy. Louis Blériot was also present, with Henry Kapferer and a dozen other aeronautical enthusiasts less renowned. If Blériot had been stunned by Wilbur's first flight, what he was about to see would leave him dumbfounded.

Around the catapult were congregated dozens of newsmen, many from other countries, and at some distance to one side a motion picture camera had been set up to make newsreels for the Paris nickelodeons. Wilbur now had no objection to pictures, either stills or movies, made at a distance, or of the Flyer in the air (realistically, he could not have prevented such in any case). He prohibited only close-up photographs that might be used to study details of the machine's construction. An announcement to this effect was again made by Berg.

At a sign from Wilbur in the pilot's seat, the catapult weight was released. Down it plummeted and the Flyer shot skyward. Again after a few seconds it banked left, circling before the cheering grandstand. This time he made a very wide circle and as he cruised past the excited crowd he held a straight path a little too long—another mistake. Looming ahead he saw the sideline trees. He had misjudged their position and now saw that they were just too high to fly over, the distance being too short to gain altitude. He was also too high in the air to make a sudden landing. To avoid the trees he would have to make a very sharp turn. Throwing both the elevator and the warping handles, he put the machine into a steeply descending left bank, so steep that a roar of consternation went up from the stands. The Flyer veered sharply round, the diameter of its circle fast diminishing to an incredible thirty yards. Then, wings level once more, it landed. For Wilbur the maneuver was not really extraordinary, though he would not often choose to put such a strain on himself and the machine. For the spectators, however, the turn in such a small circle had appeared nearly miraculous. If a police cordon had not been set up, many people, wrought to a pitch, would have broken across the field to get near the machine and its pilot.

Wilbur had not liked the sound of the engine on that flight, so he now had the Flyer trundled back to the shed where he meant to do some tinkering. On the way he took time out for a little personal police action, which was reported by the papers with appreciative gusto.

As the procession passed near the grandstand, Wilbur's eye caught a metallic glint. Looking up he spotted a man in uniform near the front aiming a camera. Hesitating not a moment, Wilbur raced toward the stands, leaped a small fence, and climbed toward the man, who turned out to be a French Army captain. As a nearby reporter wrote, Wilbur angrily demanded "that the captain should hand him his camera with all exposed plates and leave the field. The captain hesitated and made excuses, but Mr. Wright set his mouth firmly, folded his arms and waited. In face of this attitude, the captain handed over the apparatus and the plates were destroyed."

Late in the afternoon Wilbur was ready to fly again. This time he planned a maneuver that he expected would once and for all demonstrate the full capabilities of his control. In the air, when at about midfield, the Flyer banked left and headed directly toward, then past the front of the grandstand. Then, instead of continuing the left-handed circle, it banked right, zoomed all the way round in a right-handed circle, cut across midfield, then banked left again, circling toward its takeoff point, where it landed smoothly to a thunderous cheer. The figure eight that the Flyer had described had never been seen in Europe before.

When Wilbur climbed down, the more privileged visitors near the shed whirled around him. "Blériot and Delagrange were so excited," Wilbur wrote home, "that they could scarcely speak, and Kapferer could only gasp and could not talk at all. You would have almost died of laughter if you could have seen them." When Delagrange did find his voice at last, he threw up his hands and exclaimed, "We are beaten! We just don't exist!"

The next day the number of people pushing for a place inside the racecourse fence had swelled to about three thousand, with hundreds coming down from Paris by train. They were rewarded with a flight of nearly four minutes in which the Flyer, at a height of thirty feet, maneuvered between and around the few scattered trees at the center of the infield. Such absolute control, marveled the more informed watchers, was far beyond anything they had ever deemed possible. The applause and the cheering were deafening, "for this wonderful man who, in spite of a wounded arm, and not withstanding the want of practice, gave such a demonstration of his bewildering skill."

The following morning Wilbur had another surprise ready. In a ten-mile wind he flew for seven minutes and rose to a height of ninety feet, well above the tops of the tallest trees and far beyond any altitude attempted by European pilots. That afternoon he made two brief flights, both of them cut short by the strong, gusty winds that suddenly blew up. With the large crowd clogging the field he was taking no unnecessary chances.

As the duration of the flights increased, the racecourse was proving too small, both to handle the crowds and for the strain a confined space put upon the pilot in maneuvering. About ten miles distant, at a town called Auvours, there was a much larger field which Wilbur had avoided at first because it contained an installation of the French Army. Now he started negotiating for its use and found that the military would be more than glad to have him, notwithstanding his encounter with the captain. The construction of the necessary shed hangar was hurriedly begun.

A realist, Wilbur had all along admitted that accidents, particularly small ones, were probably inevitable. He still was not comfortable with the controls and too often he started to move the handles in the wrong direction before catching himself. And with the high maneuverability he had attained, control was no longer a matter of thinking in terms of three axes: longitudinal, vertical, and lateral. Now he had to think in simultaneous combinations of the three. Further complication was added by the fact that when the Flyer was steeply banked, the forward elevator acted much as a rudder, affecting side-to-side movement, as well as up-and-down. At last on August 13 he made a mistake he was not able to correct in time.

That morning he had flown "almost majestically" for ten minutes, again climbing well above the treetops. In the evening he went up for the day's second flight, meant to be a low one and brief. He had been in the air only two or three minutes when, with the Flyer banking for a left turn at a height of twenty feet, the outside wing rose higher than he intended, dropping the inside wing tip dangerously close to the ground. He shoved the warp handle forward meaning to pull back on the rudder handle. Instead, momentarily confused, he pushed both handles forward. If he had been five or six feet higher, as he said later, there would have been time to compensate for the error.

With the Flyer rushing over the ground at about thirty miles an hour the left wing tips hit hard and broke up in an explosion of wood and flapping cloth. The machine bounced flat, the left skid collapsing as the crippled Flyer skidded along the grass and then halted, without tipping. By now almost inured to such occurrences, when Wilbur's helpers and friends ran up, he just "sat for a few moments in the driver's seat, contemplating the damage," on his face a look of disgust.

Four or five days would be needed for repairs. By then the hangar at Auvours should be ready. He would make the move before resuming operations.

It had been a truly extraordinary week. Nine short flights, totaling less than a half hour of air time, had sufficed to convince the world that practical human flight was a far more remarkable thing than anyone had even remotely suspected, that it was capable of a precision never indicated by the brave but awkward efforts of other men.

A pilot, after all, was not a chauffeur, invading and warily fighting his way through a strange element in a winged cousin to the carriage or automobile. He was an integral part of a machine whose every single component was engineered toward a thoroughly integrated whole, a machine that belonged in the air and that was not itself when out of it. He was master of this machine, its soul, and master as well even of the unpredictable currents that disturbed the ocean of air in which it moved.

18

Kings of the Air

Now it was Orville's turn. Less than a week after Wilbur transferred to the field at Auvours, there arrived from America the welcome news that the trials at Fort Myer had begun.

Orville's flights, while their impact was a little dulled for Americans by the reports about Wilbur that had streamed over the ocean from Le Mans, still proved enormously moving to the large crowd that witnessed them. It was one thing to read of machines that flew. It was quite another to have the loudly rattling engine reverberate in the ears "like the clatter of a Gatling gun," to watch the two hypnotic blurs inexorably propel wings and pilot upward, to see the actual miracle passing overhead.

As A. I. Root had found five years before, it was not a sight easy to put in words, even for journalists. "How can I describe the beautiful, white, graceful, curving surfaces of this perfect and characteristic machine?" asked one writer who was at Fort Myer. "As it goes away from you and you look edgewise at the planes, they appear as the wings of a bird, with the sleigh-like runners underneath . . . as it circles over your head and you look up at the wide expanse of the surfaces, with the sun shining on them, and the dark lines made by the ribs, it looks like the sails of a trim sailing yacht. It also makes you think of some large bird in search of prey, its cry a harsh sound very much like the noise made by a mowing machine as it is driven about a hay field." Reactions to the experience were always excited, often deeply emotional. After Orville's initial flight, which occupied little more than a minute, some men in the crowd, including a newsman or two, had tears of joy welling in their eyes.

Momentarily at this juncture one of the French airmen managed to struggle briefly back into the picture. At Rome on September 6 and 7, Delagrange twice shattered Farman's endurance record, flying for a half-hour the first day and for thirty-one minutes the second. Time in the air was not the most important measure of aeronautical success, of course, but it was the easiest fact for an avid public to grasp and appreciate. Thus it was the duration of each flight that came to be hailed with the most fanfare, and when Delagrange's feat was given banner headlines it appeared that the Wrights might have a worthy rival. That notion, however, was quickly laid to rest by Orville. Wasting little time on the short practice flights favored by his brother, he suddenly launched an all-out attack on the records, determined to put them as much beyond the reach of others as possible.

At Fort Myer on the morning of September 9 he circled the large army grounds for fifty-seven minutes, climbing to an altitude of 110 feet. That was far longer and higher than any of the flights the brothers had made in secret at Huffman's pasture. In the afternoon that same day he went up again and cruised for just over an hour. Then in the cool of the evening he went up a third time, carrying a passenger, for more than six minutes, also a record. That was only the start. In the following three days he repeatedly exceeded an hour in the air, finally reaching an hour and fourteen minutes, and an altitude of 200 feet.

It was a magnificent achievement for the younger brother and it took Europe by storm, renewing the furor originally stirred up by Wilbur. To think of these two brothers, on separate continents, teaching the world to fly was dazzling. For Wilbur the effect was more personal, lifting from his harassed mind a burden of worry that had weighed him down for months. And with that, the departed worries proved to have been all too prophetic.

At Auvours on the morning of September 18 Wilbur was preparing for a long flight. It was a beautiful, cool, sunshiny day, perfect flying weather and he was eager to begin. His handling of the controls had sharpened and, with the Flyer once more in good trim, he looked forward to extending Orville's duration record. At hand was the moment he had for so long anticipated: by turns, he and his brother would set and break record after record, providing a scientific carnival the like of which had never been seen before, and firmly establishing the flying machine as a practical tool for the world's use. As he was standing by the Flyer a cablegram was handed to him. It announced that in a flight with a passenger on the previous afternoon, Orville had crashed almost head-on into the ground from a height of more than a hundred feet.

The passenger, a young army lieutenant named Thomas Selfridge, had suffered a fractured skull and had died in the hospital an hour later. Orville had sustained a broken leg, broken ribs, and a fractured and dislocated hip. His condition was not critical but his convalescence would be a long one.

Out of respect for Selfridge, who became the first fatality of powered flight, Wilbur canceled his planned activities and spent the rest of the day, as he wrote Katharine, thinking over and over, "If I had been there it would not have happened." A little later, details of the accident reached him: it had been caused by one small defect, an unnoticed hairline split along one blade of the right propeller, something that more diligent preflight inspection might have uncovered.

Orville and Selfridge had circled the Fort Myer grounds three times at an altitude of 125 feet. All appeared to be going smoothly when a tapping sound at the rear made Orville glance back. Though he saw nothing his instinct told him to land. Before he could take any action, two loud thumps sent a violent shaking through the machine, wrenching it around to the right. Then it nosed down suddenly and dove, Orville's frantic yanking at the warp and rudder controls producing no effect. Only the elevator answered, picking up the nose very slowly. Given another ten feet of altitude it might have escaped. At an angle of thirty degrees, it smashed into the ground, breaking up as it ploughed forward in a cloud of dust and dirt.

In that last fearful dive, as Orville remembered sadly, Selfridge had remained calm. He had said nothing but had turned once or twice to look into the pilot's face, "evidently to see what I thought of the situation." Only at the last had Selfridge made any sound, exclaiming almost inaudibly, "Oh! Oh!"

The split propeller blade, investigation disclosed, had flattened in flight, losing much of its thrust, and unbalancing the pressures on the two blades. This induced a vibration which permitted the propeller shaft to swing a few inches right and left. On one swing the whirling blade sliced through a wire controlling the tail rudder. Partially freed, the rudder fell over. Somehow it became fixed in that position, taking great pressure on its underside and forcing down the front of the machine.

Wilbur, determined not to allow the tragedy to halt the momentum he and his brother had already built up, was back in the air three days after receiving word of the accident, and now he too mounted an onslaught on the records. Promptly he raised the duration record to an hour and a half. Then during the next three months he flew regularly, making nearly one hundred flights, on a number of occasions exceeding an hour in the air, once with a passenger. In December he raised the altitude record to 300 feet and the duration record to an hour and fifty-four minutes. On the last day of 1908, in very cold weather, he flew round the field at Auvours for a total distance of over ninety miles, remaining in the air for two hours and twenty minutes, droning on and on as the setting sun provided the Flyer with a blazing, varicolored backdrop.

Immediately after landing he went up again with a passenger, the French Minister of Public Works, M. Barthou. Climbing off the machine after landing, Barthou informed Wilbur that the French government had decided to award to both him and Orville the Legion of Honor.

By now Wilbur Wright and his flights had become the most talked-about phenomenon in Europe. Reporters followed him constantly, setting down everything he did and nearly everything he said, on almost any subject, though they noted with some impatience that usually he did not say much. One remark of his, made at a gala banquet in Paris, caught the French fancy for epigram and was endlessly repeated. Chided for not making a longer speech at the dinner, Wilbur observed, "I know of only one bird, the parrot, that talks, and it can't fly very high."

Every day the field at Auvours (and at Pau, in the south of France, where he transferred early in 1909 to escape the cold weather) overflowed with people wanting to see things with their own eyes—including three kings: Alfonso of Spain, Edward VII of England, and Victor Emmanuel of Italy. More than a few also wanted a ride and now and then Wilbur obliged, taking selected men up for short hops, and even a woman or two. Luckily, one of these passengers wrote and published a description of his experience while it was still fresh in his mind. Behind the matter-of-fact words there still glows something of innocent wonder.

Having clambered in among various rods and wires one struggles into the little seat arranged on the front edge of the lower plane, and places one's feet on a small bar in front. A string is found crossing just in front of one's chest, and Mr. Wright gives directions that this must not be touched. It is a simple contrivance for cutting off the ignition and stopping the engine. In event of any accident the body will probably be thrown forward, and pressing against the string, immediately stops the engine. . . . All being ready, coats are buttoned, and caps pulled down to prevent being blown off. . . .

Then the driver bends down and releases the catch which holds the anchoring wire. The machine is off! It bounds forward and travels rapidly along the rail. The foreplanes are meanwhile pressed down to prevent the machine lifting prematurely, but when about half the length of the rail has been traversed, the lever is pulled back, the planes come into operation, and the whole machine rises, almost imperceptibly off the track. . . .

The ascent must be very gradual. When the machine leaves the track it glides so close to the ground that one often doubts if it is really started in the air, but then it gradually mounts. . . .

So steady and regular is the motion that it appears exactly as if it were progressing along an invisible elevated track. Only just now and again, as a swirl of wind catches it, does it make a slight undulation like a boat rising to a big wave. Mr. Wright, with both hands grasping the levers, watches every move, but his movements are so slight as to be almost imperceptible. Having soon reached the end of the ground, the machine is guided round in a large semicircle, gracefully leaning over as it turns, just as a large soaring bird would do.

Back she comes the whole length of the ground, sometimes keeping exactly on a level with the tree tops, sometimes she descends and moves along five or six feet above the ground. All the time the engines are buzzing loudly and the propellers humming so that after a trip one is almost deaf.

Wilbur's two-hour-twenty-minute flight set a record that was to stand for six months. It was also to prove the longest he would ever make. But it was not his most impressive. There was one more to come which would be hailed as the greatest of all to that time, "both in spectacular interest and personal daring," as one paper said. It would take place eight months later over the wide waters of New York harbor and would be his farewell to public flying.

William Howard Taft, President of the United States, walked into the East Room of the White House and waved to the standing audience of almost a thousand men and women. He mounted a small platform at the front and took his place between the day's two guests of honor, Wilbur and Orville Wright, greeting each in turn. Understandably he did not refer to the letter the brothers had written him while he was serving as Secretary of War, the letter he had so casually passed on to the army board.

The ceremonies were opened by Representative Herbert Parsons (being rewarded for what seemed to be his crucial part in bringing the Wrights and the government together), who reviewed the brothers' accomplishments, and then introduced the President. Speaking briefly, Taft praised the Wrights' genius, hard work, persistence, and, especially, their modesty. He closed with the hope that the flying machine would be used for the peaceful benefit of all nations and not just for purposes of war. Handing a boxed gold medal to each brother, he again expressed his admiration and gave each a hearty handshake. Then he edged his six-foot-two, 300-pound frame between the brothers and smiled down on Katharine Wright, assuring her that she had every right to be extremely proud of her brothers. "Miss Wright blushed as she shook the President's hand," reported *The New York Times,* "but her eyes were alight with pleasure."

Taft then escorted the three Wrights, along with some other distinguished guests, to the White House porch, where all posed for pictures. Asked by a reporter if he had ever thought of going up in a flying machine, the President laughingly replied that he would love it but did not think he had an "aeronautical figure." Apart from its humor, it was an interesting remark for it unconsciously reflected the fairly common belief that aviators, and the people who dared to fly with them, had to possess some of the agility and hardiness of athletes.

The Wrights' White House visit, which took place on June 10, 1909, was followed a week later by a gala two-day celebration in Dayton. There were three parades, two banquets, and a public reception attended by all the city's schoolchildren and at which Bishop Wright pronounced the benediction. Three more gold medals were presented to each brother, voted by Congress, the State of Ohio, and Dayton itself. The climax came on the second night with a grand fireworks display in which portraits of Wilbur and Orville, eighty feet high, were intertwined with an American flag.

During the two days all business was suspended—except by the Wright brothers themselves. In their spare moments they would rush back to their workshop to continue preparing for the United States Army trials, which had been rescheduled for July.

Orville, now fully recovered, did all the flying for these trials himself, rejecting his brother's offer to relieve him of at least a part of the work. He did, however, agree to proceed with more caution and at Fort Myer he spent three weeks working on plane and engine and going up for more than twenty practice flights. Then, within the space of two days, he easily satisfied the terms of the contract. In the speed tests he averaged forty-two miles an hour, earning the contract bonus for topping the minimum speed. The United States had acquired its first airplane, at a cost of $30,000.

The brothers had made their fortunes. Counting what Wilbur had earned in Europe—from prizes, awards, fees for exhibitions, contracts for the sale of single planes, and payment under the syndicate contract—and money just received from the army, the two were jointly worth nearly a quarter-million dollars in cash, with another $100,000 or so immediately in the offing, and an untold sum beckoning in the future. This was far more than anyone else had made from the budding aviation business, and appears to have been a fitting climax to all the hazards, work, and planning.

Yet whether these initial monies were indeed a sufficient return for the brothers' unparalleled achievement is a question that has often been asked. There were many who believed that it was not, including Charles Flint. "The Wrights realized substantial sums from their invention," Flint commented later, "but these were insignificant when compared with their scientific and practical accomplishments." He was perhaps thinking, especially, of those three years, 1904–6, when the Wrights, alone of all men, knew how to fly. If during those years Wilbur had used a different approach, had been less wary, had not dreamed of success on so massive a scale—but who can tell?

In early fall, 1909, New York City was girded for the greatest anniversary celebration in its history. Three hundred years before, Henry Hudson's *Half Moon* had sailed into the harbor, and just over one hundred years before, Robert Fulton had sent the city's first steamboat, *Clermont,* chugging to Albany.* To fill a program lasting two weeks there were scheduled parades, banquets, celebrity appearances, sports extravaganzas, and public festivities of all kinds including reenactments of the city's principal historical events. Buildings, monuments, and bridges were decked with flags and banners and some structures were completely outlined in festive lights—nighttime strollers could gaze upon the City Hall, the Washington Arch, and the Brooklyn Bridge ablaze with strings of color. A high point was to be the visit to the harbor of a huge fleet of naval vessels, American and foreign, and New Yorkers were agog at the prospect of playing host to one of the greatest gatherings of sea power the world had seen.

Since many other vessels, large and small, were expected to join in this grand rendezvous, newspapers were predicting that well over a thousand boats would be displayed on the waters of the lower Hudson River. There would be everything from ancient square-riggers to battleships, freighters, private yachts, excursion steamers, ferries, and luxury liners, including that modern marvel of the sea, the *Lusitania.*

As the top attraction of this massive pageant, there was to be an

* Fulton's date, of course, was 1807, but the city fathers had decided on one double-barreled observance instead of two.

exhibition of the world's newest miracle, the flying machine. Wilbur Wright himself, it was announced, had agreed to perform. The services of "the premier birdman" had not come cheap, however. For making at least one flight over the river in the vicinity of Manhattan, of at least ten miles, Wilbur was to be paid $15,000. The city fathers, aware of the difficulties of a river flight, did not consider the fee excessive. They knew that earning it would be no easy task.

While flying had, by this time, become a reality in a dozen countries, machines were still almost entirely restricted to circling over or near an open field. Cranky engines and unpredictable weather conditions made it an extremely precarious thing to venture far from the takeoff point, or to cross areas covered by natural or man-made objects. Such things as airfields, of course, did not exist, and if a hurried descent had to be made, the very low altitudes still favored by all pilots allowed precious little time for finding an open patch of ground.

Scarcely ten months before, Henry Farman had risked the first cross-country flight—from Bouy to Rheims, sixteen miles in twenty minutes, crossing woods, a river, hills, railroad tracks, and a village or two. That feat had been called foolhardy nearly as often as it was praised, and very few had bothered to emulate it. Orville at Fort Myer had made a similar though shorter flight, not by choice but for the army speed tests. The most famous such effort, important largely for its symbolism, had been made by Louis Blériot a short two months before. This was the memorable first crossing of the English Channel, from Calais to Dover, twenty-three miles in thirty-seven minutes. Blériot did not have houses, hills, and trees to worry about but water was no more inviting as a landing spot.

Wilbur's proposed flight, most observers agreed, would be even more hazardous than Blériot's. In New York harbor he would not only be flying over water, he would have to fight his way through the shifting wind gusts that even on relatively calm days swirled between the high Palisades on the New Jersey shore and the tall buildings on Manhattan. And the surface of the river would not be clear. Spread beneath the Flyer would be that immense, scattered flotilla, with many of the larger ships creating thermal updrafts to add to the problems of control.

While Wilbur was to be the star of this aerial show, a second aviator had been invited as insurance, Glenn Curtiss, who had only recently garnered some authentic fame of his own. In August he had entered an aviation meet at Rheims, the only American present. Given little chance, he had captured the speed trophy in a thrilling race against the clock, defeating Blériot by seconds, and thus made a timely addition to New York's commemoration. His contract called for a ten-mile flight, either up and down the river or back and forth between the shores. With other commitments to fill, he had agreed to only a week's stay. His fee was to be $5,000.

Base of operations for both men was Governor's Island, located just south of the tip of Manhattan and close to the Brooklyn shore. About two miles long by a half mile wide, the island's flat, sandy surface offered a hundred acres of open ground for takeoffs and landing and for the necessary practice flights. Here the city had erected two temporary sheds in which the aviators would assemble and store their machines. Since a certain number of people were to be allowed on the island, the shed areas had been roped off and guards assigned.

About a mile west of Governor's Island lay Bedloe's Island on which stood the Statue of Liberty, her famous lamp lifted some 300 feet above the water. A little to the north of the statue, near the Jersey shore, lay Ellis Island, and above that there stretched far into the north, in a nearly straight line, the lordly Hudson.

The flights of both pilots were to be made anytime after opening ceremonies on September 25. Since all flying would be controlled by wind and weather it was up to each of the two, separately, to choose the exact day, time, and course of his flight. Since such decisions could not always be made well ahead of time, an elaborate, city-wide system of signals had been arranged to alert New Yorkers: When either man should decide to go up, appropriate flags would be flown on Governor's Island. Watchers on rooftops in the city, especially on the tallest buildings, would then hoist other large flags and would set off loud explosions to attract attention. People could then make for vantage points on the western shores of Manhattan and Brooklyn.

Accompanied by Charles Taylor, Wilbur arrived in New York on September 19. (Orville had already departed for Germany, where he was to make demonstration flights for the new German Wright company.) After a meeting with city officials, Wilbur and Taylor took the ferry to Governor's Island where they immediately began assembly of the Flyer, which had arrived the day before.

Curtiss, just returning from France to a hero's welcome in the city, visited the island a couple of days later to check the progress of his assistants in readying his own machine. Both pilots were interviewed often and had repeatedly to deny the wild talk that had them flying over the city itself, chasing each other between the skyscrapers. Rumors of a head-to-head race were also rampant. "I am not much of a racer," admitted Wilbur, for the hundredth time denying the possibility, "I think I am worth more to myself alive than dead, and there is necessarily a large element of risk in these high speed contests."

It may have been at this time that there occurred a small incident, ephemeral in itself but lasting in the impression it made on those who witnessed it. In a way it epitomizes the whole story of Wilbur Wright. One evening while closely checking the performance of a propeller, he found that it was in some way not quite right at its canvas-covered tips. He asked Taylor for a drawknife, then "laid back the canvas covering from the blades and proceeded to do some real artistic whittling, much to the awe of Glenn Curtiss, and the marvel of all the mechanics standing around." The performance of the shaved propeller was immediately improved.

The warships of the United States, France, Italy, England, Germany, the Netherlands, and Mexico steamed into the harbor on September 22, to be greeted by loud blasts from ship's horns and screaming tugboat whistles. In all there were more than forty ships and even Wilbur stopped work to watch the stately procession glide mightily by. On Saturday, September 25, the opening ceremonies were held in lower Manhattan, with reproductions of the *Half Moon* and the *Clermont* being saluted by thunderous salvos from the big guns of the dreadnaughts. This, with the blasting and shrieking of the thousand other vessels, produced a volume and combination of noises such as New York had not heard before, and has not heard since. With the opening festivities ended, all eyes focused on Governor's Island.

Though the weather was good the next day Wilbur did not fly:

His contract contained a clause exempting him from Sunday performances. Curtiss had not yet returned to the island from a brief visit home. Disappointingly, Monday and Tuesday brought high winds and rain, but Wednesday dawned dry, with the wind at about ten miles an hour, safe enough for flying. Curtiss, who had arrived the evening before, went up for a short hop of about a minute. He came down dissatisfied with the sound of his engine and spent the rest of the day tinkering.

Wilbur had a special need for practice flights, since he had added something to the Flyer which might strongly affect its behavior in the air. This was an ordinary canoe, its top covered with canvas, that he had lashed underneath the bottom wing, pointing fore and aft. If the machine came down in the water it would quickly go to the bottom without something to keep it afloat. The covered canoe should keep it on the surface long enough for a rescue vessel to arrive. But the weight of the addition and its bulk protruding forward, would certainly alter the machine's aerodynamic reactions and he must learn how to make the necessary compensations.

The superiority of the catapult takeoff for the relatively restricted space on the island, in contrast to the long run Curtiss needed, quickly became apparent. About an hour after Curtiss' hop, the Flyer jumped into the air for a practice flight and went into a circling pattern thirty feet up. Five minutes later Wilbur came down and he and Taylor went over the machine again. At about ten o'clock Wilbur straightened from his work. He gazed around the harbor and announced to those nearby that as conditions were still good he would make another short practice flight before putting the machine away. A sharp-eyed reporter noted that as he spoke, "he looked toward the Statue of Liberty and made a significant nod, meant only for his head mechanician."

The catapult weight dropped and the Flyer lifted lightly off the starting rail. The sun stood high over the Brooklyn shore to the east, where were gathered at least a half million people, massed along the wharves, in the parks, the streets, on the rooftops, many with binoculars and telescopes, all with eyes fixed on the sun-brightened wings. Similar throngs filled the roofs and streets around Manhattan's blunt tip, and overflowed from the open space at Battery Park.

Round the island Wilbur circled once, gaining altitude, as the cheers of the small crowd below drifted dimly up to him. Leveling out at a height of 200 feet, he took up a northerly heading, the Flyer passing from the island out over the water. Below, a ferry whistle shrilled piercingly, another vessel added a deep-throated blast and within seconds the harbor was filled with a furious cacophony of sound. Apparently intending to go up the river, Wilbur proceeded straight north. Then, gently, he heeled over to the left, came around in a slow arc and took a sighting on the Statue of Liberty, about a mile away. "The huge form of the statue gleamed in the morning sunlight," wrote a reporter of the moment, "and seemed more stately and somber than ever."

Abreast of the statue at this moment was the *Lusitania,* outward bound. As soon as the ship's captain had been informed that the Flyer was in the air he had slowed his engines to give the nearly two thousand passengers crowding the decks a chance to view the unique sight.

Straight toward the colossal figure went the Flyer. For once no wind gusts disturbed the air and it was probably this absence of turbulence that prompted Wilbur to approach as close as he did. Banking sharply, he zoomed behind the statue, no more than twenty feet from the metal drapery of the waist. For an instant the machine disappeared from the startled view of New Yorkers, all of whom, it was found later, were sure the machine was headed for the most spectacular crash in history. Soaring around the waist, the tilted Flyer passed under the torch and the upraised arm, its forty-foot wings almost matching the arm in length. Around the waist he whirled once more, then with wings leveled he turned toward Governor's Island.

Down to his left, about a hundred yards away, drifted the *Lusitania,* its open main deck only a few feet below the level of the Flyer, its four huge smokestacks, painted red, towering far above. Cutting in front of the slowly moving ship, Wilbur looked down to see "everywhere on her decks whirlpools of handkerchiefs, hats, umbrellas, and even wraps and coats that the passengers had stripped from their backs and were waving in delirious joy." Suddenly there broke over the harbor a deafening blast from the proud ship's foghorn, the mightily vibrating sound drowning even the clatter of the Flyer's engine in Wilbur's ears. It was a salute, as one reporter happily put it, "from the Queen of the water to the King of the air."

Two minutes later the Flyer was back on the ground at Governor's Island. As Wilbur climbed down a wave of reporters crowded round, all wrought to unusual excitement by the daring of the flight and even more by its symbolic beauty. And again the first thing they noticed was Wilbur's extreme calm, so unlike the customary exuberance of other pilots. But this time a faint smile played on his closed lips as he "put his hands in his pockets and looked just a trifle pleased."

His next flight, he announced, would be the official one, the long one. He would go up the river to where the tomb of General Grant sat in granite dignity on a hill beside the shore. With the return, this would make a flight of more than twenty miles, double the contract distance. If the weather was right it would take place next morning.

Thursday brought high winds and dark clouds that hung, low and threatening, over the harbor, in the afternoon releasing a light sprinkling of rain. Of the two aviators, Curtiss was the more disappointed. His contract week was up on Saturday and he would have to depart for another exhibition in the South, yet he disliked intensely having to leave, a failure in the eyes of New Yorkers. On Saturday the clouds had lifted but the winds were still high; Curtiss decided to stay over one more day. The next afternoon, with the wind decreased a little, he got off, went to fifty feet, circled once and came down. "I did not like the way the air was boiling," he explained. Early the next morning he left.

During the four days of inaction Wilbur had to explain more than once to reporters why he would not fly in strong winds, why he would not be hurried by the impatience of New Yorkers. Finally he ventured an observation familiar in the mouths of those who entertain the public in hazardous performances. "Those people who do not know me," he said soberly, "would not in the nature of things care particularly if I should be hurt. They might even enjoy the excitement. Do you see those photographers? They would get better pictures if I should fall. No, I shall not fly until the wind is just right."

Monday, October 4, the day after Curtiss' departure, was bright and sunny, with little wind. At a few minutes before 10 A.M. Wilbur took off, climbed to 200 feet, and headed north toward the tip of Manhattan, cheered on his way by a numbing volume of blasts and shrieks from ships' horns and whistles. As he neared the shore he veered slightly left and flew along past low wharves and warehouses. Every available inch of ground below him, it seemed, was occupied by spectators, all waving and shouting, as were the roofs and the windows of the buildings.

At a speed of just over forty miles an hour the Flyer churned along, following the gradual curve of the shore. Once a powerful gust of wind rushing out from the canyon between the high buildings at Twenty-Third Street struck the machine, kicking it sideways and slewing the nose around slightly because of the canoe, but Wilbur quickly regained control. He kept to the line of the shore as it curved, at Thirty-Fourth Street, toward the northeast. Then it ran straight for as far as Wilbur could see. Ahead, the river stretched into the distance until it faded away between dim hills.

Where the shore was clear of structures he dropped down lower to give a better view to the spectators, at times getting as low as twenty feet, and rising again whenever a wharf or a warehouse stretched across his path. Many boats and ships, at piers or at anchor, passed beneath his wings, their occupants gaping upward.

After flying for nearly twenty minutes, he spotted the squat, square bulk of Grant's Tomb, offshore from which were anchored the British cruisers *Drake* and *Argyll*. He banked left, swept around the ships, and headed across the river. This simple maneuver sent a thrill through the watchers below, as it had thrilled people in France the year before. For almost all New Yorkers, Wilbur Wright's Flyer was the first airplane they had ever beheld in flight; to see in action, close up, the birdlike control they had read about was immensely stirring. "The most entrancing sight," recalled one man years later, "was his turning of the airship for the return flight. The machine seemed to float and run. . . ."

Straight across the river Wilbur flew until he neared the Pali-

sades, their lofty top edge looming just above him. Then he turned
left again, heading south. Along the New Jersey shore were anchored many of the American and foreign warships and Wilbur
now had the satisfaction of doing what he had planned and failed
to do two years before. Over ship after ship he flew, encountering
an occasional updraft that jostled the Flyer without seriously upsetting it. To the cheering of their crews, he passed over Italy's
Etna and *Etruria,* two French dreadnaughts, and two German. For
the first time an airplane was flying over battleships and, as the
newspapers the next day indicated, for the naval officers watching
it was not a comforting sight—it was "another indication of the important part aeroplanes would play in the next big war," as a German officer remarked.

Below, Wilbur now saw the American cruiser *Mississippi* moving downriver. He zoomed across its bow. Ahead, at anchor, was
another American cruiser, *Minnesota,* on its bridge Commander
William Simms, the man who had dramatically improved the navy's
gunnery efficiency. Over the *Minnesota's* stacks went the Flyer to a
chorus of cheers from the crowded decks. Later that day Simms
was asked what would happen if such an event should take place
in wartime. "At the height Mr. Wright was flying the ship would
probably be able to get the range and destroy the aeroplane,"
Simms replied confidently. "At a greater altitude and going at the
speed Wright flew, the aviator's chance of dropping anything on a
battleship would be small." It would take a decade and a half of
arguing, and the efforts of General Billy Mitchell, to disprove that
theory.

This was not only Wilbur's last public flight, it was his last of any
length. He would go up again only to help in training pilots. Since
the day when he told his father that he thought aeronautics offered
a slight chance for fame and fortune, nine years had passed. Now
he had wealth and his name was known in every civilized country
on the globe—a globe his genius had made infinitely smaller. But he
would not have much time in which to enjoy his triumph. He had
less than three years to live and almost all of that would be spent
in the hurry of business affairs.

Some ten minutes after making his turn round *Drake* and *Argyll* he had reached the harbor again. Near Ellis Island he made a quarter-turn to the left and started his descent to Governor's Island, the focus of a million pairs of eyes, the object of an almost hysterical salute from the thousand vessels spread below.

Overhead, shining full on Flyer and pilot, the unclouded sun was reaching toward its meridian.

Notes and Sources

All sources are given in shortened form: usually author's last name, publication, and date. They may be fully identified by reference to the bibliography. For four sources, repeatedly cited, the following abbreviations are used:

Papers   *The Papers of Wilbur and Orville Wright*, edited by Marvin Mc-Farland, with Notes, Commentary and Appendices, New York, McGraw-Hill Company, 1953. 2 vols., 1278 pp.

Kelly,   Kelly, Fred C., *The Wright Brothers: A Biography Authorized by*
Wrights   *Orville Wright*. New York, Harcourt, Brace and Company, 1943. 340 pp.

Miracle   *Miracle at Kitty Hawk, The Letters of Wilbur and Orville Wright*, edited [with Notes and Commentary] by Fred C. Kelly, New York, Farrar, Straus, and Young, 1951. 481 pp.

First   *First Rebuttal Deposition of Wilbur Wright*, pp. 473–614, com-
Rebuttal   plainant's record, *Wright Company* v. *Herring-Curtiss Company and Glenn H. Curtiss*, United States District Court, Western District of New York, vol. 1, 1912.

CHAPTER 1
THE LONG SILENCE

The facts of Wilbur's illness, death, and funeral are from Bishop Wright's diary, *Papers*, 1043–46; *The New York Times*, May 31, June 1, 2, 1912; also obituaries in the *World, Sun, Tribune, Herald,* and *American,* all of New York, for May 31, 1912.

On first falling ill, Wilbur said he believed he had contracted typhoid by eating some contaminated fish in Boston a few days before. The family always felt that he might have fought off the disease had he not been exhausted from his involvement in half a dozen lawsuits against patent infringers which kept him traveling, studying, conferring with lawyers, testifying, and making long technical depositions. Careful as ever, a week after the illness began Wilbur made his will, leaving $50,000 each to Reuchlin, Lorin, and Katharine, which represented his cash holdings at the time. His share of the patents and the Wright Aeronautical Company went to Orville.

On the day of Wilbur's death his father wrote in his diary: "This morning at 3:15 Wilbur passed away, aged 45 years, 1 month and 14 days. A short life, full of consequences. An unfailing intellect, imperturbable temper, great self-reliance, and as great modesty. Seeing the right clearly, pursuing it steadily, he lived and died. . . ." *Papers,* 1046.

"Father of Flight"—*New York Herald,* May 31, 1912.

"Conqueror of the Air"—*Outlook Magazine,* June 8, 1912.

"The Man Who Made Flying Possible"—*Collier's,* June 15, 1912.

"The father of the great new . . ."—*New York Herald,* May 31, 1912.

See also, for similar expressions regarding Wilbur: "Death of the Dean of Birdmen," *Hearst's Magazine,* July 1912; "Inventor Who Solved the Problem of Flight," *Current Literature,* July 1912; "Passing of a Great Inventor," *Scientific American,* June 8, 1912.

"It is not known how . . ."—*New York Sun,* May 31, 1912.

"More than any other man . . ."—*New York Times,* October 4, 1913.

"In memory and intellect there . . ."—*Papers,* 1046.

Orville's life and work after Wilbur's death. In a short preface to the official biography Kelly explains that the book does not cover "the scientific researches and numerous inventions by Orville Wright since the death of his brother." That Orville did much aeronautical research, especially during World War I and just after, is undoubted, but the result of all this work remains largely unknown, and what the numerous inventions may have been is not discoverable anywhere in the existing literature. The listing under "Patents" in *Papers,* 1228–32, allows him only one new aeronautical device, but gives as coinventor a certain J. M. H. Jacobs, an employee of the Wright Aeronautical Company. Outside aeronautics he patented a toy and a decoding machine. So little is known of Orville's later life, especially his last twenty-five years, that the only definite activities attributed to him are private consultant to the Wright Company and member of the National Advisory Committee for Aeronautics, which held periodic meetings in Washington.

The automatic stability device for which Orville was awarded the Collier trophy in 1913. Drawings for this had been prepared by Wilbur as early as 1907. *Papers,* 771, 1025, 1039. The *Journal of the Royal Aeronautical Society,* Dec. 1953, 784, records the fact that Wilbur was at work on the device as early as 1904; McMahon, *Wright Brothers,* 291, supports this date. Patent on the device was applied for in February 1908 but was not granted until October 1913, seventeen months after Wilbur's death. *Papers,* 1228. It is possible, of course, that Orville did contribute substantially to it from the start.

"Tell them I'd rather have . . ."—Quoted in a letter to the author from Marvin McFarland, editor of *Papers* and a friend of Findley's.

"Too personal"—Lindbergh, *Wartime Journals,* 383.

"Due to his own honesty . . ."—Lindbergh, *Wartime Journals,* 446.
"I could see that he had . . ."—Lindbergh, *Wartime Journals,* 384.

The Findley manuscript. In 1929 *Popular Science Monthly* published a brief biography of the Wrights in six parts ("The Real Fathers of Flight," January–June). Its author was John R. McMahon, the young man who in 1915 had helped write the original Findley manuscript rejected by Orville. The *Popular Science* series was a rewritten version of that work. Orville, who had no connection with the magazine publication, the following year tried to prevent a reissue of the serial as a book by the firm of Little, Brown. He failed but he did, it appears, manage to gain an accommodation. His reasons for this action are related to facts developed in my Chapter Two. See Notes, 252–53.

"No more success than . . ."—Lindbergh, *Wartime Journals,* 285.

The Kelly biography. The deficiencies of this volume, including the erroneous claims made on Orville's behalf, are discussed in various places in the text and Notes. See 252–53, 258, 261, 265, 268, 279, 285–86, 288, 290.

The disposition of the Wright papers after Orville's death is detailed in the Introduction to *Papers,* vii–xx. Orville's executors, in making publication of the more important documents a condition of the donation of the papers to the Library of Congress, offered the following rather curious explanation: "It would forestall the possible misuse of any of the material or distortion of the truth by careless or unscrupulous writers in the future . . . Orville Wright himself had long been concerned with these various possibilities." *Papers,* xv–xvi. Orville's concern with "distortion,'" it is now fairly clear, centered on the possibility that other writers might reach conclusions at variance with his own.

"One man alone and unaided . . ."—*Papers,* 17.

The most immediate indication in *Papers* of Wilbur's leadership is a group of a half-dozen letters, all written by Wilbur and recording the start of his interest in the flying problem, as well as his plans for experiment. Even by themselves they offer almost startling indication of his primacy, startling also in that their long-delayed publication called forth so little comment. In all six letters Wilbur writes as if Orville did not exist, constantly referring to "my plans," "my observations," "my experiments," "my machine." Just before the start of his first trip to Kitty Hawk he had this to say: "For some years I have been afflicted with the belief that flight is possible to man. My disease has increased in severity and I feel that it will soon cost me an increased amount of money if not my life. I have been trying to arrange my affairs in such a way that I can devote my entire time for a few months to experiment in this field." *Papers,* 15. A little later in a letter to his father he explains: "I am certain I can reach a point much in advance of any previous workers in this field." *Papers,* ix. At the time of the writing of this letter, the first great discovery, the principal of lateral balance, had already been made, and the first glider constructed. Again to his father: "My idea is merely to experiment and practice with a view to solving the problem of equilibrium. I have plans which I hope to find much in advance of the methods tried by previous experimenters." *Papers,* 26.

It was not until after the first season of experimenting at Kitty Hawk that Wilbur's references change from singular to plural. "I" becomes "we" and "my" becomes "our." Judging from the brothers' subsequent extreme care in maintaining a united image, some sort of pact or agreement may have been made at Kitty Hawk—the advantage to Wilbur of having the close assistance of his brother's considerable mechanical skills and the alert sympathy growing from long association is obvious. Even this retreat into the plural, however, fails to disguise the facts plainly evident in *Papers*. Through the first thousand pages, up to his death, Wilbur's presence is overwhelming. Literally all the serious correspondence, much of it involving pioneer mathematical analysis on aeronautical concepts that were as yet only in vague focus, was handled by Wilbur—and the voice that speaks from these letters is clear, controlled, and *single*. Orville's presence in the first 240 pages of *Papers* is due to the use of extracts from a deposition he made eight years after his brother's death, and to his chatty letters to his sister. Through the next 800 pages or so he is represented only by his Kitty Hawk diary entries and by an occasional letter. It is no answer to this remarkably revealing situation to say, as Kelly says, that Orville disliked letter writing, or that Wilbur had a "habit of saying or writing 'I' when he meant 'we.' " *Miracle*, 8.

From the above facts alone, Orville's secondary role is apparent, a conclusion that is made certain by extended analysis of the documents themselves, as presented throughout my narrative and in the Notes, and by the collateral research recorded herein.

"The spirit of his brother, Will . . ."—the observation occurs in a page-one interview with Orville, *New York Times Magazine*, July 17, 1927.

CHAPTER 2

WILBUR WRIGHT'S LOST DECADE

Details of the brothers' schooling in Dayton would be of particular interest now, but I am informed by the Dayton Board of Education that a search of the files has failed to turn up any records for either brother. From various mentions in early literature it appears that both attended Steele High School, yet a story in the *Dayton Daily News*, December 18, 1927, also places Wilbur at Central High School, on 4th Street and Wilkinson Avenue. The story is by John Feight, Dayton tax appraisal agent, who recalls that his classmate, Wilbur, played backfield on the school football team, and describes him as a fast runner, but quiet. Before Dayton, the brothers had attended school in Cedar Rapids, Iowa, and Richmond, Indiana, where the father's duties had taken the family.

Wilbur's youthful decision to enter the ministry is in Charnley, *Wright Brothers*, 17, and Sullivan, *Our Times*, vol. II, 569. The manuscripts of both these writers were checked by the Wright family. The girl who interested Wilbur is in Charnley, *Wright Brothers*, 24.

The hockey accident. The first pointed mention of this, and of the resulting invalidism, was made in McMahon, *Popular Science*, January 1929, which, as noted, was derived from the Findley manuscript. About a year before this, Charnley's *Wright Brothers* told the story more briefly, saying the accident had been a shock to Wilbur's nervous system, had kept him at home for four years, forced him to give up his plans for Yale, and that this change in plans had "shaped his whole career." Kelly, *Wrights*, 26 (1943) refers to the accident so briefly and vaguely, and then fills in the years 1885–92 so generally, that the reader derives no sense at all of the eight-year gap in Wilbur's working life—and this was thirty years after Wilbur's death, when it might have been expected that there would no longer be any reason for concealing his long invalidism, if there had ever been.

There is little reason for doubting that it was Orville who suppressed the facts of his brother's lost decade and a specific instance can now be documented. When Orville attempted to block republication in book form of McMahon's *Popular Science* series (see Notes, 251) he charged unauthorized use of private materials. Since many of McMahon's facts had indeed been derived from the Wrights' private collection through Findley, the charge should have carried decisive weight, and yet the book *was* published. That some sort of agreement was reached is evident and it can be shown that at least a part of the agreement concerned alterations in the text, some of which are relevant here. The first change relates to Wilbur's long period of invalidism and its role in turning his thoughts to flight. In the magazine text, in discussing the hockey accident and its consequences, McMahon writes:

> . . . his athletic activity led to an accident without which the world would have no airplane today.

In the book this plain statement has been altered and softened so that its meaning is not only obscure but equivocal:

> . . . his athletic activity led to an accident that was not less than fateful, at least this is a statement of high probability.

And then the text of the book fails to say just how this accident was "fateful." In the same connection two other revealing sentences were dropped entirely: "How could this boyish misfortune promote a world discovery?" and "The effect in poor health kept Wilbur at home for years." What remains in the text of McMahon's book is only the fact of the accident and the vague statement that Wilbur was in delicate health for "a long period." This is the same way the incident was handled later in the Kelly biography.

Another significant change in McMahon's text between magazine and book is the addition of a short passage to the book which does not appear, is not even implied, in the magazine, and that firmly sets Orville far above his brother. "Despite a popular belief to the contrary," reads the interpolated passage, "he had more initiative than Wilbur. He was the prime mover and originator. He looked first into the unknown." Nowhere else, not even in the Kelly book, did Orville permit himself to be so elevated, and all the evidence shows that Wilbur was looking into the "unknown" for more than a year before Orville joined him.

Still another change obscured the authoritative nature of much of the material in McMahon's book. The following sentence was deleted: "It was my privilege to study the unpublished documents of the Wright brothers, their diaries, letters, and family records, as well as to talk at length with Orville, his father and sister, while staying for several weeks at their home." Thus McMahon's book was left to enter the world as an orphan. (His visit to the Wright home took place in June, 1915, when he remained, with Findley, for some two weeks. Bishop Wright's diary, transcript of unpublished pages.)

"It seemed to everyone . . ."—McMahon, *Popular Science*, February 1929.

"Several times in the years . . ."—*Papers*, 187.

"What does Will do?"—Ivonette Miller (daughter of Lorin Wright) in a letter to the author, quoting from Reuchlin's letter in her possession. Mrs. Miller remembers her uncle Wilbur very well, having been sixteen at his death. To-day she is one of the very few people still living who flew with him. In 1911 she went up with him a number of times at Huffman's pasture. She is also one of the few still living, perhaps the only one, who witnessed the secret flights at Huffman's in 1904–5.

"She seems to have had . . ."—*American Magazine*, June 1909.

"Could not support a wife . . ."—Sullivan, *Our Times*, vol. II, 571.

"Will kept saying he didn't . . ."—Saunders, *Collier's*, December 25, 1948.

The Ten Dayton Boys. Information provided by Ivonette Miller, who also supplied a menu (printed by Orville) for one of the club's annual dinners, dated "November 1st. 1890." The card also carries the legend: "Fifth Annual Banquet of the T. D. B. at the Residence of Lorin and Wilbur Wright." The club is also mentioned in *World's Work* magazine, August 1910, where there is a photograph showing some of the club members outside the Wright home after Wilbur's triumphant return from France. The quotation about Wilbur's "fine bass" is also from this article, as are the facts about Orville's newspaper, *The West Side News.*

"Intellectual activity is . . ."—*Miracle*, 9.

"When he had something on . . ."—Ivonette Miller to the author.

"This man is strange and . . ."—quoted in *New York Times*, June 1, 1912.

"Mr. Wright will go down . . ."—New York *Herald*, August 7, 1908.

"Wilbur did not suffer in . . ."—Brewer, *The Aeronautical Journal*, July–Sept., 1916, 133; this is an obituary article reprinted from the same magazine's issue of July 1912.

"Fine-drawn, weather-beaten face . . ."—Harper, *Fifty Years in Flying*, 110.

"Who would apparently say . . ."—Ruhl, *Collier's*, May 30, 1908.

"Without a trace of vanity . . ."—*Scientific American*, June 8, 1912.

"unable to engage in much . . ."—Kelly, *Wrights*, 26.

"I think there is a slight . . ."—*Papers*, ix.

"It is the only great . . ."—*Miracle*, 27.

CHAPTER 3

THE DREAM BEGINS

The Wrights stated repeatedly that their first interest (meaning Wilbur's first interest) in the problem of flight was generated by an article on Lilienthal appearing in some newspaper or magazine, the exact source not given. Date was specified as about 1895–96. My search has turned up only three possi-bilities that fit, not counting ordinary news items which were always brief. First was the *McClure's* article, with the author identified only as "Vernon." The second was a shorter piece in *The New York Times* for February 23, 1896, entitled "When We Take to Flying—What Has Been Done So Far in the Way of Aeronautics." In this the work of Lilienthal is presented rather briefly and with little detail, along with some facts about such other experi-menters as Maxim and Chanute. The third was by Lilienthal himself, "Prac-tical Experiments for the Development of Human Flight," *Scientific American*, March 7, 1896; though of fair length, it talks mostly of his latest experiments with a biplane glider, explaining his weight-shifting technique for stability, and has nothing to say on the actual construction of the machine or the principles underlying it. I am satisfied that the *McClure's* article, if it was not Wilbur's first knowledge of Lilienthal, was the primary source of his permanent interest in aeronautics. Perhaps he did not come across it until some months after its publication in September 1894.

"A passive interest which . . . "—*Papers*, 103.

The toy helicopter was recalled by Wilbur in a letter of May 30, 1899, *Papers*, 4. It is also referred to by the brothers in *Century Magazine*, September 1908, and Kelly, *Wrights*, 8.

"Darting through the air . . . ."—Newcomb, *McClure's*, September 1901.

The first recorded attempt at powered flight with a full-size machine was that by Félix Du Temple in France in 1874, when Wilbur was seven years old. Steam-powered, the machine was a total failure. Ten years later a Russian, A. F. Mozhaiski, made the second try, also with steam and also failing. Both men launched their machines from long down-ramp runs. In 1890 a Frenchman, Clément Ader, became the third man to fail, though he later claimed that he had achieved a "flight" of about 150 feet. If true, this would make Ader, and not Maxim, the first man to lift a heavier-than-air machine from level ground by its own power. The records on this attempt are very obscure, however, and some later claims of Ader's have been proved false (at a second trial in 1897, a secret one under the patronage of the French army, Ader's machine definitely failed to lift). Then followed Maxim's attempt in 1894. None of the four came close to understanding the true principles of flight.

Maxim told the story of his abortive 1894 trial in an illustrated article in *Century Magazine*, January 1895. *The New York Times* reports appeared on August 3, 19, and 26, 1894.

"A flying squirrel"—*New York Times*, February 23, 1896.

"The apparatus worked well . . . ."—*New York Times*, August 12, 1896.

"Great influence"—*Miracle*, 380.

Langley. It is interesting that Langley's concern with flight, unlike da Vinci, Cayley and others, arose from observation of the *gliding* action of birds. In his article in *McClure's*, June 1897, he recalls that as a youth, "when lying in a New England pasture, I watched a hawk soaring far up in the blue, and sailing for a long time without any motion of its wings, as though it needed no work to sustain it, but was kept up there by some miracle . . . I saw it sweep, in a few seconds of its leisurely flight, over a distance that to me was encumbered with every sort of obstacle which did not exist for it . . . there was not a flutter of its pinions as it swept over the field, in a motion which seemed as effortless as its shadow. . . . After many years and in mature life I was brought to think of these things again . . ."

"The Pinnacles"—McMahon, *Popular Science*, February 1929. The brothers' habit of observing birds is variously reported in early literature. See "When the Wright Brothers Were Boys," *American Magazine*, June 1909.

CHAPTER 4

SOMETHING IN THE WING TIPS

"I am an enthusiast . . . ."—*Papers*, 5.

"One of the most remarkable . . . ."—*Aero Club of America Bulletin*, April

1912, in an article by Wilbur, "What Mouillard Did." The Mouillard quotations in my text are also from this article, a more accessible source for which is *The Aeronautical Journal* (London), July–September 1916.

Da Vinci, Cayley, and other pre-Wright experimenters. Surprising as it may sound, to date there exists no *definitive* history of the pre-Wright era, or I should say that if such a book exists I have been unable to find it though I have cast a fairly wide net. Hundreds of volumes are available which purport to tell this fascinating story, but none does much more than accumulate a mass of facts. Little attempt is made to show lines of development or to relate facts and ideas to one another. Inevitably, this void has left the way open for a number of basic errors and distortions, two leading examples of which are Leonardo da Vinci and Sir George Cayley.

For most of his life, to his death in 1519, da Vinci periodically took up the study of birds and manned flight, and left in manuscript a number of drawings and speculations. From these it is clear that his interest was entirely in flapping-wing flight. Though he was interested in the soaring and gliding of birds, he never envisioned even the possibility of the fixed-wing glider. He understood nothing of the real problems involved in flight, never considered the requirements of control or of wing lift. Neither is there any evidence that he ever attempted to fly (a favorite idea in popular presentations of his story) nor that he ever actually built wings or a machine, full-size or model, of any kind. Further, he was not a beginning but a culmination, refining and extending the more timid speculations of such earlier students as Albertus Magnus, Roger Bacon, and Albert of Saxony, perhaps also the Italian mathematician Danti and the Englishman Damian, both of whom may have actually tried gliding.

Of most interest is his manuscript treatise *On the Flight of Birds*, which shows an incisive mind at work. Even here, however, it can be seen how little he understood of the true principles of flight. And his remarks on the action of air are not based on direct observance, but are mostly transposed from the action of water. It is glory enough for da Vinci that he took a detailed and intense interest in the subject at a time when most men thought of the ability to fly as somehow supernatural. The clearest statement of all these facts may be found in Ivor Hart, *The World of Leonardo da Vinci*, Viking, 1961, and C. H. Gibbs-Smith, *Da Vinci's Aeronautics*, Science Museum, London, 1963.

A much more arresting figure than da Vinci is the Englishman Sir George Cayley, though claims on his behalf have also been exaggerated. To call him "the father of the Aeroplane" (Pritchard) or to say that he produced "the first manned—but not piloted—glider flight in history" (Gibbs-Smith) is going too far and such excesses only serve to cloud his real worth. Cayley was a wealthy baronet who dabbled in science, among other things, and as so often with such desultory studies left no permanent mark in any field. His interest in heavier-than-air flight lasted, intermittently, for about fifty years and he did manage some valuable, if generalized, insights. His hopes for a powered machine, however, always centered on wing flapping—even after the propeller-drive concept had become public.

For Cayley's biographer to say that he was "the first man in the world of flight to lay down the basic mechanical principles of heavier-than-air flight," is simply not true. Since Cayley knew nothing of the facts of wing lift, aspect ratio, longitudinal and lateral control, or the movable rudder, and was mistaken on the question of camber, it is hard to see just what "basic mechanical principles" he could have laid down. His ideas on superposing wings to gain structural strength, his observations on the dihedral, and his interest in camber, may have influenced later students, such as Henson and Stringfellow, and in that lies his real claim to distinction.

To credit Cayley with being the first man to attempt manned, fixed-wing glides is not only to distort the evidence, but it is to take that honor from the man who really deserves it. Cayley's so-called manned glides consisted of one trial in which a boy, sitting in a wheeled, boatlike contraption, under wings that were nearly square, was lifted for about ten yards after a downhill roll. A later attempt, supposedly, carried his reluctant coachman a few hundred feet across a depression in the ground, but this claim is based wholly on the recollections of Cayley's granddaughter, set down some seventy years afterwards. Cayley himself made no record of such a glide. Many years after this he did make some experiments with *unmanned* gliders, whose wings had an aspect ratio near unity, almost square. And it must be pointed out that his glider experiments, whatever they actually involved, accomplished nothing and led nowhere. Nevertheless, it is a fascinating experience to read his writings, marking as they do a sudden and fresh departure in aeronautical thought. Had he not allowed himself to be distracted by other interests he might indeed have gone far toward producing manned glider flight.

The man who, from present records, really does deserve to be called the first to attempt glider flight, risking his life in the process, was the French naval officer Jean Marie le Bris. His name can be found in all the histories of flight, yet little is known of him. Though he did not succeed in making true glides, his attempt was reasoned and sincere, not to say spectacular. Fascinated by the albatross, which he had studied many times on his cruises to the south Atlantic, in 1855 he built a full size glider that closely resembled a sea gull, with rigid wings whose angle of attack could be altered by a lever. He made a number of trials and did manage to become airborne briefly, too briefly for a true glide, and ended by breaking a leg. How much did le Bris know of Calyey's work, how much of Henson's? Did le Bris influence later men such as Du Temple, who patented his first designs in 1857? Was le Bris a formative influence on Lilienthal, who began his bird studies in the early 1860's? For that matter, what did Lilienthal know of Cayley? If a link here could be established, then Cayley might indeed be entitled to more direct credit and a higher rank. But such questions, in the present incomplete state of aeronautical history, must remain unanswered.

"At the time there was no . . ."—*First Rebuttal*, 476–78.

"These lateral tiltings . . ."—*First Rebuttal*, 481.

The pigeon incident. In telling of his pigeon sighting, Wilbur says "we noticed," employing the disguising plural that had by then become habitual with him. But it is possible to show that the observation and the conclusion from it were due to Wilbur alone. In the Wrights' Notebook A, *Papers*, 34–37, there is a series of bird observations, fifteen in all, followed by a series of twelve observations on glider flight. These notes, all of them in Wilbur's handwriting, supposedly were made during the first weeks at Kitty Hawk in September 1900—*Papers* so dates them and prints all twenty-seven observations as a continuous series. However, in the Notebook itself between the fifteen bird notes and the twelve on the glider there occur two blank pages, both numbered, suggesting that the bird notes may have been made some time earlier. (Above the bird notes there is a date, "1900," but it is in pencil, where the same date over the glider notes, and the notes themselves, are in ink.) And this possibility is made certain by the fact that the tenth bird note records, in very similar language, the same pigeon sighting that Wilbur described in his *First Rebuttal* and assigned to the summer of 1899. I give the entire passage, from photostats of the original Notebook A, so that it may be compared with the passage from the *First Rebuttal* quoted in my text:

> A pigeon moving directly from the observer oscillates very rapidly laterally, especially when moving slowly, just before lighting. The wings are not drawn in to any perceptible extent first on one side and then on the other as would be the case if the bird were balancing by increasing or decreasing the area of either wing alternately. Moreover, the oscillations of lateral balance are so rapid that gravity alone could not possibly produce them. The bird certainly twists its wing tips so that the wind strikes one wing on top and the other on its lower side, thus by force changing the bird's lateral position.

One further point: in their records concerning Kitty Hawk, the brothers mention many kinds of birds—eagle, buzzard, brown thrasher, wren, sparrow, hawk, gannet, sea chicken, "and dozens of birds which I do not know by name." But nowhere do they mention seeing pigeons. I believe that the fifteen bird observations in Notebook A were all originally made no later than June 1899 in the vicinity of Dayton, perhaps at The Pinnacles, where the two are reported to have spent so much time watching birds.

The Kelly biography says nothing at all about Wilbur's pigeon observation, but instead gives credit to Orville for the first conception of the principle of wing-tip angle variance, from which wing warping was derived. As Kelly explains it, the idea appears to have leaped into Orville's mind from nowhere: "Why, he asked himself, wouldn't it be possible for the operator to vary the inclination of sections of the wings at the tips, and thus obtain force for restoring balance from the difference in lifts of the two opposite wing tips?" (48–49). Just this bare statement is offered, without any elaboration or background. In view of the information above, perhaps there is no need to comment further, except to say that if Orville did make such a suggestion, then it must have been *after* Wilbur had deduced the principle of wing-tip angle variance from the pigeon sighting.

One question regarding the pigeon sighting continues to goad me. Through what process of logic did Wilbur conclude that the bird was controlling its balance by moving its wing tips? He could not have observed this directly (I have spent hours studying flocks of pigeons and can vouch for the impossibility of following their wing movements, even when I knew what to look for). In his recollection he states that the conclusion did not come until some unspecified time after the sighting. What other studies took place in the interim? I suggest that Wilbur may have received some hints from two books he is known to have read: *Animal Locomotion,* by J. B. Pettigrew (1874), and *The Flight of Birds* by E. J. Marey (1890). While neither book offers any precise statement of the way in which birds achieve lateral balance, each does offer some material that could have at least set Wilbur on the right track.

In Pettigrew, p. 219, there is a passage which calls attention to the flexibility of the bird wing and the way in which it can assume different angles (the italics are Pettigrew's):

> The wing of a flying creature, as I have taken pains to show, is *not rigid* . . . on the contrary, it is capable of moving in all its parts, and attacks the air *at an infinite variety of angles.* . . . If anyone watches an insect, a bat or a bird when dressing its wings, he will observe that it can incline the undersurface of the wing at a great variety of angles to the horizon. This it does by causing the posterior or thin margin of the wing [rear edge] to rotate around the anterior or thick margin [front edge] as an axis.

When Wilbur read that passage, his mind made fertile by three years of concentrated effort, did he perhaps see again in his mind's eye that rapidly oscillating pigeon, this time with a sudden close-up of the angled wing tips, the thin rear edges subtly rotating round the thick leading ones?

Pettigrew adds to his above remarks a sentence that, at first glance, seems to be a full anticipation of Wilbur but which turns out to refer to something else entirely: "As a result of this movement the two margins are forced into double and opposite curves and the wing converted into a *plastic helix or screw.*" If these "two margins" are taken to be the rear edges of left and right wings—an interpretation not unlikely at a first reading—then Pettigrew here offers a perfect description in brief of Wilbur's "torsion" principle, indicating not only the flexible twisting action of the tips, but its simultaneity. As the context makes clear, however, Pettigrew was not referring to the rear margins of right and left wings. He had in mind the front and rear edges of the same wing, and was explaining his personal theory of bird propulsion.

A little further on in Pettigrew's text Wilbur would have encountered another reference to lateral control in the bird—one which, rather strangely, describes the *result* of the torsion action without bothering to explain how it happens. No one, Pettigrew told his readers, had yet made provision in the wing of a flying machine for "conferring elasticity upon it, or of giving to it that infinite variety of angles that would enable it to seize and disentangle itself from the air with the necessary rapidity." That simple eight-word phrase —"to seize and disentangle itself from the air"—may still be taken as a good short description of the aerodynamic principle that underlies lateral control. In maintaining its lateral balance an airplane's wings really do "seize" the air; they really do "disentangle" themselves, slipping as it were from an unwelcome embrace. But again, whether all this made any impression on Wilbur is now beyond knowing.

With the Marey book it is not a matter of text, but of pictures—stunning pioneer photographs of *pigeons* in flight. In one sequence there are a half-dozen stop-action shots in which the wing torsion, the angle variance at the tips, can be seen, even if vaguely. To a desultory reader Marey's pictures might have revealed little. What might they not have told a student who came to them with a mind fully prepared to analyze, and with eyes to notice?

For either of these books to have played a part in Wilbur's pigeon deduction, he would have had to encounter them by early summer 1899, and there is no direct evidence to that effect. However, according to his own recollection (*First Rebuttal, 474*) he did at that time read "a book on ornithology" which, as he said, further stimulated his interest in the problem of flight. The book was not named but the reference to ornithology could fit either Pettigrew or Marey.

Admittedly, all of this is a playing with possibility. In the end it must be conceded that certain knowledge of the precise way in which the all-important torsion principle "came" to Wilbur was lost at his death. If he did find some clues in Pettigrew or Marey, it is only fair to point out that those same clues had long been available to anyone else who cared to make use of them.

"If the rear edge of the . . ."—*Papers*, 18.

The wing-torsion principle before Wilbur. It is sometimes charged that this idea was anticipated by one or another of the men who in their writings had specified something vaguely similar—Le Bris (1855), P. D'Esterno (1864), M. Boulton (1868), R. Goupil (1884), L. P. Mouillard (1887), A. F. Zahm (1890), C. Ader (1897), and one or two others of dimmer recollection. The attempt to prove such anticipation was the main legal thrust of all the Wrights' opponents in court. But it was firmly and repeatedly established, first by Judge Learned Hand, that there existed "no prior art."

The box-warp incident. This story has been given many times, first in the depositions Wilbur made for various court cases in 1911–12. It can be found in Charnley, McMahon, Sullivan, and Kelly, as well as any number of magazine articles. In these retellings, most of which came under the eye of Orville, the superficial details are not always identical but there is no contradiction in essentials. My description of it is based on *Testimony of Wilbur Wright*, 781–82, Complainant's Record, *Wright* v. *Herring-Curtiss*, 1912, and his *Deposition*, 46–49, in the case of *Charles Lamson* v. *Wright Company*, U.S. District Court, Southern District of Ohio, 1912, as modified and expanded by the probable elements in the other sources named above. None of the accounts states that the customer entered the store wheeling a bicycle or that Wilbur fixed it on the spot. Yet this seems certain from the fact that the customer (fortunately!) left the empty box behind. If the customer had purchased the tube to take home and do the repairs himself it is not likely that the tube would have been removed from its box.

Date of the box-warp incident. Wilbur said that this occurred during "the latter part of July 1899," while Katharine's friend Harriet Silliman was a guest at the Wright home, and that the kite was tested before the end of the month. Bishop Wright's diary shows that Miss Silliman arrived on Thursday, July 20 (transcript supplied by Mrs. Miller; see also *Papers*, 8) and remained until July 29. The day of the incident, Wilbur recalled, Miss Silliman, Katharine, and Orville had gone visiting, but Miss Silliman was ill for three or four days beginning on July 24. Thus, probable dates for the incident become July 20–22 (July 23 being a Sunday when Wilbur would not have been at the shop). Wilbur also said that the making of both the bamboo model and the experimental kite occupied only five or six days, thus the probable dates for the kite trials become July 28–31. *Testimony of Wilbur Wright*, 782, *Wright Company* v. *Herring-Curtiss; Deposition of Wilbur Wright*, 50–51, *Charles Lamson* v. *Wright*, 1912.

"I flew this apparatus . . ."—*Testimony of Wilbur Wright*, 783 (as above). According to some testimony of Orville, same source, two of the boys who witnessed the kite experiments were their neighbors, Walter and John Reiniger. The bamboo model is also from this record.

That the experimental kite of 1899 had an arced camber and not a parabola can be seen in the drawing Orville supplied with a 1920 deposition. *Papers*, 9.

I have omitted describing a second control element built into the experimental kite, the ability of the upper surface to shear forward, either the entire surface or one corner at a time, as a means of gaining longitudinal control. This was an effort to imitate what was at first thought to be the bird's action, but it was quickly dropped in favor of a forward elevator.

CHAPTER 5

KITTY HAWK 1900

The Wrights kept no diary of the six weeks spent at Kitty Hawk in 1900, but their letters home and to Chanute afterwards, *Papers*, 23–46, supply the basis for a fairly exact chronology as well as a nearly day-by-day reconstruction of their work. When these are analyzed in conjunction with Wilbur's 1901 lecture, *Papers*, 99–119, and his various legal depositions of 1911–12, a coherent picture begins to emerge. I have also drawn on such sources as Kelly and McMahon when they are not in contradiction with the primary documents. It is not feasible to record here, in every instance, the details of the analysis by which all my facts were derived but a few examples of the process will be found below. Full sources for the more important facts are given.

I do not claim to have recovered every hour and every action of those historic forty-one days (and the same may be said for the three succeeding visits to Kitty Hawk). All possibility of that was lost when Wilbur died and Orville chose to keep silent.

The fifteen-gauge measurement for the truss and warping wires is in a letter of Wilbur's, *Papers*, 41. Engineering manuals of the day supplied the thickness.

"The beach here is about . . ."—*Miracle*, 25.

"You would find here nearly . . ."—*Miracle*, 26.

The uncertainty about Orville's joining his brother at Kitty Hawk is in a letter of Katharine to her father: "If they can arrange it, Orv will go down . . ." *Papers*, 23.

The storm on Albemarle Sound and the difficulties with the schooner are in a long memorandum by Wilbur, *Papers*, 23–5.

"There may be one or two . . ."—*Papers*, 26.

The elevator. The first suggestion for the use of this device is attributed by Kelly, *Wrights*, 53, to Orville. No mention is made of the fact that the bare idea of an elevator was old or that Maxim had made the most prominent use of it before the Wrights, though unsuccessfully. Since Wilbur had been studying aeronautics for some time before Orville joined him, he must have been familiar with it. In his 1901 lecture, using his habitual "we," he says the elevator was settled on only "after long study." *Papers*, 104. Neither of the brothers, however, recorded much about it. One feature that I have chosen to pass over was its initial flexibility. At first only the rear portion could be moved, being bent up or down as the situation demanded. It was retained in this form through the experiments of 1901, then changed to its final form, a rigid surface with both front and rear edges free, pivoting on a fulcrum.

"I do not expect to rise . . ."—*Papers*, 26.

"When once a machine is . . ."—*Papers*, 26.

"Have any strong expectation . . ."—*Papers*, 27.

Camber in the 1900 glider. The only explanation for using a parabola, initially, occurs in Wilbur's 1901 lecture: "To be on the safe side, instead of using the arc of a circle we made the curve of our machine [in the wings] very abrupt at the front so as to expose the least possible area to this downward pressure [on the leading edge]." *Papers*, 110.

The Chanute truss. This was Chanute's adaptation of a standard bridge-building bracing technique, the Pratt Truss.

Date of the first kite trial at Kitty Hawk. The chronology of the 1900 experiments is nowhere given explicitly. I reached the October 6 date as follows: In a letter of Sunday, October 14, *Papers*, 29, Orville says they had already been out with the kite-glider "on three different days." He then places the third trial on Wednesday afternoon, October 10. The brothers started living in the tent on October 4, at which time the glider was not yet complete. Since the 7th was a Sunday, and Tuesday, the 9th, had winds of 36 mph, that leaves the 5th, 6th, and 8th for the other two days. Wilbur said the first kite trial was made on the day the machine was completed. This was most probably not the 5th, since the brothers would then have been out on the 5th, 6th, 8th, and 10th, making four days instead of the three Orville mentioned. Thus October 6 seems certain.

"Let me down!"—McMahon, *Popular Science*, February 1929; *Papers*, 927.

"No one can realize . . ."—Vernon, *McClure's*, September 1894.

The lift deficiency found in the wings on October 6 is given in Wilbur's 1901 lecture, *Papers*, 105, which also supplied other details of the day's work.

"Some feats which almost . . ."—*Papers*, 30.

The glider wreck of October 10 is in a letter of Orville, *Papers*, 29–30.

"Will is 'most sick . . ."—*Papers*, 31.

"Til they sound like . . ."—*Papers*, 32.

Extracts from Orville's letter describing Kitty Hawk are in *Papers*, 29–33.

"When we got through . . ."—*Papers*, 38.

The semiglides were made on October 20. They are recorded in a letter of Wilbur's, *Papers*, 43; his 1901 lecture, *Papers*, 106; and his *First Rebuttal*, 484–85.

"Although in appearance . . ."—*Papers*, 43.

"The ease with which . . ."—*Papers*, 44.

The Tates' use of the discarded glider is in McMahon, *Popular Science*, February 1929, and Kelly, *Wrights*, 66.

CHAPTER 6

KITTY HAWK 1901

Again in 1901 the brothers spent just forty-one days at Kitty Hawk. On seven of those days, starting on July 7, Wilbur made entries in his diary, all too brief, in some cases also referring to work that had preceded, and summing up. A diary kept by Huffacker for Chanute supplements the record for an additional seven days. Both diaries are quoted on scattered pages of *Papers*, 71–83. Letters of both Wilbur and Orville, from Kitty Hawk and afterwards, add to the store of information. *Papers*, 68–120, 158. In addition there are Wilbur's legal depositions of 1911–12, as well as Kelly and McMahon and the various other sources cited below. Once more, it is not feasible to describe here how all this material was analyzed and cross-checked, except for the more pertinent items.

"We considered it . . . ."—Wilbur's 1901 lecture, *Papers*, 107.

Wilbur's first letter to Chanute, written on May 13, 1900, is in *Papers*, 15–19.

"We believed that . . . ."—*Papers*, 538.

Charles Taylor's reminiscences of his work with the brothers were given in two articles: "My Story of the Wright Brothers," *Collier's*, December 25, 1948; and "Building the Original Wright Motor," *Slipstream*, May 1928. The event that called forth the *Collier's* article was the death of Orville the preceding January. Taylor was then eighty.

The experiments with the V-arm are described in Orville's 1920 deposition, partially quoted in *Papers*, 547.

"If you were not about to . . . ."—*Papers*, 57.

"Unless you feel that . . . ."—*Papers*, 64.

"We could not permit you . . . ."—*Papers*, 64.

The two articles written by Wilbur were "Angle of Incidence," *The Aeronautical Journal* (London) July 1901, and "The Horizontal Position During Gliding Flight," *Illustrierte Aeronautische Mitteilungen* (Berlin) July 1901. Both are reprinted in *Papers*, 58–63.

"We reached Kitty Hawk . . . ."—*Papers*, 70.

"The building is a . . . ."—*Papers*, 73.

The plague of mosquitoes is vividly described in Orville's letter of July 28, *Papers*, 73–75.

The collapsible Chanute machine was tried out on two or three days and proved worthless, its longest glide covering only fifty feet. *Deposition of Wilbur Wright*, 97, *Wright* v. *Herring-Curtiss*, 1912. Finally, when it was caught in the rain, its paper tubing fell apart.

Not much is known about George Spratt or his experiments. My description of him is based on a letter from his son, some incidental references in the Wrights' letters, and an obituary in *The New York Times*, November 26, 1934.

"Sufficiently guarded against . . . ."—*Papers*, 110. Huffaker also, Wilbur said, warned against the reversal of the center of pressure.

"The full power of the . . . ."—Wilbur's 1901 lecture, *Papers*, 108. He specified that the thought occurred to him at the time of the glide, so I have felt it permissible to quote it at this point.

"This was the position . . . ."—Wilbur in his 1901 lecture describes the entire incident, *Papers*, 108–9. It is also reported in a letter of Orville's, written the day after, *Papers*, 75.

"At a speed of 18 miles . . . ."—*Papers*, 71. Wilbur recorded his doubts about Lilienthal's tables in the same place.

The center-of-pressure experiments and their results are described in Wilbur's 1901 lecture, *Papers*, 110–11. They are also recorded in the diary for August 7, *Papers*, 80–81.

"At first we felt . . . ."—Wilbur's 1901 lecture, *Papers*, 111.

The glides of August 9 and the accident. Wilbur's own table of this day's glides is in *Papers*, 158. Huffaker's diary for this day describes two of the glides as "curving sharply to the left," both covering 280 feet, *Papers*, 81. In Wilbur's table the two 280-foot glides are given as the second and the fifth, which was also the last. Since the day's gliding was ended by the accident, it therefore occurred during an attempt to make a turn. The details of the glide and the accident were provided by Huffaker's diary entry, Wilbur's *First Rebuttal*, 485–86, and his 1901 lecture, *Papers*, 108–9.

"Upturned wing seems to fall . . ."–*Papers*, 82.

"Our machine does not . . ."–Wilbur in a letter to Chanute after the return from Kitty Hawk, *Papers*, 84.

"When we left Kitty Hawk . . ."–*First Rebuttal*, 486. Wilbur's disappointment is variously recorded: see Kelly, *Wrights*, 72, and *First Rebuttal*, 486. My quotation combines the two versions of the reported remark.

"The boys walked in . . ."–*Papers*, 84. Katharine also says that Wilbur was sick with a cold.

On several days while the brothers were at Kitty Hawk a tripod camera was set up to take pictures of the camp and the glider. Some of these pictures (and others taken the following year) show Wilbur aboard the airborne glider dressed in white shirt, collar, and tie. This sartorial incongruity today often provokes amusement, but that is only because the customs that prevailed in our grandfathers' day have been forgotten. The turn of the century was a highly exacting period in matters of dress and deportment. A professional man, especially a scientist, was expected to dress the part and to carry at all times at least a semiformal air. If he didn't, if he donned rougher garb and soiled his hands with physical work, he risked having his credentials called in question and might suffer the ignominy of being mistaken for a mechanic. This was a point on which the Wrights in later years were to become very sensitive, when it was claimed by some that they were indeed only mechanics who had deftly lifted ideas from the scientific work of their betters. (See, for instance, an early book, *Discovery: The Spirit and Service of Science*, by Sir Richard Gregory, 1916, where the brothers are credited only with "mechanical ingenuity" in making selections from the work of "true" scientists, particularly Langley.) Dressing the part was one way to combat this prejudice, but it is also probable that at Kitty Hawk the brothers donned white shirt, collar, and tie only when Chanute and the others were present, or when photos were to be taken. They might not in the first place have paid much heed to the matter had it not been for their sister, who kept her brothers up to snuff. This is evident in a later remark of Wilbur's, when he was enjoying his first fame in France. An artist had been drawing a picture of him, he reported to Katharine: "I fear you will raise an awful fuss when you see it. It is worse than shirt sleeves! We will soon have a picture you cannot kick about on the score of shirt sleeves. Yesterday it was rather cold and to shut out the wind during the flight I slipped on a blue jumper or overhaul jacket. It left about two inches of my coat sticking out at the bottom. After the flight Mr. and Mrs. Weiller and Mr. Deutsch came up to congratulate me and the *Vie au grand air* photographer slipped up and snapped us. Mrs. Weiller laughed heartily when I told her how you objected to shirt sleeve pictures, and how pleased you would be to see that I had on two coats." *Papers*, 923–24.

CHAPTER 7
THE PROMISE OF $P_{(\text{tang. a})}/P_{(90)}$

"The present muddled state . . ."—*Papers*, 85. Though the brothers felt, just after the return from Kitty Hawk, that they had failed, Wilbur discussed the season's work in correspondence with Chanute because "we could not keep our minds off the puzzling things we had observed, nor keep from studying possible solutions." *First Rebuttal*, 487.

The Simon Newcomb article in McClure's, September 1901. While the Wrights make no reference to reading this, they appear to have been fairly regular readers of the magazine and certainly would have been concerned to hear Newcomb's opinion. If they had missed it, assuredly Chanute would have called it to their attention.

Kelly, *Wrights*, 73, credits the "proddings" of Chanute with reviving the brothers' determination to go on. Perhaps the encouragement of Chanute played its part, but the evidence of ten letters by Wilbur scattered through *Papers* 85–138, suggests that the decision to persevere became firm only as he approached the idea of the wind tunnel.

"Get acquainted with some . . ."—*Papers*, 92. The other quotations from Katharine, in this paragraph and the next, are from this same place.

On September 11 Katharine reminded her father in a letter that Wilbur's speech was only a week away, and added: "We asked him whether it was to be witty or scientific and he said that he thought it would be pathetic before he got through with it." *Papers*, 95.

"You never saw Will looking . . ."—*Papers*, 99.

Chanute's remarks introducing Wilbur's speech accompany its printing in the *Journal of the Western Society of Engineers*, December 1901. They were omitted from the reprinting in *Papers*, 99–118.

Extract and quotations from Wilbur's 1901 lecture: *Papers*, 100, 105, 116.

The speech as printed in the engineering *Journal* contains material added later, after Wilbur made some preliminary wind tests at home. The fact is evident in the printed text, and an explanation accompanies its reprint in *Papers*, 114.

The bicycle wheel experiment is described by Wilbur in a letter to Chanute, *Papers*, 121. He specifies that the test was for checking on the "Lilienthal coefficients." The results are in another letter to Chanute of October 6, *Papers*, 123–28. In this letter, a long one, he also mentions the "trough" test, records his certainties about Lilienthal's errors, and describes his plan to make an "apparatus" (the wind tunnel) for testing different model surfaces. Recording as it does the first reference to the pivotal experiments that were to lead to successful flight, there can be few other letters in history to equal this one in interest and importance.

In light of the above it would seem unnecessary to comment at length on the claim in Kelly, *Wrights*, 74, that it was Orville who, while Wilbur was in Chicago, conceived and carried out the first wind tunnel experiments. He used an old wooden box, says Kelly, in which a curved surface was balanced against a flat plane, "in an air current passing through the box." No record of this exists outside of Kelly's pages and, to mention only one objection, if Kelly is correct then the brothers were certainly wasting their time, after Wilbur's return, in bothering with the rougher tests involving the bicycle, the weather vane, and the trough.

My information about wind tunnels prior to the Wrights, including the large tunnel of A. F. Zahm, comes principally from a Smithsonian pamphlet, *Pioneer Wind Tunnels*, by N. H. Randers-Pehrson, 1935, 24 pp., illus. (reprinted from *Smithsonian Misc. Coll.*, vol. 93, No. 4).

The Wrights' wind tunnel. Details of the conception, construction, and use of the tunnel and its balances, and the results derived therefrom, are from four main sources: letters and other documents of the brothers, *Papers*, 123–81; an Appendix in vol. I of *Papers*, "1901 Wind Tunnel," 547–77, written by Fred Howard; an article in *The Smithsonian Report for 1950*, "The Wright Brothers as Aeronautical Engineers," by M. P. Baker; a second article, "The Wright Brothers as Researchers," by George Lewis, *Aviation*, August 1939.

"We spent nearly a month . . ."—*Papers*, 186.

The making of the model surfaces is described by Wilbur in a letter of January 23, 1902 to George Spratt, *Papers*, 208.

The second balancing device for the wind tunnel was based on an idea of Spratt's, mentioned to Wilbur at Kitty Hawk in 1901, well before the brothers began their wind tunnel experiments. It did not concern an actual wind tunnel and was not a fundamental technique, but it offered a refinement for saving time and effort. Yet Spratt, who like Chanute did not fully understand what the brothers had done in their wind tunnel work, later complained to Wilbur that he had not received "fair compensation" for his contribution. Wilbur in a letter to Spratt of October 16, 1909 (when the Wrights' infringement lawsuits were in full swing), *Papers*, 968, readily admitted that the idea had come from him, though used in a balance of different construction, and he put the truth of the matter exactly in saying that it was merely "a more convenient method" for making the measurements. He reminded Spratt that he and his brother had given much advice and help in return, "and I cannot help feeling that in so doing we returned the loan with interest." Tables from the Wrights' tunnel had been supplied to Spratt, and Wilbur offered to continue giving aid. "Has your idea yielded you yourself tables as comprehensive and accurate," Wilbur asked, "as those you received from us?" Unmollified, Spratt about a month later became a witness against the brothers in an infringement suit. He claimed in an affidavit that Chanute had introduced him to the Wrights "in order that I might communicate the results of my work to them for the purpose of helping and furthering their work, which I then did." The brothers, he asserted, "at once availed themselves of my methods," leaving the impression that the whole wind tunnel operation had been appropriated from him. Affidavit of George Spratt, December 2, 1909, *Wright Company* v. *Louis Paulhan*. In court, the letters that had passed between Chanute and the Wrights, and Spratt and the Wrights, along with some precise testimony by Wilbur, disproved Spratt's unfortunate claim.

The first and second stages of the wind tunnel experiments are clearly set forth by Wilbur in two letters to Chanute, November 22 and December 1, 1901, *Papers*, 159–64, 168–71.

"Accurately measuring the . . ."—*Papers*, 164.

"It is perfectly marvelous to . . ."—*Papers*, 156.

"Far in advance of the . . ."—Lewis, *Aviation*, August 1939.

"The accuracy of these . . ."—Baker, *Smithsonian Report* 1950.
"Unless I decide to devote . . ."—*Papers*, 180.
"I happen to know Carnegie . . . "—*Papers*, 183. The offer of the $10,000 a year is made in this same letter.
"Superior to those of any . . ."—*Papers*, 203.
"A very few years . . ."—*Papers*, 198.

CHAPTER 8

KITTY HAWK 1902

In 1902 the Wrights spent sixty-two days at Kitty Hawk. This year the diary was kept by Orville, who made detailed entries for a total of fifty-three days, *Papers*, 245–80. Analysis of this diary in conjunction with the various other sources cited below permits a quite exact and nearly day-by-day reconstruction of their work during the period.

"It was our experience . . ."—*Papers*, 237–38.

Specifications of the 1902 glider are in *Papers*, 1185–87. That the new wings incorporated factors from a number of the model surfaces is noted in *Papers*, 551.

The fixed tail. Wilbur in his *First Rebuttal*, 487–89, describes the reasoning that led to adoption of the *fixed* tail. He neglects to say when this was, but it may have been as early as January 1902, since in a letter of February 7 he says that in the matter of steering and lateral stability, "I now have hopes that we have a solution . . . the great trouble will be to obtain proper skill." *Papers*, 212.

"We are convinced . . ."—*Papers*, 255.

The brothers' satisfaction with the new glider after the glides of September 19 is in the diary, *Papers*, 255.

The accident of September 20 is described in the diary, *Papers*, 256. Wilbur later provided a more extensive picture in his second lecture (June 24, 1903) to the Western Society of Engineers, *Papers*, 321. He does not give the date but says it happened "on the second day" of work, which was the first day of "regular gliding."

Orville's first glide. On September 23 Orville wrote in the diary that the glider was taken to the big hill, and "I here took my first free glide." *Papers*, 259. Nowhere in the preceding pages of *Papers*, or in any other source, is there any indication that he had been airborne in the glider before this. The pictures taken in 1901 show only Wilbur as operator.

"Sliding one way then . . ."—*Papers*, 260.

Orville's accident of September 23 is described in the diary, *Papers*, 260, and in Wilbur's 1903 lecture, *Papers*, 322–23. Some details are added by Wilbur in a letter written the evening of the accident, *Papers*, 261.

"Maintained that the trouble . . ."—*Papers*, 270.

"They would watch the gannets . . ."—John Daniels, in Saunders, *Collier's*, September 17, 1927.

The glides of September 29, 30, and October 1 are listed in the diary in tabular form, with the operator for each trial indicated, *Papers*, 264–68.

"We often considered ourselves . . ."—*First Rebuttal*, 489.

"Taking the chance over and . . ."—*First Rebuttal*, 489.

The movable rudder. The genesis of this all-important feature became, in the later infringement suits, one of the most closely analyzed elements of the Flyer. Wilbur described the process in his *First Rebuttal,* 489–91, and earlier had responded at length to counsel's cross-examination on the subject, *Deposition of Wilbur Wright, Wright* v. *Herring-Curtiss,* September 1911, Defendant's Record, U.S. District Court, Western District of New York, pp. 91–125. In all his testimony Wilbur clearly says that the idea of converting the fixed rudder to a movable one was reached by close observation of the glider in flight and by taking repeated risks, after which "we finally began to notice the conditions under which the difficulty was liable to occur." Then, after deciding on a movable rudder as the solution, "we spent several days in experimenting to make sure that this was the real cause of the difficulty."

But that is not the way Kelly, *Wrights,* 81–82, recounts the process. According to Kelly it was Orville who, while unable to sleep after retiring one night, "figured out" the need for a movable rudder. The claim deserves some analysis.

On the morning after conceiving the improvement, says Kelly, Orville explained the idea to his brother. At this point in his text Kelly supplies a paragraph of technical explanation (beginning "When the machine became tilted . . ."), with which, he says, Wilbur agreed. Kelly is specific in attributing the technical explanation to Orville, yet it proves to be not Orville's but Wilbur's, lifted intact from the *First Rebuttal,* 489–90. Kelly goes on to explain how Wilbur promptly suggested the rudder-warp linkage to simplify operations. Yet in his *First Rebuttal,* 490, Wilbur took pains to attribute this refinement to his brother, the only time anywhere in his records that he does this: "Meanwhile, my brother in thinking about the matter . . ." (the passage continues with an explanation of the aerodynamic factors that made the rudder-warp linkage feasible).

For some reason Kelly avoided quoting a phrase from the diary kept by Orville which might seem to have bolstered Orville's claim: "While lying awake last night I studied out a new vertical rudder." *Papers,* 269. The reason for Kelly's oversight perhaps was the fact that the entry was made on October 3, referring the dawning of the idea to the night of October 2, a day on which Wilbur had already written his father that "we now believe that the flying problem is really nearing its solution." *Miracle,* 80. There was also the inconvenient fact that the next day's diary entry, October 4, specified that Orville's new rudder was "one that is operated at the same time as the end tips," *Papers,* 270, a direct reference to the rudder-warp linkage. Finally, in a deposition Orville made in 1920 he explained that it was only "after a good deal of thought" that the idea of the movable rudder occurred to "us." This admission goes back comfortably to Wilbur's assertion that "several days" of experimenting had passed between the first conception of the movable rudder and its installation.

What appears to have happened is this: On five days between September 20 and September 30 the brothers made about a hundred glides. During this time the nature of the problem became clear and the solution finally dawned on Wilbur, perhaps by September 30. During October 1–2 the brothers discussed a movable rudder and the complications it would impose on the pilot. Orville, unable to sleep during the night of October 2, thought of making the function of the movable rudder automatic by wiring it into the wing-warping action. This idea the two discussed and tested on October 3, then decided to give it a try, and on October 4 began the alterations.

The glides of October 2–3, with the operator indicated, are listed in a table in the diary, *Papers*, 268–69. The erratic progress of Wilbur's 550-foot glide is noted in the same place.

The work of altering the tail is in the diary for October 4, *Papers*, 270. The change to a single vane is recorded in the same place.

"The day opened with . . ."–*Papers*, 272.

The glides of October 10 are in the diary, *Papers*, 272–73. In the same place Orville mentions his troubles with the controls.

Details of the glides made in the final two weeks at Kitty Hawk, frequently interrupted by bad weather or lack of wind, are in the diary and a letter of Orville's, *Papers*, 274–80. A review of the period was provided by Wilbur in his 1903 lecture, *Papers*, 324–26.

The walk to Kitty Hawk in the rain is mentioned in a letter of Wilbur's, *Papers*, 284.

CHAPTER 9
THE FLYER IS BUILT

For the Wrights' propeller work I have relied mainly on an appendix in vol. 1 of *Papers*, "The Wright Propellers," 594–640, and for their motor work on an appendix in vol. 2, "1903 Motor," 1210–14 (both written by Fred S. Howard). Other sources for both and for various incidents of the period are cited below.

"At the time the Wrights . . ."–*Papers*, 595.

"It is hard to find . . ."–Orville, in *Flying*, December 1913.

The loud discussions between the brothers over the propeller are described in a number of places: Kelly, *Wrights*, 89; McMahon, *Popular Science*, April 1929; *Flying*, December 1913; Charles Taylor in *Collier's*, December 1948, to name a few. Subsequent writers have forgotten that these heated arguments took place only in regard to the propeller, and have tended to picture them as a constant habit of the brothers during all their work.

"I don't think they really . . ."–Taylor, *Collier's*, December 1948.

"One morning following the . . ."–Taylor, *Collier's*, December 1948.

"Discussion brings out . . ."–Wilbur in a letter, *Papers*, 306.

"If you don't stop arguing . . ."–McMahon, *Popular Science*, April 1929.

"The thrust generated by a . . ."–Orville, in *Flying*, December 1913.

"We had been unable to . . ."–*Papers*, 313.

"Enthusiastic and efficient . . ."–Orville in *Flying*, December 1913. This praise of Taylor by Orville was carefully measured. The complete passage runs: "In just six weeks from the time the design was started we had the motor on the block testing its power. The ability to do this so quickly was largely due to the enthusiastic and efficient services of Mr. C. E. Taylor, who did all the machine work in our shop for the first as well as the succeeding experimental machines." In later years Taylor, who continued to work for Orville after Wilbur's death, began to claim more than a mechanic's function in the construction of the motor, implying he had had a hand in the design as well. This produced a coolness between the two men that was eventually reflected in Orville's will. Out of an estate probated at more than a million dollars, Orville left Taylor an annuity of $800, less than the wage he received when he first went to work for the brothers. Taylor died in San Fernando, California, on January 31, 1956, aged 87. His obituaries gave him the last word, saying he was both designer and builder of the original Wright motor.

"An attempt to repair . . ."—Taylor, *Collier's*, December 1948. The two quotations from Taylor in the following paragraphs are from this same source.

"The state of the art . . ."—Hobbs, *Beehive*, Fall 1954.

"Ignorant of what a motor . . ."—Orville in *Flying*, December 1913.

That Chanute had prior knowledge of Langley's intention to test his machine in fall 1903 is recorded in an article in a French magazine, *La Locomotion*, April 11, 1903, translated in *Papers*, 654–59; see 658. I am assuming, safely I feel, that Chanute would have passed the information on to the Wrights.

"It would be interesting to . . ."—*Papers*, 345.

"Airship as a Submarine"—*New York Times*, August 9, 1903. The other quotations relating to Langley's model are from this same source.

The coin flip is mentioned by Orville in *Flying*, December 1913.

CHAPTER 10
HIGH NOON AT KITTY HAWK

The Wrights' stay at Kitty Hawk in 1903 extended for ninety-two days. The diary was again kept by Orville and he made entries daily, except for the seventeen days he was back in Dayton preparing new shafts, *Papers*, 356–98. The letters of the brothers, in *Papers*, and in *Miracle*, and the documents cited below, add to the store of information for reconstructing these remarkable three months.

The practice glides with the 1902 machine occupied ten scattered days during October. They are in the diary, *Papers*, 358, 360–62, 368, 370, 373–74.

"We made tail so as to . . ."—*Papers*, 360.

The description of Langley's October 7 trial is from *The New York Times*, October 8, 1903. I have also read accounts in the New York *Herald*, and New York *Sun*, and in Sullivan, *Our Times*, vol. II, 560–62.

"I see that Langley . . ."—*Papers*, 364. Three weeks later Orville referred to Langley's failure in a letter to Katharine: "I suppose you have read in the papers the account of the failure of Langley's big machine. He started from a point 60 feet in the air and landed 300 feet away, which is a drop of 1 foot for every 5 forward. We are able, from this same height, to make from 400 to 600 feet without any motor at all, so that I think his surfaces must be very inefficient. They found that they had no control of the machine whatever, though the wind blew but 5 miles an hour at the time of the test. That is the point where we have a great advantage. We have been in the air hundreds and hundreds of times, and we have pretty well worked out the problem of control." *Miracle*, 106. This letter was perhaps intended more as reassurance to the worried family back in Dayton, a crash on sand being likely to produce more damage than one on water.

The terrific storm of October 9–11 was described by Wilbur in a long letter to Katharine, *Papers*, 365–67. For him the storm conjured up biblical associations: ". . . about two o'clock in the afternoon a storm hove into view that made the storm that followed the prayers of Elijah look small in comparison. . . . As the new building was not quite complete as to bracing, etc., we expected it to go first so we lay there rocking in the billows waiting for it to crash. Toward morning we could hear the water sloshing around on the floor of our old building . . . Orville got up to investigate (he being the expert on night alarms at home, you know) and reported the floor under water at the north end, but the south end embracing the kitchen, library, etc., still dry. 'And the evening and the morning were the first day' . . ."

Chanute's letter of October 24 to Wilbur is in *Papers*, 372. A footnote quotes the clipping that was enclosed. The fact that Chanute's letter was received at Kitty Hawk on November 1 is noted in the diary for that day, *Papers*, 375.

That the brothers intended to test the Flyer first as a glider, without the motor, is mentioned a number of times in their letters. As late as Sunday, November 1, Orville wrote to Katharine: "Of course we are going to thoroughly test the control of it on the hills before attaching the motor." *Miracle*, 106. Since the diary for November 2–4 shows the two in the act of hurriedly mounting the motor, I feel confident in concluding that there was a discussion in the afternoon or evening of November 1, prompted by the arrival of Chanute's letter, which led to the decision to skip the glide testing and go right to the first powered attempt. Spratt's opposition to that decision is clear from a later letter of Chanute's in which he says: "You know now that you were in error in your apprehension of disaster to the Wrights. It would have been safer to test their new machine thoroughly as a glider before launching it with the motor aboard, but they took the risk and won." The letter was written after the first flight; it is quoted in a footnote in *Papers*, 377. I take it that Spratt would have first voiced his doubts on the evening of November 1.

"We got the machine ready . . ."—*Papers*, 376.

The $4 cost of the starting track is mentioned by Wilbur in a letter, *Miracle*, 109. He dubbed the track "The Junction Railroad," *Miracle*, 121.

"We had to come down . . ."—*Papers*, 383.

"5 blankets and two . . ."—*Papers*, 383.

Chanute's departure from Kitty Hawk on November 12 is noted in the diary, *Papers*, 379.

"He doesn't seem to think . . ."—*Miracle*, 107.

The test for power loss in the transmission, prompted by Chanute's caution, is mentioned by Orville in a letter to Taylor, *Papers*, 387, in his 1913 *Flying* article, and by Wilbur in a letter to Chanute, *Papers*, 402.

The grounding of the submarine *Moccasin* was widely reported. My facts are from the New York *Herald*, December 4–10, 1903.

For Langley's second failure I have drawn mainly on *The New York Times*, December 9, 1903, and Sullivan, *Our Times*, vol. II, 565–67.

"We did not have enough . . ."—*Papers*, 391.

The entry in the diary for Sunday, December 13, when the brothers could have made their first trial had they been willing to overlook their promise to their father, reads: "Wind of 6 to 8 meters blowing from west and later from north. Air warm. Spent most of day reading. In the afternoon Mr. Etheridge of L. S. Station, with wife and children, called to look at the machine." *Papers*, 391.

The details of the December 14 power trial are in the diary, and in a letter of Wilbur's to his family that same evening, *Papers*, 391–92. Orville, in *Flying*, December 1913, refers only briefly to this trial and, rather strangely, ends by saying that the test "had shown nothing as to whether the power of the motor was sufficient to keep the machine up." This contrasts with Wilbur's belief that the test had given ample indication of the machine's capability, *Papers*, 393. At various other times Orville seems to have forgotten what actually occurred at that December 14 trial. In a 1920 court deposition he makes it seem that the machine failed even to rise: "Through a mistake in handling it at the start the machine was broken slightly, so that repairs had to be made before another attempt could be undertaken." Seven years after that, in a newspaper interview, he was more explicit on the failure to lift, saying Wilbur "smashed the ground runners at the end of the run. The machine never left the track." *New York Times* Magazine, July 17, 1927.

"As the machine had . . ."—*Papers*, 393.

"The machine would undoubtedly have . . ."—*Papers*, 393.

The casual stroller who paused to inquire about the machine on December 16 is recorded by Orville in his 1913 *Flying* article, and is also in McMahon, *Popular Science*, April 1929.

The first flight. The diary contains a long entry covering the four trials of December 17, giving the exact time for the start of each as well as other details, *Papers*, 394–97. My other sources were a letter from Wilbur to Chanute, December 28, 1903, *Papers*, 401–3; the brothers' statement to the Associated Press of January 5, 1904, *Papers*, 409–11; Orville's article in *Century Magazine*, September 1908; Orville's article in *Flying*, December 1913; McMahon, *Popular Science*, April 1929; the recollections of John Daniels in Saunders, *Collier's*, September 17, 1927. These make up the whole available primary source material for the events of December 17. Kelly in his biography of the Wrights made no effort of his own to describe the trials but was content with reprinting a portion of Orville's 1913 *Flying* article.

In the diary and their letters at the time the brothers did not specify which of the four trials they considered to be the first true flight, but Wilbur later stated that a flight under 300 feet could not be taken seriously—"less than this is nothing," he wrote, *Papers*, 734–35. Analysis of the four trials leads inevitably to the conclusion that, while the first three attempts were valuable and heartening, not until the fourth attempt could they be sure that the machine had sustained itself. But it is clear that the brothers were not particularly concerned about differentiating among the four trials, and in their first detailed published description of them (*Century Magazine*, September 1908, written by Orville with Katharine's help after Wilbur had sailed for France), Orville's twelve-second effort is called "the first flight . . . in the history of the world." While there is no record that Wilbur ever publicly disagreed with this, the honors later shifted to the fourth trial. At Wilbur's death *The New York Times*, June 2, 1912, stated that the first three attempts were merely "jumps" and that Wilbur's flight of 852 feet in 59 seconds was "the first real flight by man in an aeroplane." A year later, at a dinner given by the Aero Club of America in Orville's honor, the principal speaker made the following observation: "The record of the first flight, made by the late Wilbur Wright, in the conquest of the air, is recorded in the books kept by the Wrights, which show that on the fourth test, with the wind blowing twenty miles an hour, Wilbur Wright flew 852 feet . . ." *New York Times*, December 18, 1913.

Any doubts as to which of the four should be considered the first flight are erased by a visit to the original grounds at Kitty Hawk, with the appearance and size of the Flyer fixed in the mind (an easy task, since a full-size replica of the Flyer reposes in a small museum nearby). This I have done for hours at a time, studying the markers at the takeoff point and at each landing spot, walking off the distances, feeling the wind, imagining the rattling Flyer rising, speeding forward, dipping, landing. On paper or in print the numbers denoting the length of each flight—120, 175, 200, 852—are merely numbers, for most people telling little of the reality of that day seventy-one years ago. To an observer on the spot, however, the first three numbers are indeed seen as reflecting jumps or hops, while the 852-foot distance, stretching far from the takeoff, is at last felt and appreciated as a proper distance for a first flight to have covered, convincing beyond cavil.

"With all the knowledge . . ."—Orville, in *Flying*, December 1913.

"After a while they shook . . ."—Daniels, in Saunders, *Collier's*, September 17, 1927. This article, unfortunately, is rather brief. Daniels was found by Saunders running a ferryboat along the North Carolina coast; he had retired from the lifesaving service in 1918 (he died on January 31, 1948, the exact same day as Orville Wright, *New York Times*, February 1, 1948). Wilbur's telling the five witnesses to shout and clap hands is also from Daniels' recollections.

The accident that ended the day's flights is reconstructed from a short account in the diary, *Papers*, 397, a longer description by Daniels in the *Collier's* article, and *Flying*, December 1913.

It appears that there may actually have been seven witnesses to the first flight. One man who remained at the Kitty Hawk lifesaving station that day, Captain S. Payne, later said he watched the proceedings through a spyglass. The same claim was made by another man at the Kill Devil Hill station, R. L. Westcott, who had been present for the December 14 trial. *Papers*, 394.

CHAPTER 11

THE STORY OF THE CENTURY—ALMOST

Carrie Grumbach's recollections of the arrival of the telegram are in *Miracle*, 118. Bishop Wright, she recalled, "was always calm and showed no excitement. But he looked pleased."

The time of the telegram's arrival in the Dayton Western Union office is stamped on its face: 5:25 P.M. *Papers*, Plate 71. It would certainly have reached the Wright home less than a half hour later.

Lorin's visit to the *Journal* office is in Kelly, *Wrights*, 106. The criticism of Tunison here (after forty years!) is a part of Kelly's overall effort to depict the press as slow-witted and blind on the subject of flying, strengthening his later assertion that the newspapers simply ignored the flying experiments of 1904–5. My interpretation of the incident, I feel, is somewhat nearer the mark, particularly since the Dayton *Daily News* eventually did pair the Wrights' flights with the balloon feats of Santos-Dumont. See Kelly, *Wrights*, 107.

Wilbur's desire for secrecy. In a letter from Chanute to Wilbur, January 20, 1904, *Papers,* 417, there is this remark: "You talked while I was at camp of giving your *performance,* if successful, all the publicity possible, and you know that I would not divulge the *construction* of your machine . . ." (italics Chanute's). In another letter Chanute wrote a friend a few days earlier, he says: "The Wrights are immensely elated. They have grown very secretive and nobody is to be allowed to see the machine at present." *Papers,* 413. Further evidence is in the text of this chapter and the chapters following, with their Notes. It is curious that no one has ever remarked on the best evidence of all: The brothers did not invite even one reporter to the trials at Kitty Hawk. Two months before the first flight Chanute remarked in a letter to Wilbur: "It is a marvel to me that the newspapers have not yet spotted you." *Papers,* 372. Wilbur knew what he was doing when he picked the remote Outer Banks for his experiments.

Photographs of the 1901 glider appeared in the *Scientific American,* February 22, 1902, with credit to the *Journal of the Western Society of Engineers.*

Details of the sending of the telegram from the Kitty Hawk weather station are in Kelly, *Wrights,* 102–4. No earlier primary source with like detail is available. That the brothers stopped long enough to have lunch before sending the wire is in the diary, *Papers,* 397.

Coverage of the first flight by the Norfolk Virginian-Pilot. My view of this is based on analysis of three principle sources: Sullivan, *Our Times,* vol. II, 592–94; Kelly, *Wrights,* 104–6; and an article in *Editor and Publisher,* February 14, 1948, "Wright Death Recalls Coverage of First Flight," by Hillier Krieghbaum.

The various publications that telegraphed the brothers at Kitty Hawk requesting stories and pictures are listed in the diary for December 19, *Papers,* 398.

The fact that reporters were calling at the Wright home even before the brothers returned from Kitty Hawk—that is, December 18–22—is in *Papers,* 398–99.

"Suppressed" the newsmen—*Papers,* 400.

"As all the experiments have . . ."—*Papers,* 411. The first sign of a parting of the ways between Chanute and the Wrights cropped up at this time as a result of what Wilbur had said in his Associated Press release, ". . . without assistance from any individual or institution." No sooner had Chanute read this statement in some paper than he wrote Wilbur: "Please write me just what you had in mind concerning myself when you framed that sentence in that way." *Papers,* 414–15. Wilbur's answer, deliberately, was kept vague, he not wanting to offend Chanute, though he already saw that his friend was tending to accept more credit than was due him: Wilbur wrote that he had found in newspapers a "somewhat general impression that our Kitty Hawk experiments had not been carried out at our own expense, etc. We thought it might save embarrassment to correct this promptly." *Papers,* 415. The significance of that "etc." was overlooked by Chanute and he was for a while placated—there is no doubt, it might be noted here, that Chanute was convinced he had contributed substantially to the Wrights' success, though as he was to admit later he could not say precisely what his contribution had been. See his letter in *Papers,* 940–41.

"Without exploiting the invention . . ."—This thought was expressed repeatedly. See *Papers*, 679, 686, 712.

Wilbur's decision to develop the Flyer in secret. Through the rest of his life Orville denied that he and his brother had indulged in any secrecy, even in the operations at Huffman's in 1904-05. (See, for instance, Kelly, *Wrights*, 123, 134–35; Sullivan, *Our Times*, vol. II, 599; *New York Times* Magazine, July 17, 1927.) His insistence on the point has had its influence. To give one example: *Encyclopedia Britannica* (1974), in a long article under "Flight, History of," insists that in the experiments of 1904-5 "The Wrights were not secretive about their work. It was there in the open for anyone to see" (Vol. VII, 388). In refutation of that myth I offer my Chapters 12, 13, 14, with their Notes.

CHAPTER 12

THE GOINGS-ON AT HUFFMAN'S PASTURE

The chronology and background for this chapter are derived principally from analysis of the diary and letters of the brothers, *Papers*, 426–71, and Wilbur's *First Rebuttal*, 493–98. Other sources are cited below.

"So far we have not been . . ."—*Papers*, 433.

Specifications for Flyer No. 2 are in *Papers*, 1189-90, in scattered letters of Wilbur, *Papers*, 424–34, and in Kelly, *Wrights*, 121.

My description of Huffman's pasture and its environs is based on a sketch in Wilbur's 1904 diary, reproduced in *Papers*, 456; two of Wilbur's letters, *Papers*, 426, 441; and study of some maps of the period, as well as the brothers' photographs of the field. (Today Huffman's pasture is part of the Wright Patterson Air Force Base.)

Timing of the Interurban trolleys. That the brothers timed their flights so as not to be in the air when a trolley passed is clearly stated in Kelly, *Wrights*, 135, though the qualification is made that this was only "at first." The fact that they were successful in this until the eighty-second flight of 1904, then were caught by an unscheduled special, and were not caught again until the end of the 1905 season, when their flight time had lengthened beyond a half hour, indicates that it was a permanent and carefully observed policy. But the fact can be made even more obvious. My calculations show that the Flyer was actually in the air on sixty different days during 1904–5. For each of those days the brothers stayed at the field about six hours, for a total of 360 hours, frequently making four flights during that time. Since four trolleys passed about every hour, two going east and two west, there were well over a thousand chances that the Flyer would have been seen. And yet, until the flights became too long to allow such management, they were not seen. And two days after the flights were first spotted by trolley passengers in October 1905, the work was terminated.

The "failed" flights of May 25–26. That these first public demonstrations at Huffman's pasture were deliberately rigged to fail is strongly indicated by the circumstances, even apart from Wilbur's remark about how "neatly . . . we fooled the newspapers." When the brothers, a short time later, did begin to fly regularly they were careful to maintain secrecy, never once during six months inviting the press to return—and in fact refraining from any discussion of the subject even when face to face with a newspaperman (see Kelly, *Wrights*, 139–40). Further evidence is in the text of this chapter, the Notes below, and in Chapter 14 and its Notes. My reconstruction of these two days is based on four sources: Orville's account in *Century Magazine*, September 1908; Kelly, *Wrights*, 123–25; Bishop Wright's diary and a letter of Wilbur's, both *Papers*, 436–37.

In the *Century* article and the Kelly biography, of course, the failures are presented as sincere attempts to fly, and once more blindness is implied on the part of the reporters who, unfortunately, were now "convinced that the age of flight had not yet come." Needless to say, Kelly does not face the obvious question of why the press was not reinvited when the real flying started.

"Which we are sure will baffle . . ."—*Miracle*, 164.

"The newspapers are friendly . . ."—*Papers*, 439.

The flights of June 10–December 9 at Huffman's are recorded in continuous diary entries and letters, *Papers*, 439–72. In the Notes below I give specific citations only for the more outstanding incidents—the dates provided in the text will allow any fact not so cited to be easily located in *Papers*. The brothers customarily recorded times in fractions of seconds. For simplicity I have rounded these off to the nearest whole second.

Orville's accident of August 24 is in the diary, *Papers*, 452. He had been in the air less than eight seconds, covering about two hundred feet against an eleven-mile wind.

The diary for 1904, kept by Wilbur, gives the operator's initials with each flight. From September 7, when the catapult was first tried, to September 20 only Wilbur went up, *Papers*, 453–56. I interpret this to mean that he was testing the new device. As the diary shows, Orville was present at all these trials, either his initials are noted as a timer, or two times are given—one by Taylor, the other by Orville.

A. I. Root. The Wrights' connection with Root is one of the more obscure facets of their Huffman's pasture experiments, but it is more than probable that there was previous contact. Root first took notice of the brothers soon after the first flight, with an article in his magazine, *Gleanings*, March 1, 1904. He was a Sunday school teacher in addition to his bee business, and the article tells how he discussed the news accounts of the Wrights' success with his class. Kelly, *Wrights*, 142, says that he arrived at Huffman's by automobile on September 19 and put up at the Beard farm. He implies that Root was given the freedom of the field. The diary for September 20, the day of the first circle, notes "Root present," and he is again noted as present on November 22, suggesting his continued presence during the intervening two months. That he was also a guest in the Wright home is made certain by a passing observation in *Gleanings:* "When I first became acquainted with them . . . they showed me a library [of aeronautical literature] that astonished me!" Afterwards, the brothers did not lose contact with him. As late as January 1908 they thought of allowing him to buy stock in their projected company, *Papers*, 855.

The first circle. My description of this is based on the diary entry accompanied by Wilbur's rough sketch, *Papers*, 456, along with a letter of Wilbur's written two weeks later, *Papers*, 459–60; Root's article in *Gleanings*, January

1, 1905; Wilbur's *First Rebuttal,* 493; and Kelly, *Wrights,* 142–43. The Root quotations are from his article in *Gleanings,* a more accessible source for which is Gibbs-Smith, *The Aeroplane,* 1966, where it is reprinted in an appendix.

The turning difficulty is described by Wilbur in *First Rebuttal,* 495–96, and in Kelly, *Wrights,* 131.

"Intelligence of what we . . ."—*Papers,* 460.

"The strain upon the human . . ."—New York *Herald,* November 22, 1906.

The presence of the two accidental spectators, Brown and Reed, is recorded in the diary for November 9, *Papers,* 463. They are identified in Kelly, *Wrights,* 135, as officers of the line. This fact and the absence of any mention of passengers indicates that the car was a special.

CHAPTER 13

FLYING MACHINE FOR SALE

My information about Congressman Nevin is from Kelly, *Wrights,* 149–50; *Biographical Directory of the American Congress, 1774-1961;* and an obituary, *New York Times,* December 18, 1912.

Wilbur's January 3 visit to Nevin is in Bishop Wright's diary and a letter of Wilbur's, *Papers,* 494.

Wilbur's decision to keep the Flyer under wraps until he had a signed agreement is stated or implied in a number of places, perhaps clearest in two letters to Chanute. May 28, 1905: "We have felt serious misgivings about the advisability of any further experiments prior to reaching an understanding with some government. At present our machine is a complete secret, but it may not remain so if we attempt further experiments." *Papers,* 494. October 19, 1905: "We have never had any intention of showing the machine in advance of a definite understanding in regard to its purchase." *Papers,* 517. The text of this chapter and succeeding ones supplies further evidence on the point.

Wilbur's letter of January 18 to Nevin does not appear in *Papers,* but it is included in *Miracle,* 135–36, and Kelly, *Wrights,* 149–50. General Gillespie's answer is in Kelly, *Wrights,* 150.

"Flat turndown . . ."—*Papers,* 495.

"A good clear knock on . . ."—*Papers,* 495.

Nevin's subsequent role in the Wrights' first contact with the U.S. government is clouded. It is said that when the letter reached him in Washington he was ill and so did not make personal contact with anyone. *Miracle,* 142. Whether the letter passed though the hands of Secretary of War Taft is not known, nor is it known just how it reached the War Department. Nevin served in Congress until March 1907, and the fact that he played no further part in the Wrights' story may indicate that his faith in the brothers' claims was minimal. After leaving Congress he returned to the practice of law in Dayton and died on December 17, 1912.

The many letters received in these years by the army board, offering flying machines, is the subject of a contemporary article in *The New York Times,* April 7, 1906, Section 3, p. 8: "Inventors Solving the Problem of Aerial Flight Every Day." In the article, Langley's failure is mentioned along with the comment, "Since then, both Congress and the War Department have been somewhat more conservative on the subject of flying machines." The same admission is made in Kelly, *Wrights*, 150.

Here is the complete text of the Wrights' first letter to the U.S. Army, written January 18, 1905. Today's reader should view it against the background of its own time, when it was generally assumed that if the impossible ever did come to pass, and man did fly, the news would immediately carry, like wildfire, round the world.

> The series of aeronautical experiments upon which we have been engaged for the past five years has ended in the production of a flying machine of a type fitted for practical use. It not only flies through the air at high speed, but it also lands without being wrecked. During the year 1904 one hundred and five flights were made at our experimenting station, on the Huffman prairie, east of the city; and though our experience in handling the machine has been too short to give any high degree of skill, we nevertheless succeeded, toward the end of the season, in making two flights of five minutes each, in which we sailed round and round the field until a distance of about three miles had been covered, at a speed of thirty-five miles an hour. The first of these record flights was made on November 9th, in celebration of the phenomenal political victory the preceding day, and the second on December 1st, in honor of the one hundredth flight of the season.
>
> The numerous flights in straight lines, in circles, and over S-shaped courses, in calms and in winds, have made it quite certain that flying has been brought to a point where it can be made of great practical use in various ways, one of which is that of scouting and carrying messages in time of war. If the latter features are of interest to our own government, we shall be pleased to take up the matter either on a basis of providing machines of agreed specification, at a contract price, or of furnishing all the scientific and practical information we have accumulated in these years of experimenting, together with a license to use our patents; thus putting the government in a position to operate on its own account.
>
> If you can find it convenient to ascertain whether this is a subject of interest to our own government, it would oblige us greatly, as early information on this point will aid us in making our plans for the future.

Imagine the U.S. Secretary of Defense, in 1975, receiving out of nowhere a letter in which the writer announces he has constructed a rocket in which he has already visited Mars and returned safely to earth, and is willing to make the rocket available to the government on contract. But even that would not adequately express the army board's depth of puzzlement, for in 1975 rockets are facts of life, while in 1905 flying machines, for all but the Wrights, were still in the realm of Jules Verne. Wilbur Wright, as his hundreds of letters show, possessed a sophisticated understanding of human nature. It is hard to believe that in choosing this approach he was not fully aware of the response it would evoke.

On June 6, 1905, Chanute wrote Wilbur: "I think that you should, however, endeavor to protect the interests of the United States in your deal with the British. I fear that this will be difficult. . . ." Two days later Wilbur replied: "We have no intention of forgetting that we are Americans, and do not expect to make arrangements that would probably result in harm to our native country." *Papers*, 497–98.

The financial terms offered to the British are in Kelly, *Wrights*, 151–52. The British reply concerning Colonel Foster is in the same place.

"Secret formulas."—The phrase occurs in a letter of Wilbur to Chanute, *Papers*, 677.

That Wilbur in 1905 believed he could make a 500-mile flight is stated in a small book, *Navigating the Air*, published in 1907 by the Aero Club of America. To this Wilbur contributed a brief article, "The Relations of Weight, Speed and Power of Flyers," in which he offers the following sensational conclusion: "Even in the existing state of the art it is easy to design a practical and durable flyer that will carry an operator and supplies of fuel for a flight of over 500 miles, at a speed of fifty miles an hour." His purpose in this article was to soften the general disbelief that had hampered his business negotiations, disbelief that was the inevitable result of the secrecy. It contains affidavits from four of the Huffman's pasture witnesses.

That Wilbur's initial offering to the British was made on January 10, 1905, which was a week before the first offer to the United States, is in Kelly, *Wrights*, 148, and *Papers*, 495. Kelly makes no explanation of this, and does not mention the visit Wilbur paid to Nevin on January 3, recorded in *Papers*, 494.

CHAPTER 14

A SENSATION OF PERFECT PEACE

The flights at Huffman's pasture in 1905 are recorded in detail in Wilbur's diary and letters, again with the operator's initials included. *Papers*, 499–519. They are also described in *First Rebuttal*, 495–98.

The refinements incorporated in Flyer No. 3 are given in an appendix in *Papers* 1190–92, the diary, *Papers*, 492, and Kelly, *Wrights*, 133–34.

The first day of flying in 1905 was June 23; the accident occurred less than ten seconds after takeoff, *Papers*, 499.

Orville's accident of July 14 occurred after he had flown about 600 feet. My description of it is based on the details given in the diary, *Papers*, 501, and in passing mentions in some letters.

Wilbur's eighteen-minute flight of September 26 is in the diary, *Papers*, 512. This was an important accomplishment, being about three times as long as any previous flight, but Kelly, *Wrights*, 137, merely lists it with other flights, not specifying the pilot.

The thorn-tree incident of September 28. This is reconstructed from the diary, *Papers*, 512; Wilbur's *First Rebuttal*, 496–98; *Century Magazine*, September 1908; and Kelly, *Wrights*, 131–32. For some reason Kelly gives a different interpretation of the incident, contradicting Wilbur's analysis in *First Rebuttal*, 498. Obliquely, he denies that the technique of stall recovery—diving—was learned from this near-accident, and says the recovery from this was "from an entirely different cause, the great difference in speeds of the two wings." But this explanation leaves the Kelly biography without any reference to the manner in which the brothers worked out their method of stall recovery. Kelly merely says that diving to recover speed in a stall had been their "practice."

Most of the names of the people invited as witnesses to flights late in October are listed in the diary, *Papers*, 513–14. On September 29 Torrance Huffman was present with Taylor and the two Wrights. The next day there were three witnesses, named, along with Lorin and his son Milton. On October 3 four witnesses, named, were there with Taylor and the brothers, and the next day there were eight witnesses, all named. For the last flight of the season, Wilbur's thirty-eight-minute effort, four witnesses are named along with "about a dozen others" not named.

"Our most acute sensation . . ."—New York *Herald*, November 25, 1906.

"When you know, after . . ."—New York *Herald*, November 25, 1906.

Orville's description of a ride in the Flyer is from *Century Magazine*, September 1908.

Wilbur's hope of flying for an hour is stated in a letter to Chanute, October 19, 1905, *Papers*, 517.

William Fouts is singled out by Orville, in Kelly, *Wrights*, 145, for blame as the one who broke silence to the newsmen about the long flights. According to the diary, *Papers*, 513, the druggist had witnessed Orville's long flights of September 30 and October 3.

During fourteen weeks of flying at Huffman's in 1905, the brothers had been airborne a total of just under four hours, according to the diary, where the time of nearly every flight is recorded. The aggregate distance was about 130 miles. Orville's totals were the greater—he had over two hours of airtime for about eighty miles, to Wilbur's hour and a half for about fifty miles.

CHAPTER 15

THE TROUBLES OF SELLING A SECRET

"We are waiting for them . . ."—*Papers*, 511.

Wilbur's letter of October 9 to the Secretary of War, his second approach to the U.S. government, is in *Papers*, 514–15. Once more, it should be read in the light of the time, keeping in mind the spectacular flights just concluded at Huffman's pasture.

> Some months ago we made an informal offer to furnish the War Department practical flying machines suitable for scouting purposes. The matter was referred to the Board of Ordnance and Fortification, which seems to have given it scant consideration. We do not wish to take this invention abroad, unless we find it necessary to do so, and therefore write again, renewing the offer.
>
> We are prepared to furnish a machine on contract, to be accepted only after trial trips in which the conditions of the contract have been fulfilled; the machine to carry an operator and supplies of fuel, etc., sufficient for a flight of one hundred miles; the price of the machine to be regulated according to a sliding scale based on the performance of the machine in the trial trips; the minimum performance to be a flight of at least twenty-five miles at a speed of not less than thirty miles an hour.
>
> We are also willing to take contracts to build machines carrying more than one man.

Making such an offer on such a subject, no more inept and unconvincing a letter could be imagined. Its very brevity marks it as inviting rejection. Why were the long flights not listed along with the names of witnesses? Why did Wilbur not explain how it had all been done in purposeful secrecy? Why was Chanute's name, which would have carried weight on such a subject, excluded? The real purpose of the letter, of course, occurs in the third sentence where the foreign negotiations are put on record. With this letter in the War Department files, it could never be said that the Wrights had not given fair warning of their intentions.

The army's reply to the Wrights' second letter is in Kelly, *Wrights*, 153–54. Here is Kelly's comment on the passage quoted in my text: "In other words, the Board would have to see drawings and descriptions to determine if the machine the Wrights had been flying could fly!" Even a little reflection would have shown that this was not the purpose of the board's request.

The Wrights' response to the army's reply is in *Papers*, 518. The army board's answer to this is in Kelly, *Wrights*, 155.

Chanute's offer to approach President Roosevelt is in a letter to Wilbur, December 6, 1905, *Papers*, 531. Wilbur's refusal was written two days later— that is, on the very day he received Chanute's letter, *Papers*, 532. Obviously surprised, Chanute the next day wrote that if Roosevelt remained uninformed "he may blame you hereafter . . . for not calling his attention to your recent achievements." *Papers*, 532. Wilbur made no answer to this warning.

The breakdown of the British negotiations is detailed in Kelly, *Wrights*, 156–57, and in *Papers*, 528. Rather disingenuously, Kelly says that the Wrights refused to show Colonel Foster a flight only because "experiments for that year had been concluded."

Details of the negotiations with the French and with Arnold Fordyce are in various letters in *Papers*, 529–44, 577–709, and in Kelly, *Wrights*, 182–89. The signing of the contract is recorded in Bishop Wright's diary, *Papers*, 540.

The cause of the reawakening of French interest in aeronautics was first explained by Wilbur in a letter to his brother, June 28, 1908, from France, *Papers*, 903–4. He was supplying data to be included in the *Century* article but the published article does not contain it. Further detail is provided by an appendix of *Papers*, 654–73, and Kelly, *Wrights*, 166–70.

"After thinking the matter over . . ."—*Papers*, 527.

Wilbur's letter to the Aero Club of America, reporting the long flights of October, is in *Papers*, 699–702.

The involvement of Senator H. C. Lodge on behalf of the U.S. Army is in Kelly, *Wrights*, 157–58, and in *Papers*, 716–18, 723, 728.

The exchange between Wilbur and Chanute over Wilbur's delaying tactics is in *Papers*, 729–32.

CHAPTER 16

COMPETITION

Santos-Dumont. On October 23, 1906, the Brazilian hopped his machine about 150 feet. Chanute in a letter to Wilbur expressed his belief that this put Santos-Dumont "very nearly where you were in 1904." Wilbur corrected this notion in a letter of November 2, 1906: "From our knowledge of the subject we estimate it is possible to *jump* about 250 feet, with a machine which has not made the first steps toward controllability and which is quite unable to maintain the motive force necessary for flight. By getting up good speed a machine can be made to rise with very little power, and can proceed several hundred feet before its momentum is exhausted." *Papers,* 733–34. He reminded Chanute that "Maxim made a machine lift 12 years ago and immediately quit in despair."

The 700-foot flight of Santos-Dumont took place on November 12. It received page-one coverage in most American newspapers the next day. For a week afterward there were almost daily stories about the feat and its implications, including much French skepticism about the mysterious Wrights.

"The real disturbing element . . ."—*Papers,* 756.

The Sherman Morse articles in the New York *Herald,* November 22 and 25, 1906, are unsigned, but Kelly, *Wrights,* 191 identifies Morse as the author.

My information on Charles R. Flint comes from his autobiography, *Memories of an Active Life,* and the *Dictionary of American Biography.* Whether it was the Wrights or Flint who made first contact cannot be documented from the existing record, nor can my suggestion that it was the flight of Santos-Dumont which prompted the move. However, it is a matter of record that Flint was in touch with the brothers about two weeks after Santos-Dumont's November 12 flight, hardly a coincidence. Writing to Chanute on December 1, 1906, Wilbur says that Flint's "representative visited us here a few days ago," *Papers,* 741. I believe that the representative was there at Wilbur's invitation and not, as in Kelly, *Wrights,* 194, on his own intiative, though the point is not a critical one.

The Wright-Flint negotiations are detailed in a series of letters by Wilbur, *Papers,* 743–52, and in Kelly, *Wrights,* 194–96. The $10,000 drawing account for the Wrights' expenses is mentioned by Flint in an interview, *New York Times,* June 6, 1909. Corroboration of the arrangement is in a letter of Orville's, *Papers,* 899, where he says "I have just received another $1000 from F[lint] and Co."

Regarding the contact with Lord Haldane, Flint in his autobiography says that, to overcome all hesitations, at one point he offered to "exhibit the Flyer to England's Ambassador Bryce, at a place an hour from Washington." The exhibition was not made and it must have been Wilbur who objected.

Flint says nothing in his autobiography about the proposed flight at Hampton Roads, but it is just the sort of demonstration he would have counseled. Since it came up immediately after his connection with the brothers began, and since the Wrights never gave any indication of using such an approach before this, I think it must have been Flint's idea. The plan for the flight is in Kelly, *Wrights,* 160–61, and is recalled in a 1926 letter of Orville's, *Papers,* 1137–39. The brothers were at work on designs for the pontoons ("hydroplanes," they called them) perhaps by early February 1907, and were experimenting with them on the Miami River by March, *Papers,* 753. They had five weeks between the start of their actual experiments and the naval parade of April 26, and it is obvious that the time proved insufficient.

The renewed army negotiations are detailed in several letters in *Papers,* 754–55, 757, 760–61, 765–66, and in Kelly, *Wrights,* 162–65.

The brothers' frustrating six-month stay in Europe in 1907 may be followed in detail in their letters and Wilbur's diary, *Papers,* 772–834. Kelly, *Wrights,*

196–206, adds some further information and clarifies some of the references in *Papers*.

"We doubt whether an . . ."—*Papers*, 824.

The bribe offer. This is mentioned in Kelly, *Wrights*, 201, and is corroborated by a letter and diary entry of Wilbur's, *Papers*, 781, 809.

"Rather warm heart to heart . . ."—*Papers*, 809.

That Wilbur witnessed Farman's flights of November 9 is recorded in a letter he wrote the day after, *Miracle*, 240 (misdated November 19 in the volume, an obvious error) and in a second letter written after his return, *Papers*, 851, which also offers criticism of Farman's machine.

The army contract. In order to satisfy some obscure law or tradition the army was forced to advertise for bids on a flying machine rather than simply make an exclusive contract with the Wrights. The terms, however, were framed according to the capabilities of the Flyer, and it was expected that this would discourage anyone else who thought to respond. In addition a good-faith bond was required amounting to ten percent of the stipulated price. Unexpectedly a total of forty-one applications was received, with the bids ranging from a thousand dollars up into the millions. Most of these, of course, were the hopeless gestures of cranks, publicity seekers, and deluded inventors. Soon all were eliminated except two: the Wrights and Augustus Herring, the man who had been at the Kitty Hawk camp in 1902 as Chanute's assistant. Both of these bids were accepted, though it was believed that Herring would not be able to fulfill the requirements. Herring's idea, it appears, was either to use his knowledge of the Wrights' 1902 glider to build a similar machine with a motor, or else to force the brothers to make some sort of accommodation with him—his bid was $5,000 under that of the Wrights. This, he expected—incorrectly—would gain him an exclusive contract, which he would then sublet to the Wrights. He even visited Dayton to propose joining forces but was summarily dismissed. When Herring could not deliver a machine by the stipulated time he was eliminated and the Wrights at last had the field to themselves. Further information on this almost comic-opera incident can be found in Kelly, *Wrights*, 211–12, and in *How Our Army Grew Wings*, by C. D. Chandler and F. P. Lahm, Ronald Press, 1943 (the book, incidentally, accepts the old myth of the army's blindness toward the brothers, not suspecting the true situation as set forth in my chapters 13, 15, 16). About Herring, one of the strangest figures in early aviation, it is difficult to discover much additional information. The fullest source, especially on his later connection with Glenn Curtiss, is C. R. Roseberry, *Glenn Curtiss, Pioneer of Flight*, 1972.

"It was the most wonderful . . ."—*New York Times*, November 19, 1907, quoting from an unnamed French journal.

The Wrights' official army bid, submitted January 27, 1908, is in *Papers*, 856–57. It was accompanied by sketches and a photograph of the 1905 machine, with the statement that these were to be kept confidential.

The French contract. It is probable that Wilbur, having an American contract in hand, reduced his French asking price in order to bring agreement, putting him in a position to make worldwide disclosure, a move that was made easier by the competition that had arisen in France. No other reason is on record for his suddenly accepting half of the million francs originally asked. The French terms are in a letter of Wilbur's, *Papers*, 861.

The Kitty Hawk practice flights of May 1908. My principal sources for reconstruction of this period were four: the diary kept by Wilbur, *Papers*, 860–81; Kelly, *Wrights*, 218–24; Sullivan, *Our Times*, vol. II, 602–13; and a contemporary article, "History at Kill Devil Hill," by Arthur Ruhl, *Collier's*, May 30, 1908, which also contains the story of the "attacking party."

"There was something weird . . ."—New York *World*, December 16, 1923, as quoted in Sullivan, *Our Times*, vol. II, 611.

Wilbur's accident of May 14 is described in his diary entry, *Papers*, 878. It occurred after he had been in the air for seven minutes, twenty-nine seconds.

The aileron. As a variation of the warping wing, the aileron was first experimented with in 1904 by a French group led by R. Esnault-Pelterie. In trying to build a Wright-type glider, Esnault-Pelterie and his associates decided that a warping wing put too much strain on the working wires, so they concluded to keep the wings rigid, making a small section at each tip movable. The results in gliding were satisfactory, though not as powerful as the warping. Before long the idea was taken up by many others, at least partly in the hope that the new mechanism would be held outside the Wright patents. In time, of course, various improved forms of the aileron replaced warping altogether. For Esnault-Pelterie's own statement see *Papers*, 735, which reprints part of his article from *L'Aerophile*, June 1905.

The flights of Curtiss, Delagrange, Blériot, and Farman in the summer of 1908 may be found in most general histories of aviation. I have used *Histoire de l'Aeronautique*, by Charles Dollfus and Henri Bouche, Paris, 1932, and *Flight Through the Ages*, by C. H. Gibbs-Smith, New York, 1974, among others, as well as a number of contemporary newspapers.

CHAPTER 17

WILBUR WRIGHT'S TRIUMPH

For Wilbur's operations in France during May 29–August 13, 1908, I have drawn principally on his diary and letters, *Papers*, 883–913; Kelly, *Wrights*, 233–53, and the various newspapers and magazines cited below. I have not felt it necessary to give more precise references for minor background facts.

"Mr. Wright deserves better . . ."—*Automotor Journal*, August 1908, quoted in Freudenthal, *Flight into History*, 184.

"However, we must take things . . ."—*Papers*, 886.

Wilbur's worry over leaving Orville to undertake the Fort Myer trials alone is first evident in a letter of May 20, 1908, *Papers*, 883, but is most clearly expressed in a letter he wrote to Katharine after Orville's accident, *Papers*, 925–26. In this he tells how he had more than once almost decided to return to America to help his brother.

"They are such idiots! . . ."—*Papers*, 985.

"I opened the boxes . . ."—*Papers*, 900.

The impact of Wilbur's personality and habits is very evident in all that was written at the time on both sides of the ocean; good summaries may be found in Kelly, *Wrights*, 235, 241, and in a contemporary article, "Veelbure Reet—American," by Frederick Palmer, Collier's Weekly, May 15, 1909.

The scalding accident. Details of this are in a letter of Wilbur to his father, *Papers,* 905; New York *Herald,* July 5–6, 1908; and Kelly, *Wrights,* 234–35.

The nighttime move from the Bollée factory to the racecourse hangar was followed by, among others, the New York *Herald* reporter, whose account appeared on August 5.

"His arm is really bad . . ."—New York *Herald,* August 7, 1908.

"It is up to you now . . ."—New York *Herald,* August 8, 1908.

Farman's first flight at Brighton Beach, Brooklyn, was made on July 31, and appears to have been a disappointment to the crowd of about a thousand, which expected higher and longer flights—the machine rose some twelve feet in the air and flew about 300 yards. The next day some three thousand people were on hand, at fifty cents each, but high winds kept Farman on the ground. On August 2 another crowd of three thousand saw him fly for 600 yards at a height of twenty-five feet. On the next two days he slightly bettered these figures, also racing and beating an automobile. He attempted no turns, the field being too small for the wide, lumbering circle his machine required. By August 5 the flights at Brighton Beach were terminated and the announcement made that a larger field was being sought. The new location had not been found when on August 9 the sensational news of Wilbur's flights in France reached the American public. Farman shortly after returned to France, having failed to draw large enough crowds, threatening his backers with a suit for payment of the $25,000 guarantee. Facts from New York *Herald* and *The New York Times,* August 1–15, 1908.

That the Wrights were worried about Farman as competition can be seen in a letter Orville wrote Wilbur just before Farman began his flights: "Farman was expected to arrive in New York today. If you don't hurry he will do his flying here before you get started in France." *Papers,* 911.

Wilbur's flights in France August 8–13. For some reason there are no diary entries covering these, nor do Wilbur's letters home give much detail; evidently he was too preoccupied for writing. My reconstruction relies on one letter of Wilbur's, *Papers,* 911–12, reports in the New York *Herald* and *The New York Times,* August 9–15, Kelly, *Wrights,* 236–40, and Harper, *Fifty Years in Flying,* 109–14. An article by C. H. Gibbs-Smith, "How Wilbur Wright Taught Europe to Fly," *American Heritage,* February 1960, is brief and without much detail.

For the August 8 flight, Wilbur's first in France, the New York *Herald,* particularly, is very full and detailed. I have also drawn on *The New York Times* and the New York *American,* both for August 9, 1908. The account in Kelly, *Wrights,* 237–38, is very brief and incorrectly has Wilbur making a figure eight. In *Papers,* 911, there is only a passing reference to the flight. None of the other literature gives it more than a few sentences or a paragraph, and yet in a very real sense it can be said that this flight marks the birth of world aviation—it was the first public flight of the first practical airplane. But the rush of succeeding events managed to obscure its significance.

"He called to one of . . ."—Harper, *Fifty Years in Flying,* 111.

The remarks of Blériot and Gasnier are from the *Herald,* August 9, 1908.

One of the very curious things in the Kelly biography is the statement that the American newspapers paid almost no attention to what Wilbur was doing in France. The accounts were brief, says Kelly, and "not treated as important," The day after Wilbur's August 8 flight, he asserts, "*The New York Times* had no mention of the event" (227). In reality the *Times* of August 9 gave the story a half column on its front page, telling of "wildly cheering spectators." Despite Kelly, American newspapers gave full coverage to all of Wilbur's French flights. It might be noted that Kelly's comments in this area are related to the importance he assigns Orville's Fort Myer flights, which began a month later. Kelly's presentation of the events of this period is, in fact, extremely clumsy, to say no more. First come Orville's Fort Myer flights in a chapter headed "End of Disbelief." Then in the next chapter are recounted Wilbur's European operations, under the heading "When Wilbur Wright Won France." It takes more than a casual reading to see that Kelly has gotten the two events the wrong way round, both as to time and significance.

Wilbur's tight circle of August 10 round a diameter of only about thirty yards is recorded in a letter, *Papers*, 912, where Wilbur explains that it was caused by the proximity of the trees. It is also mentioned in the New York *Herald*, August 11, 1908.

Wilbur's going into the stands to confiscate a camera is from the New York *Herald*, August 11, 1908. This incident had a slightly more violent repetition a year later at the second Fort Myer trials when Wilbur again went after a cameraman. In landing from a flight Orville sustained some damage that left the Flyer lopsided against a tree. By this time Wilbur had no objection to photographs of the Flyer but he did not want pictures made of an accident of this sort, and he so informed the crowd. Outside the hastily thrown up rope that held back the group of onlookers he spotted a camera being aimed. He threw something directly at the camera, then started for the offender, evading his brother's grasp. Jumping the rope he grabbed the photographer and wrenched the camera away. It developed that the man was an army photographer, taking pictures on orders for the Signal Corps, to which the machine was to be sold. Wilbur returned the camera with apologies. The incident is told in Charnley, *Wrights*, 271.

"Blériot and Delagrange were . . ."—Wilbur in a letter to Orville, *Papers*, 912.

"We are beaten! . . ."—Villard, *Contact*, 54. The precise circumstances under which Delagrange made this admission are not given, but it obviously followed his first sight of the Flyer, and that was on August 10. The same or similar remarks are quoted for Delagrange in a number of other books and articles, always in a general way, however.

"For this wonderful man . . ."—New York *Herald*, August 12, 1908.

Wilbur's accident of August 13. In a letter written two days later, *Papers*, 912, Wilbur admits that the smashup was caused by his lack of familiarity with the controls: "I have not yet learned to operate the handles without blunders." The New York *Herald*, August 14, quotes him as saying, "The mistake I made this morning is a stupid mistake." His own analysis of how his mishandling caused the accident is in a letter to Orville, *Papers*, 919. While he was castigating himself, however, others felt differently. "The predominant sense was one of wonder," Griffith Brewer wrote later, "that the same man could calmly invent such a mechanism and yet fly it with consummate skill." *The Aeronautical Journal*, August–September 1916, 130.

"Sat for a few moments . . ."—New York *Herald*, August 14, 1908. Wilbur's bad arm may have had something to do with the crackup. Two days later in a letter to Orville he writes, "My arm is still sore." *Papers,* 913.

CHAPTER 18
KINGS OF THE AIR

Orville's Fort Myer flights of 1908 are recorded in a U.S. Signal Corps log, *Papers,* 916–25; the New York *Herald,* September 2–18, 1908; and Kelly, *Wrights,* 226–32.

"How can I describe . . ."—*World's Work,* October 1909.

The Delagrange flights of September 6–7 at Rome made page-one headlines in most newspapers. I have used the New York *Herald,* September 7–8, 1908.

By September 3 Wilbur had resumed regular flying, now on the new field at Auvours, with the result that the brothers were in the air on the same day five different times before Orville's accident ended their remarkable intercontinental exhibition—September 3, 4, 10, 12, 17 (Wilbur's flights for those days have been determined by analysis of his letters in *Papers,* 919–20, and accounts in the New York *Herald,* September 4–18, 1908). And on at least three of those days it is possible they were in the air at precisely the same moment, allowing for an approximate three-hour time difference. The starting times for Orville's flights are listed in the Signal Corps log, showing he usually went up between five and six in the evening. I have not been able to determine the exact time of day for all Wilbur's September flights but they were usually in the afternoon or early evening. I think it possible that both were in the air at the same moment on September 3 when Orville flew for over an hour, starting at five, and Wilbur went up in late afternoon for ten minutes. Again on September 10 Orville flew for over an hour starting at 5:09, and Wilbur was up for twenty-two minutes, apparently taking off about two. On September 12 both men made two flights, though Wilbur's lasted only four minutes and six minutes, being forced down by fog, while Orville was up for ten minutes with a passenger, then for more than an hour by himself. Finally, Orville's accident on September 17 may have happened while his brother was in the air in France. Before the crash Orville had been up for some five minutes, beginning in early evening, while Wilbur was up for a half hour just before sunset. The idea of both brothers being airborne simultaneously, three thousand miles apart, is an interesting possibility that further research in French papers might settle definitely.

Orville's Fort Myer accident is described and analyzed in Kelly, *Wrights,* 229–30; in a letter of Orville to Wilbur, *Papers,* 936–39; and in the New York *Herald,* September 18, 1908.

"If I had been there . . ."—*Papers,* 925.

"Evidently to see what I . . ."—*Papers,* 937.

Wilbur's flights of September–December 1908 have been compiled from references in *Papers,* 925–47, especially 942–43, and Kelly, *Wrights,* 241–50.

"I know of only one bird . . ."—widely quoted; see Kelly, *Wrights,* 245.

"Having clambered in . . ."—Baden-Powell, *Aeronautics,* December 1908.

For the Wrights' White House visit and the Dayton celebration I have used *The New York Times* and the New York *Herald,* June 11, 18, 1909.

The 1909 Fort Myer trials are recorded in the U. S. Signal Corps log, *Papers*, 956–61.

My estimate of nearly a quarter-million dollars for the brothers' earnings by fall 1909 is based on scattered references in *Papers*, 931–64. Of this sum, $116,000 came from the French syndicate, $30,000 from the American government, and various smaller sums from prizes, awards, and business arrangements in Italy, Germany, England, and France—see, for instance, *Papers*, 947, where $10,000 is mentioned, and *Papers*, 951, where an English order for a half-dozen Flyers is recorded. That the brothers could have done better than this is only a feeling on my part, though a strong one. If they had, in 1905, arranged a secret demonstration for the U.S. Army it is hard to believe that Congress would not have appropriated some millions of dollars to acquire the only airplane in the world, with its secrets. If then the brothers had been barred from selling elsewhere, it is unlikely the prohibition would have lasted more than a few years. By contrast, in a commercial way the aircraft industry did not begin to have earnings in the millions until the start of World War I.

Wilbur's Hudson River flights. The general background of the city's celebration I have taken from the *Times* and the *Herald*, September 15–October 5, 1909. Wilbur's contract, setting a fee of $15,000, also provided that in the event of failure to make the specified flight only the sum of $2,500 for expenses would be allowed. In his negotiations with the Aeronautical Committee for the celebration, Wilbur had promised a flight "which would be a notable achievement, and quite as difficult as Blériot's flight across the English Channel." This was reported at the committee's meeting of August 18, 1909. At the following week's meeting it was announced that the contract had been signed. All the above from *Official Minutes of the Hudson-Fulton Celebration Commission*, compiled by H. Sackett and E. Hall, J. B. Lyon Co., 2 vols., Albany, 1911; see pp. 1396–97, 1413, 1449.

Henry Farman's pioneer cross-country flight took place on October 30, 1908, stealing a little of Wilbur's thunder in France—it may in fact have been done for just that purpose, Farman not being content to surrender the limelight. On the day following, Blériot made a similar journey, for the second cross-country trip. Kelly, *Wrights*, 260, overlooks these two when he says that Orville at Fort Myer in July 1909, in the speed test, "made the first cross-country trip yet made in an airplane, a total distance of about ten miles to Alexandria and return."

Glenn Curtiss' contract terms and fee are given in Roseberry, *Curtiss*, 208. My other information on Curtiss' involvement with the celebration also comes from this book, along with the news accounts cited below.

"I am not much of a racer . . ."—New York *Herald*, September 20, 1909.

"Laid back the canvas . . ."—McSurely, *Beehive*, 53. The author refers the incident to the Belmont Air Meet of 1910, but it does not appear that Wilbur was at Belmont, and Governor's Island in 1909 is the only other possibility.

The Statue of Liberty flight. My description of this and the five quotations in my text are from the New York *Herald*, September 30, 1909. Wilbur's nonchalant attitude never failed to fascinate the crowds and even the reporters present at his flights. After he landed from circling the statue, *The New York Times* reported with relish how he climbed calmly down from the little seat and casually remarked to Taylor, "Goes pretty well, Charlie." To which the mechanic, equally matter-of-factly, responded, "Looks all right to me, Will."

"Those people who do not know . . ."—*American Magazine,* February 1910.

An unusual portrait of Wilbur survives from this time which, though it contains some of the condescension that was then typical of the professional class, is one of the few surviving records of a face-to-face encounter. Cass Gilbert, famed architect and then engaged in the design of the Woolworth Building in New York, was introduced to Wilbur in the latter's room at the Park Hotel on October 5, 1909. This was the day after Wilbur's twenty-mile flight and he had already met hundreds of people eager to shake hands and talk with him. In his description, Gilbert does not seem to realize that Wilbur, as usual, desired nothing more than to get away from well-wishers and celebrity hunters. Looking with a cool eye from the height of his own fame and success, Gilbert could find nothing "romantic or distinguished" in the man before him. Yet in his description, despite the usual reference to the Wrights as "mechanics," he shows awareness that there was a difference:

> His personality interested me very much. He is a man a little below average height, very slender and wiry in build. He is smooth shaven and his face is wrinkled and without much color. His eyes are a greenish-blue. He occasionally looked straight at me with a very frank, clear expression but more often looked slightly to the right and downwards. He seemed to be quite unostentatious and without any pose of manner. Very simple and direct and of few words, modestly spoken. He smiled occasionally with a sort of half smile that did not give the impression of much exuberance of spirit but rather of a provincial boy who had an underlying sense of humor and perfect confidence in himself but with a slightly provincial cynicism as to how seriously the other man might regard him or his views. He was totally impassive and I should say unimpressionable so far as the surface went, but probably very keenly sensitive, and on the whole rather the type of high grade, intelligent and well read mechanic whom I occasionally meet in connection with building work. He looked like the student and shop man rather than the man of affairs or the pushing administrator of a factory. . . . In answering my questions or replying he would look directly into my face and a sort of wan, half-cynical but kindly smile would flit across his countenance and disappear.

Gilbert's memorandum, jotted down the same night, did not come to light until it was published in *Minnesota History,* September 1941.

Two days after Wilbur's Statue of Liberty flight, Orville in Germany broke into the headlines by shattering the world altitude record, reaching a height of over 1600 feet, far beyond any competitor. New York *Herald,* October 2, 1909.

In reconstructing Wilbur's twenty-mile flight of October 4, I have drawn on the New York *Herald* and the *Times,* October 5, 1909. Both papers carried the story on page one, the *Times* giving it the lead position under a headline which proclaimed, "Wright Flies Twenty Miles."

"The most entrancing sight . . ."—*The New York Times,* June 8, 1924. The remark is made in a letter to the editor, Sec. 8, p. 17.

"Another indication of the . . ."—*The New York Times,* October 5, 1909.

"At the height Mr. Wright was . . ."—*New York Times,* October 5, 1909.

The New York Times gave exact times for the flight's duration: takeoff from Governor's Island, 9:45; abreast of Grant's Tomb, 10:13; return landing at Governor's Island, 10:26. The faster time downriver was the result of a tailwind and having fewer obstacles to rise over. Also, on the upward leg Wilbur kept his speed low to give spectators a more leisurely view.

It is worth noting that in Kelly, *Wrights,* 265, Wilbur's Hudson River flights are recorded in a single paragraph, while Orville's flights in Germany during that same time, which were unspectacular except for the 1600-foot altitude, are allowed four pages. Wilbur's flight, of course, was the most important made up to that time and some idea of its epic proportions may still be glimpsed in the unconscious hyperbole of the *Times* reporter. The flight was made, he wrote in the excitement of the moment, under conditions "such as no aviator in the history of the world has ever attempted before."

Acknowledgments

Certain friends were kind enough to read and comment on the manuscript, or portions of it, and to these I return my thanks: Wallace J. Franklin, Hugh Rawson, Walter Hunt, Edward Zeigler, Sherwood Harris. For his faith in the project from the beginning I am grateful to Paul Fargis. Mrs. Harold S. Miller of Dayton (the former Ivonette Wright), and Marvin McFarland of the Library of Congress, were both kind enough to answer certain questions in correspondence. Mr. McFarland's sure hand as editor of *The Papers of Wilbur and Orville Wright*, the basic document for the Wrights' story, made my task infinitely easier; the appendices in these volumes, particularly those by Fred S. Howard, are indispensable to anyone attempting to unravel the Wrights' motor, propeller, and wind tunnel work.

For various sorts of timely assistance I thank the staff of the Wright Brothers Museum and Monument at Kill Devil Hill, Mr. Anthony P. Grech and the staff of the library of the Bar Association of New York City, and the staff of the Wertheimer Study of the New York Public Library at Forty-second Street. Some answers to certain obscure questions were supplied by George G. Spratt, as well as by Phyllis B. Greer and William P. Chamberlin, both of the Dayton Public School Board, and by Stanley C. Wylie of the Dayton and Montgomery County Library.

I am keenly aware of how much I owe to all those newsmen and journalists, in their own time either anonymous or named, who in pursuing their daily tasks sixty and seventy years ago became the sole historians of many things in the Wright story that would otherwise have been lost.

Bibliography

The following list of sources consulted might easily have been more than doubled in length. But such an indiscriminate compilation would serve no good purpose. While the literature on the Wrights is very large (one bibliography published in 1968 runs for 187 pages) much more than half of it, perhaps seventy or eighty percent, is merely a reshuffling of old facts and surmises, and a perpetuation of errors and distortions. The items I have chosen to list are those that contain the primary materials on which I have drawn in reconstructing the story, and those that have helped me, in one way or another, to understand the subject and its historical background. This understanding has gained almost as much from reading things that are not true as from those that are. Hence, some of the items listed are now worthy of remembrance only as curiosities. For complete bibliographical coverage of aeronautics and the Wrights, see the entries under Pritchard and Renstrom.

Anon., "The Wright Aeroplane and Its Fabled Performances," *Scientific American,* January 13, 1906.
———, "The Wright Aeroplane," *Scientific American,* April 7, 1906.
———, "Inventors Solving the Problem of Aerial Flight Every Day," *New York Times,* Sec. 3, p. 8, April 7, 1906.
———, "Wright Aeroplane," *Scientific American,* June 13, 1908.
———, "How America Lost the Wright Aeroplane," *New York Times,* Sec. 10, p. 1, June 6, 1909.
———, "When the Wright Brothers Were Boys," *American Magazine,* June 1909.
———, "Impressions of American Inventors," *Scientific American,* June 12, 1909.
———, "Wrights Yesterday and Today," *World's Work,* October 1909.
———, "Sketch of Wilbur Wright," *American Magazine,* February 1910.

————, "Wilbur Wright, Conqueror of the Air," *Outlook*, June 8, 1912.

————, "Passing of a Great Inventor," *Scientific American*, June 8, 1912.

————, "Death of the Dean of Birdmen," *Hearst's Magazine*, July 1912.

————, "Inventor Who Solved the Problem of Flight," *Current Literature*, July 1912.

————, "Ten Years' Marvels Since the Wrights' First Aerial Flight," *The New York Times*, Sec. 6, p. 1, October 12, 1913.

————, "Fifty Years of Aviation," *The New York Times*, Sec. 10, pp. 1–28, October 11, 1953.

Bacon, G., *Balloons, Airships and Flying Machines*, New York, Dodd, Mead, 1905.

Baden-Powell, B. F., "A Trip with Wilbur Wright," *Aeronautics*, December 1908.

Baker, M., "The Wright Brothers as Aeronautical Engineers," *Smithsonian Report for 1950*, in *Smithsonian Annual*, 1951.

Berget, A., *The Conquest of the Air*, N.Y., G. P. Putnam's Sons, 1911.

Brewer, G., "The Life and Work of Wilbur Wright," *The Aeronautical Journal*, July–September 1916.

Bruce, R., *Alexander Graham Bell and the Conquest of Solitude*, Boston, Little, Brown Co., 1973.

Casson, H., "At Last We Can Fly," *American Magazine*, April 1907.

Cesare, O., "The First Man to Fly Works On," *New York Times Magazine*, July 17, 1927.

Chandler, C., and Lahm, F., *How Our Army Grew Wings*, New York, Ronald Press, 1943.

Chanute, O., *Progress in Flying Machines*, New York, Forney Co., 1894.

————, "Aerial Navigation," *Cassier's Magazine*, June 1901.

————, "A History of the Wright Flying Experiments," *Scientific American Supplement*, June 1, 1907.

Charnley, M., *The Boys Life of the Wright Brothers*, Harper & Brothers, New York, 1928.

Clayton, H., "Wilbur Wright's Successful Flight in a Motor Driven Aeroplane," *Science*, January 8, 1904.

Coffyn, F., "Flying with the Wrights," *World's Work*, December 1929.

Davy, M., *Henson and Stringfellow*, Science Museum, London, 1931.

Dollfus, C., and Bouche, H., *Histoire de l'Aeronautique*, L'Illustration, Paris, 1932.

Durand, W., "Orville Wright 1871–1948," *Biographical Memoirs, National Academy of Sciences*, vol. 25, 1948.

Findley, E., "The Wrights and the Reporter," *Beehive*, February 1953.

Flint, C., *Memories of an Active Life*, New York, G. P. Putnam's Sons, 1923.

Freudenthal, E., *Flight into History*, Norman, University of Oklahoma Press, 1949.

Gibbs-Smith, C., "How Wilbur Wright Taught Europe to Fly," *American Heritage*, February 1960.

————, *Sir George Cayley's Aeronautics*, Science Museum, London, 1962.

————, "The Wright Brothers and Their Invention of the Practical Aeroplane," *Nature*, June 1, 1963.

————, *The Wright Brothers, A Brief Account*, Science Museum, London, 1963.

————, *The World's First Aeroplane Flights,* Science Museum, London, 1963.

————, *The Invention of the Aeroplane,* London, Faber and Faber, 1966.

————, and Brooks, P., *Flight Through the Ages,* New York, Thomas Y. Crowell Co., 1974.

Gilbert, C., "Notes and Documents: Cass Gilbert and Wilbur Wright," *Minnesota History,* Sept. 1941.

Goldstrom, J., *A Narrative History of Aviation,* New York, Macmillan Co., 1930.

Grahame-White, C., *The Aeroplane: Past, Present and Future,* Philadelphia, Lippincott, 1911.

————, *The Story of the Aeroplane,* Boston, Small, Maynard, 1911.

Gregory, Sir R., *Discovery: The Spirit and Service of Science,* New York, Macmillan Co., 1916.

Harper, H., *My Fifty Years in Flying,* London, Assoc. Newspapers Ltd., 1956.

Harrison, M., *Airborne at Kitty Hawk,* London, Cassel, 1953.

Harris, S., *The First to Fly,* New York, Simon and Schuster, 1970.

Hart, I., *The World of Leonardo da Vinci,* New York, Viking Press, 1961.

Hildebrandt, A., *Die Bruder Wright,* Berlin, Otto Elsner, 1909.

Ingells, D., "Wilbur and Orville—Student Pilots," *Flying,* April 1954.

Kelly, F., "How the Wright Brothers Began," *Harper's Magazine,* October 1939.

————, *The Wright Brothers: A Biography Authorized by Orville Wright,* New York, Harcourt, Brace and Co., 1943.

———— (ed.), *Miracle at Kitty Hawk: The Letters of Wilbur and Orville Wright,* New York, Farrar, Straus, and Young, 1951.

Krieghbaum, H., "Wright Death Recalls Coverage of First Flight," *Editor and Publisher,* February 14, 1948.

Langeweische, W., "What the Wrights Really Invented," *Harper's Magazine,* June 1950.

Langley, S., "The Flying Machine," *McClure's,* June 1897.

Lewis, G., "The Wright Brothers as Researchers," *Aviation,* August 1939.

Lindbergh, C., *Wartime Journals of Charles Lindbergh,* New York, Harcourt, Brace, Jovanovich, 1970.

McClarren, R., "Wright Brothers Collection at the Franklin Institute," *Franklin Institute Journal,* August 1951.

McFarland, M. (ed.), *The Papers of Wilbur and Orville Wright,* 2 vols., New York, McGraw-Hill Co., 1953.

McMahon, J., "The Real Fathers of Flight," *Popular Science Monthly,* January–June, 1929.

————, *The Wright Brothers, Fathers of Flight,* Boston, Little, Brown, 1930.

McSurely, A., "The Wrights and the Propeller," *Beehive,* spring 1953.

————, "The Horsepower at Kitty Hawk," *Beehive,* spring 1953.

Magoun, F., and Hodgins, J., *Sky High,* Boston, Little, Brown, 1935.

Marey, E., *Animal Mechanism,* New York, Appleton, 1874.

————, *The Flight of Birds,* New York, Appleton, 1895.

Marshall, A., and Greenly, H., *Flying Machines: Past, Present and Future,* London, Marshall Co., 1907.

Maxim, H., "A New Flying Machine," *Century Magazine,* January 1895.

————, *My Life,* London, Methuen and Co., 1915.

296   [Bibliography]

Meynell, L., *First Men to Fly*, London, Lauri and Co., 1955.
Mingos, H., "Thus Man Learned to Fly," *Saturday Evening Post*, July 7 and 14, 1928.
Moore, P., "Octave Chanute's Experiments with Gliders in the Indiana Dunes," *Indiana Magazine of History*, December 1958.
Newcomb, S., "Is the Airplane Coming?" *McClure's*, September 1901.
Page, A., "How the Wrights Discovered Flight," *World's Work*, August 1910.
Palmer, F., "Veelbure Reet—American," *Collier's Weekly*, May 15, 1909.
Pettigrew, J., *Animal Locomotion*, New York, Appleton, 1874.
Peyrey, F., *Les Premières Hommes-oiseaux*, Paris, H. Guiton, 1908.
Pritchard, J., "A Bibliography of the Wright Brothers," *Journal of the Royal Aeronautical Society*, London, March 1948.
———, "The Wright Brothers and the Royal Aeronautical Society, A Tribute," *Journal of the Royal Aeronautical Society*, London, December 1953.
———, *Sir George Cayley, Inventor of the Aeroplane*, New York, Horizon Press, 1961.
Randers-Pehrson, N., *Pioneer Wind Tunnels*, Washington, D.C., Smithsonian Institution, 1935.
Renstrom, H., *Wilbur and Orville Wright, A Bibliography*, Library of Congress, 1968.
Roseberry, C., *Glenn Curtiss: Pioneer of Flight*, New York, Doubleday and Co., 1972.
Rotch, L., *Conquest of the Air*, New York, Moffat, Yard and Co., 1909.
Ruhl, A., "History at Kill Devil Hill," *Collier's Weekly*, May 30, 1908.
Saunders, H., "Then We Quit Laughing," *Collier's Weekly*, September 17, 1927.
Sherman, D., "The Bishop's Boys," *Flying*, December 1959.
Stick, D., *The Outer Banks of North Carolina*, Chapel Hill, University of North Carolina Press, 1958.
Stillson, B., *Wings: Insects, Birds, Man*, Indianapolis and New York, Bobbs-Merrill Co., 1954.
Sullivan, M., *Our Times*, vol. II, Chapter 28, New York, Charles Scribner's Sons, 1927.
Sutton, Sir G., *Mastery of the Air*, New York, Basic Books, 1965.
Taylor, C., "Building the Original Wright Motor," *Slipstream*, May 1928.
———, "My Story of the Wright Brothers," *Collier's Weekly*, December 26, 1948.
Todd, F., "The Airship is Here." *World's Work*, September, 1908.
———, "The Man in the Air," *World's Work*, October 1908.
Turner, G., "The Men Who Learned to Fly," *McClure's*, February 1908.
Valentin, A., *Leonardo da Vinci*, New York, Viking Press, 1938.
Vernon (pseud.), "The Flying Man," *McClure's*, September 1894.
Villard, H., *Contact! The Story of the Early Birds*, New York, Thomas Y. Crowell Co., 1968.
Woodhouse, H., "Wilbur Wright, The Man Who Made Flying Possible," *Collier's Weekly*, June 15, 1912.
———, "History of the Conquest of the Air," *Flying*, March 1916.
Wright, O., "The Wright Brothers Aeroplane," *Century Magazine*, September 1908.
———, "How We Made the First Flight," *Flying*, December 1913.

Wright, W., "Some Aeronautical Experiments," *Journal of the Western Society of Engineers,* December 1901.

———, "Experiments and Observations in Soaring Flight," *Journal of the Western Society of Engineers,* August 1903.

———, "The Relations of Weight, Speed and Power of Flyers," in *Navigating the Air,* New York, Doubleday, Page and Co., 1907.

———, "Flying as a Sport," *Scientific American,* February 29, 1908.

———, "Our Aeroplane Tests at Kitty Hawk" (in 1908), *Scientific American,* June 13, 1908.

———, "Flying from London to Manchester," *London Magazine,* February 1909.

———, "The Earliest Wright Flights," *Scientific American,* July 16, 1910.

———, "What Mouillard Did," *Aero Club of America Bulletin,* April 1912.

———, "What Clement Ader Did," *Aero Club of America Bulletin,* May 1912.

———, "Otto Lilienthal," *Aero Club of America Bulletin,* September 1912.

———, "First Rebuttal Deposition," *The Wright Company vs. the Herring-Curtiss Company and Glenn H. Curtiss, Complainant's Record, United States District Court, Western District of New York,* 1912, pp. 473–614. Also in the same volume, "Second Rebuttal Deposition of Wilbur Wright," pp. 615–690, and "Testimony of Wilbur Wright," pp. 780–799.

———, "Deposition," *Charles H. Lamson vs. the Wright Company, Defendant's Record, In Equity No. 6611, the United States District Court, Southern District of Ohio, Western Division,* Springfield, Ohio, the Young and Bennett Co., Printers, 1913, pp. 13–76.

(Note: printing of the Wrights' various depositions, testimony, and affidavits was an automatic part of the process of appeal in litigation. This was done for six of the lawsuits in which Wilbur was involved, a full listing for which may be found in *Papers,* 1233–34.)

Zahm, A., *Aerial Navigation,* New York, Appleton and Company, 1911.

———, *Early Powerplane Fathers,* South Bend, University of Notre Dame Press, 1945.

———, *Aeronautical Papers, 1885–1945,* 2 vols., South Bend, University of Notre Dame Press, 1950.

Index

(References are to the main text only; for further treatment of selected topics consult the Notes under the appropriate chapter heading.)